Treating Mental Disorders

Treating Mental Disorders
A Guide to What Works

Peter E. Nathan

Jack M. Gorman

Neil J. Salkind

New York Oxford
Oxford University Press
1999

#40200099

Oxford University Press

Oxford   New York
Athens   Auckland   Bangkok   Bogotá   Buenos Aires
Calcutta   Cape Town   Chennai   Dar es Salaam   Delhi   Florence
Hong Kong   Istanbul   Karachi   Kuala Lumpur   Madrid
Melbourne   Mexico City   Mumbai   Nairobi   Paris   São Paulo
Singapore   Taipei   Tokyo   Toronto   Warsaw

and associated companies in
Berlin   Ibadan

Library of Congress Cataloging-in-Publication Data
Nathan, Peter E.
Treating mental disorders : a guide to what works /
Peter E. Nathan, Jack M. Gorman, Neil J. Salkind.
p. cm. Includes index.
ISBN 0–19–510228–2
1. Mental illness—Popular works. 2. Mental illness—
Treatment—Evaluation—Miscellanea. 3. Consumer
education. I. Gorman, Jack M.   II. Salkind, Neil J.   III.
Title.
RC480.515.N38   1999   616.89—dc21   98–49355

Printed in the United States of America
on acid-free paper

1 3 5 7 9 6 4 3 2

Dedication

This book is dedicated first, to those people who everyday face the challenges we describe in the following pages and to those people who help them. The book is also dedicated to the authors' families, who bore with great forebearance and understanding the substantial time demands these efforts imposed. So, to Anne Helene and Siri; Lauren, Rachel, and Sara; and Leni, Sara, and Micah, our thanks and love.

Forward

We're writing this forward for one important reason. It's our chance to write a more personal note to our readers about why this book is important and why it is valuable. Mental disorders are often "hidden" from the person who suffers from them, from the person's family and friends and, sometimes, from both. Yet, when mental illness is not openly addressed, understood, and treated, it can become an unwelcome addition to every facet of life. Work, family, school and social relationships are affected—most often, not for the better.

In *Treating Mental Disorders: A Guide to What Works*, we have created a set of vital questions and informed answers designed to address the most important issues facing persons with a mental disorder and those who care about them. The questions and answers address all-important issues, like how the disorder manifests itself, how often and under what circumstances it occurs and, most important, the best way to treat it, based on the most current, best-informed scientific findings. Based on our clinical experience, as well as an analysis of authoritative research findings, including the information contained in our Oxford companion volume, *A Guide to Treatments That Work*, we are convinced that, with appropriate treatment, most persons with most mental disorders can lead healthy and productive lives. But, in many cases, they will be able to do so only when their disorder is recognized and treated.

It is our hope that this book will be read and used not only by the mental health professionals who work with persons with the mental disorders we describe but, even more important, by those who need assistance in seeking out treatments that work—those that can help return them or their loved ones to lives of productivity and fulfillment.

Contents

Acknowledgments

The authors would like to thank Joan Bossert, Editorial Director at Oxford University Press for the opportunity to work together on this project, Janet Majure for her editing expertise, and Traci Bunkers for designing the book.

Introduction

Treating Mental Disorders: A Guide to What Works is a book for people who want to know about how mental disorders are treated and how well these treatments work. The book is based on the original text titled *A Guide to Treatments That Work*, also published by Oxford University Press, which was edited by Peter E. Nathan and Jack M. Gorman. They and Neil J. Salkind have collaborated in this book to provide a reliable and easy-to-read source of information for educated consumers who are not mental health professionals. This book, which is organized by major mental disorders, is not a self-help book or self-treatment guide; the mental disorders that are discussed are serious and should be diagnosed and treated only by professionals. The book, however, is intended to provide family and friends of those with a mental disorder — as well as physicians, social workers, nurses, administrators, lawyers, and other professionals — the information they need to better understand mental disorders and how they might be treated.

    Treating Mental Disorders discusses major mental disorders in a question-and-answer format. Anyone needing information about treatment decisions should be easily able to understand the pros and cons of a particular treatment. While family and friends should not make treatment decisions on their own, this book will help them understand the issues involved when working with a mental health professional.

    Each chapter contains information about the definition and diagnosis of a particular mental disorder, its prevalence, and the effectiveness of the various treatments. A summary table of disorders and effective treatments can be found at the end of this introduction.

The Different Types of Treatments for Mental Disorders

Treating Mental Disorders: A Guide to What Works has organized the various treatments into two general categories: psychosocial and pharmacological.

    Psychosocial treatments are based on the assumption that a mental disorder reflects an illness rooted in the individual's unique characteristics and his or her interactions with the environment, including family, school, work, and other people. To treat the disorder, one of many different types of psychosocial treatments that focus on the individual and his or her daily interactions might be used. Psychosocial treatments can take on many different forms, such as behavioral therapy where patients learn new ways to deal with old situations. Other approaches include cognitive-behavior therapy, relaxation techniques, education, and vocational therapy where job training and job-obtaining skills are emphasized.

Pharmacological treatments (sometimes called psychopharmacological treatments) involve the use of medication to treat a mental disorder. The assumption underlying the use of these medications is that some type of chemical imbalance in the brain exists that the medication can correct. For example, antidepressants help alleviate depression by regulating important chemicals in the brain. Modern psychiatry has made tremendous advances in the last 30 years in this area of research and treatment.

Are there treatments where both the psychosocial and pharmacological treatments are combined? Yes, and when that is the case, these combinations are discussed in the chapter as well.

How Do We Know What Works?

This book is all about treatments that have been shown to be effective for mental disorders. How does one know what works and what doesn't? The answer is that these treatments have been subjected to numerous and rigorous studies conducted in such a way that there is reasonable certainty that the treatment is effective.

Researchers who conduct such studies have what they call a *gold standard* of research. These gold standard studies have certain characteristics that clearly contribute evidence either in favor of or against the use of a particular treatment. Thus, researchers attempt to make sure that groups being studied are as alike as possible and that they are treated as much alike as possible. The basic assumption underlying this method is that treatments can be compared to one another with all the factors that could affect the outcome of the comparison being controlled. So if there is a change in the behavior of the people participating in the research, the only thing it can be attributed to is the treatment itself and not a host of other factors such as the patient's previous history, age, or social class.

For example, researchers might want to investigate the question, "Are antidepressants an effective treatment for depression?" They will follow several steps, which can generally be applied to studying any treatment for any mental disorder, to achieve the gold standard.

Step 1 would be the selection of a group of people who have a depression disorder, making sure that there are as few as possible other conditions or factors that interfere with the disorder. For example, if the researcher wants to test the effectiveness of a particular treatment for depression, he or she includes those patients who are depressed and have no other mental illness.

Step 2 is to divide the patients into two groups. Each person will be either in the treatment group (where patients in the group receive the treatment) or in the control group (where patients in the group receive everything the treatment group receives except the treatment). To ensure this research is useful, patients will be placed in one of the two groups using random assignment. Random assignment means that people are separated into groups at random and there is no pattern as to why a person is in one group or the other. This technique helps assure that at the beginning of the experiment, both groups are as equal as possible. In some experiments, the control group (or even an additional group) receives a placebo, an inactive treatment. For example, if each person in the experimental group receives some type of medication, participants in the control group might receive a similar pill that has no psychopharmacological activity.

This process of random assignment is especially important to eliminating any possible contaminating factor that might affect a person's behavior, other than (of course) the treatment. So in this example, each patient with the disorder is assigned to either the control or the treatment (experimental) group. Because each person is randomly assigned, researchers can assume the groups at the beginning of the experiment are the same. If the groups are different from each other at the end of the experiment, the difference is presumably because one group (the experimental group) received the treatment while the control group did not.

Step 3 is to measure the outcome in which the researcher is interested. For studying a treatment for depression, this measurement might be a test of the degree of depression. Since every other potential factor (except group membership) is being controlled, the treatment is the only reasonable explanation for any measured differences in the groups. When researchers are confident that such differences are due to the treatment and nothing else, the difference is described as being statistically significant.

That is the way good research is designed and carried out. The better the research, the more useful the findings and the more confidence can be placed in the reported usefulness of the treatment. The gold standard is high, and the results of such well-designed experiments can form the basis for treatment. In this book, when we talk about treatments that work, we are referring to those that have met the research standards just discussed.

When the three steps discussed above are repeated, researchers get a consistent set of outcomes. In general, the more a particular treatment is tested under different conditions, the more confidence can be placed in the outcomes. The problem, however, is that in much research one or more of these three steps cannot be completed satisfactorily. For example, it might be impossible to divide a group of patients into two groups that are equal on all characteristics and qualities except for the treatment. This case is common, especially since many mental disorders occur along with other disorders. In such a case, how does the researcher know what disorder is being treated? Or perhaps the measures used to evaluate the effectiveness of a treatment are not as accurate as necessary to detect important differences between the experimental and control groups. As a result, those differences go undetected even though they really exist and may be important no matter how small.

A Summary of Treatments

Following the introduction is a multipage table that provides a summary of the treatments available for the various disorders discussed in this book. The table contains the information found in each chapter of the book as to disorders, treatments, and the page numbers for finding detailed information.

This table can be used to get a quick overview of the kinds of treatments available for various disorders. It can, also be used to discuss treatment options with a therapist. Again, it contains a summary of information that reflects the results of well-conducted and trustworthy scientific research.

However, even the most effective treatments, which work wonders for many people, will not work for everyone because patients and the conditions they have vary widely. Mental health professionals are trained to treat people as individuals, and any treatment that is selected will be tailored to the patient's individual case and needs.

How to Help Someone with a Mental Disorder

What follows is a brief description of some areas that family and friends might find useful in assisting someone with a mental disorder. First are some general guidelines about selecting a therapist, then information about medication, and finally a description of where to find more information about mental disorders.

Selecting a Therapist

When it does come time to select a therapist, consumers and professionals need to look for a person who has training and experience in the particular mental disorder for which treatment is sought. Currently, mental health professionals with many different types of training conduct therapy. These professionals include clinical social workers, clinical psychologists, psychiatrists, counselors, and trained clergy. Only physicians (including psychiatrists) can prescribe medication. Therefore, a social worker or clinical psychologist might work in conjunction with a psychiatrist when medication is required for treatment.

Selecting a mental health professional is a critical part of the entire treatment process. Consequently, some important questions should be asked. Asking some of these questions can be uncomfortable, but the answers are informative and can be helpful in making a decision:

1. What is your training, and how long have you been in practice?
2. How many patients have you treated who have this disorder?
3. Do you have any special training in treating patients with this disorder?

4. What is your basic approach to treating this disorder? Do your patients meet in individual or group therapy sessions or both? Do you believe that medication is always necessary?
5. From your experience, how long does it take for the treatment to begin working? If medication is prescribed and it is not effective, what is the next step?
6. How often can I expect to be seen and how long is each session?
7. How much does a session cost?
8. What types of insurance does your office honor, and can you help patients complete the necessary forms?

The Expense of Medication

Many medications that have been shown to be effective in treating mental disorders are very expensive. For example, risperidone (the generic name for the trade medication Risperdal), a relatively new medication for treating schizophrenia, costs about $3,000 a year. However, many drug companies sponsor programs that provide free or low-cost drugs for those who cannot afford them. Also, many insurance policies cover the cost of the medication.

If financial assistance is needed for getting a particular medication, a person can call the manufacturer and ask if it has an assistance program. Doctors and pharmacists should have the telephone number, postal, or e-mail address you need. (By law, pharmacists cannot distribute medication without a prescription and without payment, but they can help you get information.)

Following is a list of some drug manufacturers that currently provide such assistance. Of course, these companies have access only to the medications that they manufacture and support.

Ciba-Geigy Patient Support Program
800-257-3273

Lilly Cares Program
800-545-6962

Pfizer Prescription Assistance
800-646-4455

SmithKline Paxil Access to Care Program
800-546-0420

Solvay Patient Assistance Program
800-788-9277

This is a short list and surely does not contain all the manufacturers who provide assistance. Always try the specific manufacturer first. The following organizations can provide additional information about patient assistance.

National Alliance for the Mentally Ill
200 North Glebe Road, Suite 1015
Arlington, VA 22203-3754
703-524-7600, 800-950-NAMI (6264)

National Mental Health Association
1021 Prince Street
Alexandria, VA 22314-2971
703-684-7722, 800-969-6642

Generic Versus Brand Medications: Becoming Familiar with Names

Throughout *Treating Mental Disorders: A Guide to What Works*, both the generic or chemical name for a medication (such as fluoxetine), as well as the trade name for that same medication (Prozac), will be mentioned. In addition, all the generic and trade names are organized in the table at the end of this introduction.

There are several reasons why this information can be of value. First, it provides the necessary information if a patient is given the choice to buy the generic or trade version of the medication. Second, other sources of information about a mental disorder may use only the generic or only the trade names, and the table easily converts from one name to the other. Finally, the drugs are categorized by class (such as antidepressants or antipsychotics). Knowing the class of drugs into which a medication falls can be useful when talking with a therapist about the expected side effects of such drugs.

About Side Effects from Certain Medications

No medication is entirely safe, and many have side effects that vary in degree from person to person. Also, it is almost impossible to predict which side effect will affect which patient and how severe the side effect will be. Some side effects are mild and almost unnoticeable, while others can be quite severe. Throughout this book the side effects that can accompany particular medications are discussed so the patient is aware of possible complications. The prescribing physician should be contacted immediately if any uncomfortable or worrisome side effect is experienced. He or she will probably take one of the following courses of action:

1. Decrease the amount of medication. The goal is to have the patient take enough medication to be effective but not so much that the side effects cannot be tolerated.
2. Try another medication. As the field of psychopharmacology continues its research, the products being developed are much more finely tuned to the specific condition, and side effects can be dramatically reduced.
3. Prescribe a medication that helps neutralize the side effects. Since a physician cannot predict who will react in what way to a medication, a period of time is necessary to evaluate a drug's effectiveness and side effects for a particular patient.

Where to Find General Information About Mental Disorders

Each chapter in *Treating Mental Disorders: A Guide to What Works* ends with a set of specific resources you can use to find additional information. These resources are organized into three groups: books, Internet sites, and the names and addresses of organizations to which you can write for additional information.

Here is a list of general resources that you can consult that address at least part of every disorder that is discussed in this book.

Books
The New Psychiatry : The Essential Guide to State-of-the-Art Therapy and Emotional Health by Jack M. Gorman. St. Martins Press, 1996. ISBN 0312146906.

The Essential Guide to Psychiatric Drugs (3rd Ed.) by Jack M. Gorman. St. Martins Press, 1997. ISBN 0312168241.

Abnormal Psychology: An Integrated Approach by G.P. Wilson, P.E. Nathan, K.D. O'Leary, and L.A. Clark. Allyn & Bacon, 1996. ISBN 0130058025.

Internet Sites

National Institutes of Health at http://www.nimh.nih.gov/about/index.htm

Internet Mental Health at http://www.mentalhealth.com/

Yahoo! at http://www.yahoo.com (for general category searches)

Mental Health Net at http://www.cmhc.com/

Where To Write

National Institutes of Health
NIMH Public Inquiries
5600 Fishers Lane
Bethesda, MD 20892-8030
1-800-421-4211

The American Academy of Child & Adolescent Psychiatry
3615 Wisconsin Ave., N.W.
Washington, DC 20016-3007
202-966-7300

American Psychological Association
750 First Street, N. E.
Washington, DC 20002
202-336-5500

American Psychiatric Association
1400 K Street, N.W.
Washington, DC 20005
202-682-6325

National Alliance for the Mentally Ill
200 North Glebe Road, Suite 1015
Arlington, VA 22203-3754
1-800-950-NAMI (6264)

Summary of Treatments That Work

Chapter	Disorder	Psychosocial Treatments	Pharmacological or Other Treatments
Childhood Disorders	attention-deficit hyperactivity disorder		• stimulants
	conduct disorder	• cognitive problem-solving skills • parent management training • multisystemic therapy	
Eating Disorders	anorexia nervosa	• no proven treatment	
	Bulimia	• cognitive behavioral therapy	• antidepressants • appetite suppressants
	binge eating	• cognitive behavioral therapy • interpersonal therapy • behavioral weight loss programs	
Sleep Disorders	Insomnia	• stimulus control therapy • sleep restriction therapy • relaxation training • cognitive behavioral therapy	• benzodiazepines • zolpidem • selective antidepressants

Chapter	Disorder	Psychosocial Treatments	Pharmacological or Other Treatments
Sexual Disorders	Hypoactive sexual desire	• individual psychotherapy	• vasoconstrictive dilators
	Erectile dysfunction	• individual psychotherapy	• vacuum pumps • implants • sildenafil
	Premature ejaculation		• antidepressants • stop-start and start-squeeze therapies
	Female orgasmic disorder		• masturbatory training
	Male orgasmic disorder		• genital stimulation
	Vaginismus		• dilation • muscle control exercises
	Dyspareunia		• lubrication • surgery
	Paraphilias	• cognitive behavioral therapy • aversive conditioning	
Substance Use Disorders	Nicotine		• nicotine patch • nicotine gum • bupropion
	Heroin		• methadone • naltrexone
	Alcohol	• social skills training • community reinforcement • behavioral marital therapy	• naltrexone • acamprosate
	Cocaine	• no proven treatment	

Chapter	Disorder	Psychosocial Treatments	Pharmacological or Other Treatments
Somatoform and Dissociative Disorders	Somatization	• regular contact with physician • acceptance of symptoms • avoidance of unnecessary testing • stable contact with professional	
	Conversion		
	Somatoform pain		
	Hypochondria		• antidepressants
	Body dsysmorphia		
	Dissociative amnesia		
	Dissociate fugue		
	Dissociative identity disorder	• Hypnosis	
	Depersonalization disorder		
Depressive and Bipolar Disorders	Depression	• cognitive behavior therapy • behavior therapy • interpersonal therapy	• antidepressants • lithium
	Bipolar disorder	• education	• anticonvulsants • antipsychotics
Anxiety and Phobia Disorders	General anxiety disorder	• anxiety management program • relaxation with cognitive therapy • cognitive-behavioral therapy	• azapirones • antidepressants • benzodiazepines

Chapter	Disorder	Psychosocial Treatments	Pharmacological or Other Treatments
Anxiety and Phobia Disorders (cont.)	Panic disorder	• panic control treatment • cognitive behavioral therapy • relaxation therapy • bibliotherapy	• antidepressants
	Phobias	• exposure-based treatments including desensitization • social skills training • relaxation training	• antidepressants • benzodiazepines
Obsessive - Compulsive Disorder		• exposure and ritual prevention • rational emotive therapy	• selective serotonin reuptake inhibitors • neuroleptics • chlomipramine
Post-traumatic Stress Disorder		• exposure therapy • anxiety management training • cognitive processing therapy	• antidepressants
Schizophrenia		• behavior therapy • social learning programs • family education • social skills training • vocational rehabilitation • case management	• antipsychotics
Personality Disorders	Odd cluster	• exposure • social skills training • intimacy-focused training	• dopamine antagonists
	Dramatic cluster	• dialectical behavior therapy	
	Anxious cluster		• monoamine oxidase inhibitors

Chapter	Disorder	Psychosocial Treatments	Pharmacological or Other Treatments
Disorders of Aging	Alzheimer's	• no proven treatment	
	Depression and anxiety	• cognitive behavioral therapy • psychodynamic therapy • interpersonal therapy • education	• antidepressants • benzodiazepines

Generic and Trade Medications Mentioned in *Treating Mental Disorders: A Guide to What Works*

Generic Name	Trade Name	Generic Name	Trade Name
acamprosate	Campral	desipramine	Norpramin
alprazolam	Xanax	dexfenfluramine	Redux
amantadine	Symmetrel	dextroamphet-	Dexedrine
amitriptyline	Elavil or Endep	amine	
amoxapine	Asendin	diazepam	Valium
brofaromine	Consonar	disulfiram	Antabuse or
bromocriptine	Parlodel		Temposil
bupropion	Wellbutrin	divalproex	Depakote
buspirone	Buspar	donepezil	Aricept
carbamazepine	Tegretol	doxepin	Sinequan
chlordiazepoxide	Librium	fenfluramine	Pondimin
chlorpromazine	Thorazine	fluoxetine	Prozac
clobemide	Aurorix	fluphenazine	Prolizin
clomipramine	Anafranil	fluvoxamine	Luvox
clonazepam	Klonopin	haloperidol	Haldol
clonidine	Catapres	imipramine	Tofranil
clozapine	Clozaril	isocarboxizid	Marplan
cyproterone	Androcur	lithium	Lithonate
acetate		lorazepam	Ativan

Generic Name	Trade Name	Generic Name	Trade Name
maprotiline	Ludiomil	sentindole	Serlect
medroxyprogest-erone acetate	Depo-Provera	sertraline	Zoloft
		sildenafil	Viagra
methylphenidate	Ritalin	sodium amorbarbital	Amytal
mirtazapine	Remeron		
naltrexone	Revia	sodium pentobarbital	Nembutal
nefazodone	Serzone		
norpramine	Desipramine	tacrine	Cognex
nortriptyline	Pamelor or Aventyl	temazepam	Restoril
olanzapine	Zyprexa	thioridzine	Mellaril
papaverine	Pavabid	thiothixene	Navene
paroxetine	Paxil	tranylcypromine	Parnate
pemoline	Cylert	trazodone	Desyrel
perphenazine	Trilafon	triazolom	Halcion
phenelzine	Nardil	trifluoperazine	Stelazine
phentolomine	Regetine	trimipramine	Surmontil
physostigmine	Antilirium	venlafaxine	Effexor
pimozide	Orap	yohimbine	Yocon
quetiapine	Seroquel	zolpidem	Ambien
resperidone	Risperdol		

Trade Name	Generic Name	Trade Name	Generic Name
Ambien	zolpidem	Antilirium	physostigmine
Amytal	sodium amorbarbital	Aricept	donepezil
		Asendin	amoxapine
Anafranil	clomipramine	Ativan	lorazepam
Androcur	cyproterone acetate	Aurorix	clobemide
Antabuse	disulfiram	Aventyl	nortriptyline

Trade Name	Generic Name	Trade Name	Generic Name
Buspar	buspirone	Parnate	tranylcypromine
Campral	acamprostate	Pavabid	papaverine
Catapres	clonidine	Paxil	paroxetine
Clozaril	clozapine	Pondimin	fenfluramine
Consonar	brofaromine	Prolizin	fluphenazine
Cylert	pemoline	Prozac	fluoxetine
Depakote	divalproex	Redux	dexfenfluramine
Depo-Provera	medroxyproge sterone acetate	Regetine	phentolomine
		Remeron	mirtazapine
Desipramine	norpramine	Restoril	temazepam
Desyrel	trazodone	Revia	naltrexon
Dexedrine	dextroamphet- amine	Risperdol	resperidone
		Ritalin	methylphenidate
Effexor	venlafaxine	Serlect	sentindole
Elavil or Endep	amitriptyline	Seroquel	quetiapine
Halcion	triazolom	Serzone	nefazodone
Haldol	haloperidol	Sinequan	doxepin
Klonopin	clonazepam	Stelazine	trifluoperazine
Librium	chlordiazepoxide	Surmontil	trimipramine
Lithonate	lithium	Symmetrel	amantadine
Ludiomil	maprotiline	Tegretol	carbamazepine
Luvox	fluvoxamine	Temposil	disulfiram
Marplan	isocarboxizid	Thorazine	chlorpromazine
Mellaril	thioridzine	Tofranil	imipramine
Nardil	phenelzine	Trilafon	perphenazine
Navene	thiothixene	Valium	diazepam
Nembutal	sodium pentobarbital	Viagra	sildenafil
		Wellbutrin	buproprion
Norpramin	desipramine	Xanax	alprazolam
Orap	pimozide	Yocon	yohimbine
Pamelor	nortriptyline	Zoloft	sertraline
Parlodel	bromocriptine	Zyprexa	olanzapine

Treating Mental Disorders

Chapter 1

Childhood Disorders

Attention-Deficit Hyperactivity Disorder: More Than the Very Active Child

Ever since Billy was an infant, his parents have assumed his problem is a simple one—that he had much more energy than other children. Billy could not sit still and was always difficult to manage. Now that he's 8 years old, his parents keep hoping that this seemingly boundless amount of energy will be channeled into constructive activities such as sports or schoolwork. But Billy seems more out of control than ever. He still can't sit still, he does not pay attention to his teachers in school, and he often gets into trouble with his friends and even some adults in the neighborhood. When he attempts to do his schoolwork, it is clear that he cannot concentrate for more than a few minutes at a time so he rarely finishes an assignment. Things are even worse at home. Billy picks on his younger brother and fights, sometimes very aggressively, with his older sister. Also, he's come close to having some serious accidents and seems to act first and think later. His parents try as hard as they can to monitor Billy, but they are at the end of their rope. Fortunately, the family's pediatrician has dealt with many children like Billy who he diagnoses as having attention-deficit hyperactivity disorder. The doctor prescribes medication—Ritalin, a psychostimulant—which helps Billy concentrate and pay attention and alleviates a good deal of his restlessness. The doctor also recommends the family see a clinical child psychologist. The psychologist works with Billy's parents to teach them how to reward his good behaviors and punish the less desirable ones. In time, this combination of treatments allows Billy to better meet demands at home and at school and lets the family begin to feel normal.

Q *Who is the hyperactive child, and how often does attention-deficit hyperactivity disorder occur?*

A child who has an attention-deficit hyperactivity disorder (ADHD for short), usually is inattentive, overly active, and having a difficult time with self-control. At home and at school, such a child can't pay attention, does not follow instructions, is easily distracted, and can't control himself or herself in situations where other children can.

Some other symptoms looked for in the diagnosis of attention-deficit hyperactivity disorder include

- ignoring details
- trouble sustaining attention
- failure to follow instructions
- easily distracted
- forgetful in daily activities
- fidgety
- running and climbing when inappropriate
- always "on the go"
- difficulty waiting his or her turn
- often interrupting others

These symptoms must be present in two or more settings, such as home and school, and the individual must not suffer from any other mental disorder.

The effects of these symptoms on the child's home and school life are what make everyday functioning so difficult. Children with attention-deficit hyperactivity disorders are prone to serious accidents (as would be any child who is overly active and not paying attention). They also are more likely to have problems in their studies and with peer groups, have troubled feelings about themselves, and come from a family characterized by conflict. All of these characteristics tend to persist and are highly likely to continue through adolescence and possibly into adulthood.

About 3 to 4 percent of elementary school-aged boys and 1 to 2 percent of the same age girls are diagnosed as having an attention-deficit hyperactivity disorder. Other estimates place the percentage of children affected at 3 to 5 percent, and some estimates go as high as 10 percent. Given about 50 million elementary schoolchildren in the United States, some 1 million to 5 million children have this disorder. Most important, this diagnosis is responsible for between 30 and 50 percent of all referrals to mental health services for children.

Interestingly, the discrepancy between the number of boys (there are far more) and girls who are referred for clinical treatment is even greater than the difference in estimate of the number of children with the disorder. This situation is probably because boys who have an attention-deficit hyperactivity disorder tend also to have other disruptive behavior disorders. Also for unknown reasons, boys have this disorder more often.

Q *What are some of the possible causes for attention-deficit hyperactivity disorder, and what other behaviors often occur in these children?*

As with many psychological disorders, no single factor can be pointed to as the cause of attention-deficit hyperactivity disorder. More likely, the disorder is the result of an interaction among many factors.

Among the possible risk factors is genetic predisposition; male relatives of the attention-deficit hyperactivity disorder child tend to have been hyperactive when they were younger. Difficulties during pregnancy and immediately following birth, such as an infection during the first trimester of gestation or anoxia (or lack of oxygen) during birth, are risk factors, as is an environment that is overstimulating, especially during infancy and early toddlerhood. Parenting styles play an important role in the development of aggressive and antisocial behaviors that often accompany attention-deficit hyperactivity disorder. As a result, mental health professionals often focus on family-directed treatments to help the child and the family.

Q *I've heard the term hyperactivity used a lot. Is hyperactivity the same as attention-deficit hyperactivity disorder?*

No. The term *hyperactivity* was first used and became popular in the 1950s as shorthand for hyperkinetic impulse disorder, describing children who were very active, regardless of their level of social or cognitive skills. Thus, hyperactivity means excessive activity with no accompanying symptoms. During the 60s and 70s professionals recognized the condition they were seeing went far beyond excessive motor activity and also included cognitive and social components. At that time, the term *attention-deficit hyperactivity disorder* started being used in diagnostic settings.

Q *What are the ways that attention-deficit hyperactivity disorder can be treated?*

In general, two approaches have been used to treat attention-deficit hyperactivity disorder. The most effective way of treating attention-deficit hyperactivity disorder has been through medication, using psychostimulants. Home- and school-based interventions also have been used with some success.

Home- and school-based interventions represent two different types of programs. One, direct contingency management, uses rewards and punishments to help manage the child's inappropriate behaviors and usually takes place in a specialized treatment facility or in what's called a demonstration classroom (where a particular type of treatment is demonstrated). Clinical behavior therapy teaches parents and teachers to work with the child in his or her natural environment, such as the school or home. Both types of intervention are based on the observation that children can learn how to control impulses if the child's environment is structured to support appropriate cognitive and social behaviors.

Q How does a typical program work and how effective is direct contingency management?

Direct contingency management is based on the assumption that the impulsive and inattentive behaviors that characterize the child with an attention-deficit hyperactivity disorder are learned. Given the proper conditions and instruction, such behaviors can be replaced with more appropriate ways of functioning at home and at school, the theory goes. As a result, direct contingency management relies on a variety of systematically applied rewards and punishments in a rigorously controlled environment.

For example, a direct contingency management program might find the teacher designing a highly individualized reward program for specific behaviors along with negative consequences such as scolding, time-out, and the withdrawal of previous privileges or points for behaviors that are not acceptable. Most teachers combine the rewards and punishments, encouraging and rewarding behaviors that are appropriate and punishing behaviors that are not appropriate.

The results of direct contingency management have been impressive. In one study the rate of on-task behavior increased from 35 percent to 79 percent when the contingencies (the rewards and punishments) were strictly adhered to. Also, academic productivity has been found to improve along with behavioral changes, an important finding since poor performance in school is often closely tied to other difficulties, such as low self-esteem and unhappy social interactions.

While direct contingency management appears to be effective, it has several major drawbacks. First, once the contingencies are removed, the behaviors that were changed often return. This result is especially true when the child returns to a setting where the originally inappropriate behaviors were first encouraged or learned. Second, what we know about direct contingency management is based mostly on case studies and not the controlled types of studies that prove efficacy. So while direct contingency management may work on a case-by-case basis, there is no evidence using the standards of proof that we discussed in the Introduction that this is an effective treatment across a large portion of attention-deficit hyperactivity disorder children.

Treating Mental Disorders

Q How does a typical clinical behavior therapy program work, and how effective is it?

Clinical behavior therapy involves a highly structured curriculum for both parents and teachers. As in direct contingency management, parents and teachers both use contingencies to help manage behaviors. But, unlike direct contingency management, clinical behavior therapy takes place in a less controlled setting even though the most important managers of the child's behavior (parents and teachers) are directly included in the treatment.

A typical clinical behavior therapy program might work something like this example. Parents and teachers are trained to direct attention to the child. Next, goals for the child's behavior are defined, and information is collected as to how well the child regularly meets those goals. Of course, in the initial stages of creating a program the child would not be expected to meet the goals at all. Third, a highly individualized and well-coordinated school- and home-based behavior change program is implemented by the teacher and the parents including nonphysical means of punishment (such as time out or the withdrawal of rewards).

The program is highly systematic and individualized, to the extent that a teacher is taught to attend to the smallest detail in his or her student's classroom life, even including such concerns as seating arrangements. The collaboration between the school and the home seems to be a critical factor in the success of any clinical behavior therapy program. In some programs, a daily report card is sent home so parents can monitor school progress, and, if necessary, remedial steps can be quickly taken by the parents in coordination with the teacher.

Clinical behavior therapy is usually implemented over a period of 3 to 6 months, with parent and teacher training making up the bulk of the program. The hope is to train the parents to monitor and influence the child's behavior. Although studies of the effectiveness of clinical behavior therapy vary in the way they are conducted, they agree that this technique can be effective.

Q What are some of the limitations of clinical behavior therapy?

Clinical behavior therapy has several limitations. First, few highly controlled and well-designed studies of clinical behavior therapy have been completed, which means confidence in the studies is less than it might be. Second, the effectiveness of this treatment shows up more often in the judgments of teachers and parents than in the behavior of the child (which should be the main concern) as observed by a clinician. So while teachers and parents (who have an understandably heavy investment in the program) see improvements, the perceived change may be due to their own bias and how they are evaluating the child's behavior rather than to true change.

Finally, while the use of clinical behavior therapy can decrease the level of inappropriate behavior, the program rarely helps the child become like a child without attention-deficit hyperactivity disorder. Follow-up studies do not provide convincing information that clinical behavior therapy results in long-lasting changes. In other words, a child's behavior improves, but he or she still is more like a child with the disorder than without it.

Q Overall, how effective are behavioral or non-pharmacological treatments for attention-deficit hyperactivity disorder?

While they have shown to be helpful, in general neither direct contingency management nor clinical behavior therapy meets the criteria we use to qualify as an effective treatment for attention-deficit hyperactivity disorder. It's not that direct contingency management and clinical behavior therapy do not provide some benefits. They do, to a limited degree. It's just that the benefits have not been shown to be long lasting, and rarely are they sufficient for the child and his or her family to make any long-term progress at home or at school.

Q When were psychostimulants first used to treat the symptoms of attention-deficit hyperactivity disorder?

In 1937, doctors first recognized that certain types of amphetamines calmed children and adolescents who were institutionalized. It wasn't until the 1960s and 1970s, though, that the first controlled studies showed that stimulants had several positive effects. The studies found that these medications reduced the amount of defiant and oppositional behavior, helped manage seizures, and reduced many symptoms of attention-deficit hyperactivity disorder such as inattentiveness and fidgetiness. Since the first controlled "gold standard" studies in the mid 1960s, there has been an explosion of well-planned and controlled Type 1 studies in which the effects of psychostimulants have been systematically compared to other treatment options.

Q What are the most common drugs used to treat attention-deficit hyperactivity disorder symptoms? How are they administered?

Three drugs have been used: dextroamphetamine (Dexedrine), pemoline (Cylert), and methylphenidate (Ritalin). Each drug has received approval from the federal Food and Drug Administration and helps reduce symptoms within days of the start of a medication program. Of the three drugs, methylphenidate is the most widely used, accounting for over 85 percent of doctors' prescriptions for this disorder, even though methylphenidate has not been shown to be more effective than the other two drugs. The number of prescriptions written for methylphenidate quadrupled between 1990 and 1995 and is now upwards of 4 million per year.

These drugs are usually taken in tablet form (some are chewable), 2 to 3 times per day. Each dose lasts 2 to 7 hours depending on the drug and the individual child. The amount of medication a child receives is usually based on his or her weight. Because children are so different from one another, it can take weeks for a doctor to adjust the amount of medication for optimal effect. Some physicians, however, prescribe the amount of medication based on a child's behavior, rather than his or her weight. This method can be imprecise and certainly does not allow for the easy generalization to other children.

Q How do these stimulants work? It seems strange that stimulants can help calm a child with an attention-deficit hyperactivity disorder.

It's not exactly clear how stimulants work. One theory is that these drugs increase central nervous system activity in some parts of the brain that are responsible for inhibition. With the stimulants, children with attention-deficit hyperactivity disorder become more inhibited, and their levels of overactivity and impulsivity decline. Researchers believe this inhibitory effect of the stimulants makes the child less restless and more able to pay attention.

When a stimulant leads to calmness, the result is known as the paradoxical effect since you would expect children to become even more stimulated and active (as happens when children without the disorder or adults take stimulants).

Q How effective are stimulants over a long period?

No one knows for certain. Many studies clearly show the benefits of medication over a short period, but few have clearly tested the benefits of this treatment over a longer period such as months or years. The average study only lasts six weeks, while the average length of time for a child to receive stimulant treatment is 3 years— quite a difference. In fact, of the one hundred or so studies on the effects of psychostimulants completed during the last 10 years, only eighteen lasted 3 months or more, hardly time to reach any conclusion about long-term effectiveness and management issues.

The long-term studies that have been done suffer some major problems. The primary problem is that different studies use different diagnostic criteria and different outcome measures, making the results of the long-term studies less comparable with studies of a shorter duration.

Q If these drugs are so widely used, shouldn't we be concerned about side effects?

There clearly are potential dangers associated with using any drug, and the use of stimulants to treat attention-deficit hyperactivity disorder is no different. For the parent of a child with attention-deficit hyperactivity disorder, the important question is whether the benefits outweigh the risks. To complicate matters, it is nearly impossible to predict how an individual child will react to stimulants. Some children experience no negative side effects. Others have negative reactions and need monitoring if the treatment continues.

The most recent studies have associated the use of methylphenidate and dextroamphetamine with five distinct side effects: insomnia, decreased appetite, stomach aches, headaches, and dizziness. Pemoline has been associated with abnormal liver functioning, so a check by a physician every 3 months or so is recommended. Pemoline is more expensive than alternatives, one reason it may be the less likely used treatment choice.

There is also some speculation that the use of Ritalin (the commercial form of methylphenidate) can slow a child's growth. The only large controlled study did report a slight reduction in growth rate (or how fast the children grew), but growth resumed immediately when treatment was interrupted. The change in growth rate is probably related to the decrease in appetite. Since few well-designed studies have looked at growth, it's unclear what the long-term effects, if any, of methylphenidate might be. The general recommendation is that growth and weight be monitored. If a sharp reduction is seen, then the medication should be reduced or another type of medication should be sought out.

A more general warning about the use of drugs and the child with attention-deficit hyperactivity disorder is fitting here. Most children at one time or another are overactive, and many teachers and parents think these children are quick candidates for drug treatment. After all, it works fast and takes little effort on the parent's or teacher's part. However, since overactive children are not necessarily characterized by the set of symptoms we're referring to as attention-deficit hyperactivity disorder, great caution must be taken in prescribing medication. An experienced physician needs to be sure that the diagnosis fits the syndrome and that the correct amount of medication is reached as quickly as possible.

Q Side effects are one thing, but with such an active child and drug problems in schools, what other complications might arise in the use of stimulants to treat attention-deficit hyperactivity disorder?

There are important issues related to medication that parents and others need to keep in mind.

First, the behavioral benefits of a single dose of medication lasts only a few hours, 5 to 7 hours at most. If the drug is given in the morning, its effects may be gone by the afternoon. This fact can make management of medication very difficult in schools for everyone involved including the child, teacher, parents, and school health personnel. Second, almost 25 percent of children with attention-deficit hyperactivity disorder are not helped by the first type of stimulant they try. About 25 percent may also have side effects such as a headache or stomach ache that are sufficiently troubling as to halt treatment with the first drug tried.

Finally, even given the effectiveness of stimulants in treating attention-deficit hyperactivity disorder, it's still not clear what's best for each child. A doctor can't say which medication should be chosen or how often and at what dosage it should be given for any particular child. Although methylphenidate has been the drug of choice because it is relatively inexpensive it has not shown to be significantly more effective than pemoline or dextroamphetamine.

Q There seem to be lots of potential problems with the use of stimulants. Aren't there non-stimulant drugs that can be used to treat attention-deficit hyperactivity disorder? How effective are they?

Yes, there are alternatives. These alternatives are helpful, since using stimulants may not always be possible in the management of attention-deficit hyperactivity disorder.

Sometimes, school personnel prohibit the presence of stimulants at school because of their potential for abuse by children without the disorder, and sometimes adverse side effects rule out stimulants. Also, stimulants given late in the day to help school-age children with their homework can cause insomnia and interfere with sleep.

Some antidepressants have been considered the first alternative line of drug treatment for attention-deficit hyperactivity disorder. One such drug, bupropion (Wellbutrin) has been shown to be effective in the treatment of some of the symptoms of this disorder. A newer antidepressant, venlafaxine (Effexor) has also been used to treat attention-deficit hyperactivity disorder and studies have reported a reduction in symptoms of from 40 to 60 percent. This particular antidepressant has been well tolerated with few side effects. Buspirone (an anti-anxiety medication) has also been shown to reduce aggressive behaviors.

Q You've covered several different types of pharmacological treatment for attention-deficit hyperactivity disorder. In general, how well do they work?

The use of psychostimulant medications have become a primary method of treatment for the child with attention-deficit hyperactivity disorder. Their effectiveness has been demonstrated in more than 100 studies. In the majority of these studies, the results have shown that approximately 70 percent (and as many as 80 percent) of the children respond to treatment.

These results are especially true for the behavioral symptoms of attention-deficit hyperactivity disorder, but it is not necessarily true for outcomes related to learning and schoolwork. Even though medication has been shown to be clearly effective in the short run, psychostimulants, again, have yet to be adequately tested over a long period. Also, more research needs to be done on the effects of these drugs when other behavioral disorders occur along with attention-deficit hyperactivity disorder.

Q What about studies where medication and other treatment techniques such as direct contingency management or clinical behavior therapy are combined?

The next logical step for researchers is to see how well a combination of non-pharmacological and pharmacological treatments works.

One 2-year effort, the New York–Montreal study, looked at various combinations of medication and psychosocial treatments. One group of children received the optimal dose of methylphenidate. The second group received methylphenidate along with training programs targeted at parents and teachers, and the last group of children received methylphenidate and a program aimed at increasing the child's attention-paying skills. The findings are telling and further support the use of stimulants. The addition of a psychosocial program did not increase the effectiveness of the stimulants. In fact, when medication was discontinued on a trial basis, it had to be restarted shortly thereafter even though other treatments continued. Currently, the National Institutes of Health's Child and Adolescent Disorders Research Branch is funding a large multigroup study examining the effectiveness of combining treatments. The results will not be known for several years.

Q Can adults have ADHD?

Adults can definitely be diagnosed as having attention-deficit hyperactivity disorder. How frequently the disorder occurs among adults and when it should be treated are unclear, however. After all, the adult with attention-deficit hyperactivity disorder can more easily compensate for shortcomings than can a child. In addition, the disorder may not clearly manifest itself as it does with children and may easily go unidentified.

For example, it would be unusual to suspect that an adult with marital problems, poor anger control, and general unhappiness with work might be suffering attention-deficit hyperactivity disorder. It would be far easier to attribute such problems to social or interpersonal issues or even to an unlikable character rather than to a treatable disorder.

During the 1970s and 1980s, in an earlier version of the *Diagnostic and Statistical Manual* (the primary reference book for classifying mental disorders) there was a condition known as attention-deficit disorder, residual state (or ADD-R). This classification was intended to include patients over 18 years of age who had been diagnosed with attention-deficit hyperactivity disorder as children, were no longer physically hyperactive, but still had problems with inattentiveness and impulsivity. This classification was excluded from later versions of the *Diagnostic and Statistical Manual*, but a steady stream of publications and groups of patients and parents support the existence of the condition.

Q Do children with attention-deficit hyperactivity disorder become adults with attention-deficit hyperactivity disorder? How can ADHD adults be treated?

The best way to answer this question is to follow children who were diagnosed as attention-deficit hyperactivity disordered and then study their behavior as adults.

The use of a comparison group of adults who were ADHD as children without the disorder as adults is helpful as well. One study did this and found that adults who were attention-deficit hyperactivity disordered as children had higher rates of antisocial behavior, completed fewer years of education (perhaps because of the types of cognitive and learning problems we mentioned earlier), and had complaints of restlessness, sexual problems, and interpersonal problems.

However, other studies show only 3 to 5 percent of adults with a history of childhood attention-deficit hyperactivity disorder had any symptoms. Perhaps the most accurate conclusion we can reach is that some individuals will carry the behaviors and symptoms of childhood attention-deficit hyperactivity disorder with them into adulthood. While it's still an unanswered question, environmental factors as well as other influences probably determine the final course of childhood attention-deficit hyperactivity disorder into adulthood.

Treatment for the attention-deficit hyperactivity disorder in adulthood has focused on the use of stimulants rather than behavioral strategies. That is because the behavioral treatments are unrealistic. Given most adults' everyday responsibilities, close supervision and monitoring would be difficult, to say the least.

We know from the results of several studies that medication does tend to help control the characteristic behaviors associated with attention-deficit hyperactivity disorder in adults, but the findings are not as clear as for children. Other studies have shown no improvement in the reduction of symptoms, and some researchers attribute this finding to the low dose of stimulants used, which was often the same as that used for children.

Conduct Disorder: Beyond Misbehaving

If there was ever a time that Chris's parents needed help, it is now. He has gone from being simply mischievous and needing conscientious supervision to acting in dangerous ways, expressing physical aggression, and showing little respect for other people or their property. Just the other day, Chris's mother caught him stealing from her wallet. At his high school, Chris has been involved in similar incidents with classmates, and he has bullied his way to get what he wants. Chris has conduct disorder, which is quite different from the misbehavior we see in all children. Conduct disorder is a group of serious behavior problems that can threaten everyone that Chris comes in contact with, including his friends, his siblings, and his parents. Any type of parental discipline turns into a shouting and a pushing match, usually between Chris and his father.

Since his parents started working with a therapist, Chris's behavior has gotten somewhat better, but there is no guarantee that the treatment will continue to work. As the therapist tells them, conduct disorder is difficult to treat, and the prognosis into adulthood is often a source of concern. But his parents have learned how to communicate better with Chris and make clear what kinds of behavior are acceptable and what are not. That at least is a beginning.

Q What is a child with conduct disorder like?

The child who has a conduct disorder participates in a variety of antisocial behaviors such as fighting, lying, and stealing. While it's normal for children to lie once in a while or get into disagreements, the behavior of a child with a conduct disorder goes far beyond the realm of normal misbehavior. A child with conduct disorder seems to have no regard for other people's feelings, personal property, or safety.

A diagnosis of conduct disorder is reached if a child has repeatedly shown any three of the following symptoms during the past year, or any one during the past 6 months: bullying, fighting, using a weapon, being cruel to animals, stealing, fire-setting, breaking into others' property, running away, lying, and truancy. In a child with the disorder, these behaviors are persistent and occur with a greater intensity than is age appropriate.

Q How common is conduct disorder?

The prevalence of conduct disorder in school-aged youth is about 2 to 6 percent. As with other behavior disorders of childhood, the proportion of preadolescent boys being affected is much higher than girls—with rates that are almost 4 times as high. For adolescents, the total rate of conduct disorder is higher than for younger children, around 7 percent. At the later ages of adolescence, the disparity between the sexes seems to even out, and about as many girls as boys are diagnosed with the disorder.

Q What are some of the risk factors associated with conduct disorder?

Factors that place a child at risk for conduct disorder have been studied extensively. While none of these factors can be isolated as a single cause of conduct disorder, several acting together increase the likelihood of the disorder's occurring. Among these risk factors are a difficult personality, poor intellectual skills, large family size, birth-related complications, harsh and ineffective parenting practices, marital discord, poverty, and siblings who are antisocial. There is also some recent evidence of a relationship between conduct disorder and some abnormalities in brain chemistry affecting the transmission of nerve impulses.

To understand how children can be at risk for conduct disorder, several issues need to be considered about the complexity of the way the risk factors interact. First, risk factors such as poverty, poor parental supervision, and problems with the parents' marriage tend to be grouped together when children have the disorder. For example, a child in a large, poor family may be at risk for conduct disorder while the child from a large family that is financially secure may not be. Second, it seems that no one risk factor is necessary or sufficient for the onset of the disorder, and no one factor is more important than any of the others. Rather, it is the accumulation of factors and the fact that they interact that is important. Third, these risk factors become closely intertwined; they almost feed off of one another. For example, harsh punishment might make the already difficult child even more obstinate and reactive, leading to even harsher punishment.

It is important to reemphasize that these risk factors are not causes of the disorder, but rather, associated factors.

Q Are there other disorders that occur with conduct disorder? What are they?

Children whose behavior meets the criteria of conduct disorder probably have characteristics of other disorders as well. In particular, conduct disorder and oppositional defiant disorder (a similar type of disorder but less extreme) tend to occur in the presence of attention-deficit hyperactivity disorder. In some studies 45 to 70 percent of children with conduct disorder or attention-deficit hyperactivity disorder also meet the criteria of the other disorder.

It's not surprising to find that children with conduct disorder also have academic difficulties reflected in poor grades, being retained one or more grades in school, and being removed from school. These children also have poor interpersonal skills and are resentful and suspicious of others. Clearly, conduct disorder is pervasive in that it affects many different dimensions of the child's growth and development.

Q Are there specific characteristics of these children's families that makes them different from other families?

Several clearly defined family characteristics tend to occur more often in families of a child with conduct disorder than in other families. Two of the strongest indicators are a history of criminal behavior and alcoholism. Less frequent, but also common, characteristics are disciplinary practices that are harsh, lax, and inconsistent; less warmth and acceptance of children; lack of participation in activities as a family; and parental ignorance of their children's whereabouts. These characteristics taken as a group more typify the family with a child with a conduct disorder who is referred for treatment than those families who are not referred for treatment.

Other factors common among families with a child with conduct disorder also illustrate the complexity of the origin and the difficulty in treating this disorder. These other factors include poor housing, lack of transportation, and mental disorders, all of which place additional stress on parents (and the entire family) and make difficult children even more difficult to deal with. A child's misbehavior can be associated with a family issue, and likewise a family is often disrupted when it has a child with conduct disorder. Such interactions contribute to treatment difficulties.

Treatments are most effective when a disorder's cause is clear. In those cases, the cause can then be targeted. Unfortunately, this is not the case with conduct disorder.

Q What are the long-term effects of conduct disorder?

One reason why identifying and treating children with conduct disorder is so important is that their behaviors are often related to significantly more serious behaviors, including crime, later in life. Some studies have shown that antisocial behavior in childhood predicts multiple problems even 30 years later. However, keep in mind that not all criminals had this disorder as children, and not all children with this disorder go on to be criminals. However, research suggests that the majority of children who are antisocial will suffer a significant degree of risk for some type of problematic behavior over the course of their lives.

Q What are some ways that conduct disorder is treated?

Four basic treatments have been used over the past 20 years to treat conduct disorder. Cognitive problem-solving skills training focuses on the way children perceive and experience the world around them. Parent management training refers to a strategy where parents are trained to work with their children's behavior in the home. Functional family therapy is a series of interrelated therapies that focus on family interaction and communication patterns to help foster useful means of functioning. Multisystemic therapy focuses on all the members of the family, in the belief that the family is a system and how each family member behaves affects all family members.

Following is a closer look at each one of these treatments, including how they work and evidence of their effectiveness.

Q How does a typical cognitive problem-solving skills training program work?

Cognitive problem-solving skills training focuses on getting the child with a conduct disorder to more accurately perceive events rather than view them through a distorted lens. For example, the child with conduct disorder might perceive another child's looking at him or her as a personal threat. The child without the disorder would see that look as only a glance between children.

The different forms of cognitive problem-solving skills training share several characteristics. First, there is an emphasis on how children approach a particular situation and the thought processes they use to guide their behavior. Cognitive problem-solving skills training teaches a step-by-step approach to thinking through such experiences. Second, an emphasis is placed on developing the particular types of behaviors that fit the situation. Acceptable behaviors are focused on and inappropriate behaviors are not. Third, the treatment includes highly structured activities that include games, academic activities, and tasks. For example, the course of therapy progresses from simple games up through the application of the same skills in real world settings. Fourth, the therapist plays an active role in the treatment of the child with conduct disorder. Finally, treatment includes using various techniques such as role-playing and reinforcement to encourage the child to react more appropriately to everyday events in the child's world.

How effective is cognitive problem-solving skills training?

Cognitively based treatments such as cognitive problem-solving skills training are successful. The results of highly controlled studies have shown that this type of treatment reduces the amount of aggressive and antisocial behavior at home, at school, and in the community. Even more impressive is the finding that these gains have continued for up to a year following treatment.

There's hope for even more effective cognitive treatments since basic research in developmental psychology continues to add knowledge to our understanding of how cognitive processes are related to behavior. If researchers can better understand what exactly is distorted in the child's perception, cognitive treatments may become more finely tuned and targeted. An advantage of cognitive therapies is that many versions are available in specially prepared manuals. In this format, information is easily accessible and easily shared with others.

How does parent management training work?

Parent management training focuses on teaching parents how to change their child's behavior. The parents meet regularly with the therapist or the trainer. The goal is to train the parents to interact with a child in ways that promote appropriate social behaviors and decrease inappropriate or deviant ones. The rationale behind this approach is that the home is where behaviors are most often encouraged and sustained. Likewise, the home is where change can also most easily occur.

Parents are taught a variety of parenting skills such as establishing rules for the child to follow, how to use positive reinforcement to encourage appropriate or prosocial behaviors, mildly punishing those behaviors that are not acceptable, and negotiating compromises. Developing such parenting skills is a challenge for any parent, but especially for the parent with a difficult child. Having a well-structured and clearly defined treatment program helps set guidelines that are enforceable.

Don't think, however, that just because parent management training focuses on the parent, that the parent is solely responsible for the quality of the interaction between the child and the parent. Parent-child relationships go both ways, and the expression of behavior disorders such as conduct disorder often reflect that.

For example, the child's stealing could be aimed at getting the attention he needs from his parents, and the stealing might be encouraged by that attention (be it positive or negative). Also, several studies have focused on how parents interact with children who have a conduct disorder. Here, deviant behavior on the part of one person (such as the child who is lying) is rewarded by the parent, and the behavior just continues. Parent management training attempts to break that pattern by training parents how to break the cycle of a coercive interaction.

Q How effective is parent management training?

Parent management training is one of the most promising treatments for conduct disorder. A large number of well-controlled studies over the past 25 years have shown that the training works and works well. The treatment seems to affect behaviors in several settings such as the home and school, and follow-up studies show that the gains in good behavior can last 1 to 3 years.

Also, the impact of parent management training appears to be very broad. Behaviors that are associated with conduct disorder but that are not the direct targets of the treatment also are positively affected. For example, mothers experiencing depression often improve once the family has been exposed to parent management training. The siblings of children who have been referred for treatment also improve, even though they are not the direct focus of the program. That outcome is especially important since siblings of conduct-disordered children are also at risk for antisocial behavior. Both the effects on depressed mothers and siblings suggest that parent management training is far-reaching.

Effective programs need to be of long enough duration (about 50 to 60 hours) to teach all the necessary skills and give the parents time to practice. Parents need to learn specific skills including how to change behavior, and the therapist or trainer needs to be experienced in this type of work.

Treating Mental Disorders

Q *How does functional family therapy work?*

Functional family therapy is an integrated approach to dealing with conduct disorders. It looks at conduct disorder from the viewpoint that the inappropriate behaviors serve a particular function for the child within his or her family. In other words, the child gets what he or she wants by acting that way. For example, a child's aggressive behavior is how particular interpersonal needs (such as attention and intimacy) are met.

The underlying rationale of functional family therapy is an emphasis on family systems, where the behavior of any one member in the family affects all the other members. Thus, the therapist tries to point out to family members how their behaviors are clearly interrelated with those of other family members on a day-to-day basis. With this in mind, the main goals of a functional family therapy program are to increase positive reinforcement among family members in their dealings with each other, to establish clear communications so every family member understands what is being said, to specify behaviors that family members want from one another, to negotiate in a fair and constructive manner, and to work as a group on solutions to family problems.

Q *How effective is functional family therapy?*

There have been relatively few well-controlled studies of the effectiveness of functional family therapy in dealing with conduct disorders. The results of these few studies, however, showed that functional family therapy led to greater changes than other treatment programs such as traditional family therapy. Moreover, gains lasting up to $2^1/2$ years after treatment have been evident.

Q *How does multisystemic therapy work?*

One element of functional family therapy is the idea that the family operates as a system. Multisystemic therapy capitalizes on this idea and sees the child with a conduct disorder as a person who behaves within several different systems. To be effective, any therapeutic approach has to address all these systems. Multisystemic therapy is a family-based treatment approach. This therapy conceives conduct disorder as a problem involving several different domains of poor functioning including the individual, his or her family, and factors outside the immediate family such as other relatives, the neighborhood, and school. Each of these systems needs to be included in the therapy, hence the multisystemic nature of the therapy.

Different therapeutic techniques (such as role-playing) are used to identify problems, increase communication among family members, build cohesion, and change the unproductive ways in which family members interact. While multisystemic therapy draws on many of the ideas already discussed, it is not just a combination of the other therapeutic approaches. Multisystemic therapy is different because of the way the family is treated as a whole—one functioning unit—without focusing on any one individual's behavior during treatment.

Q How effective is multisystemic therapy?

Multisystemic therapy reduces antisocial and aggressive behaviors in groups of youths, while quality of family functioning increases and emotional and behavior problems decrease. That all-important criterion of how long the results last also seems to support multisystemic therapy. Youths from families treated using this type of therapy have lower arrest rates during adolescence. Parents and children also have fewer conflicts, a definite plus during adolescence when parents and children are always testing each other's limits.

Q Has anyone tried to combine different treatments for conduct disorder?

Combined treatments have not been studied sufficiently. Given the available information we have about individual treatments, it is unclear that combining them would have any significant effect. With so little known about the individual approaches, explanations about why (or whether) a combination of them works would be a guessing game. For example, if there is an effect, how would one know what aspect of the combined treatment was responsible?

Q What about medication for conduct disorder?

As far as pharmacological treatment, no strong evidence exists for its effectiveness regarding children with conduct disorder, although studies are ongoing and some initial results are promising.

Q So, what in general can you tell me about the success of treating conduct disorder in children?

All treatments for conduct disorder that we have discussed have significant promise. An absence of sufficient empirical data about them, however, makes it difficult to decide which treatment works best for which child and his or her family. You remember how we stressed the importance of such information in the Introduction. Hence, there is still considerable trial and error in picking a treatment for a child with conduct disorder.

Q Where Can I Find More Information About Childhood Disorders?

Books

All About Attention Deficit Disorder by Thomas W. Phelan. Child Management, 1996. ISBN 1889140007.
   Provides parents, teachers, pediatricians, and mental health professionals the facts and resources they need to deal effectively with attention-deficit disorder, a mental disorder like attention-deficit hyperactivity disorder.

ADHD and Teens: A Parent's Guide to Making It Through the Tough Years by Colleen Alexander-Roberts. Taylor Publishing, 1995. ISBN 0878338993.
   Practical advice to help parents deal with their teens and the challenges presented by attention-deficit hyperactivity disorder. Teens with attention-deficit hyperactivity disorder have an extremely high risk of unproductive outcomes including failing in school and breaking the law.

Attention Deficit Disorder in Adults by Lynn Weiss. Taylor Publishing, 1997. ISBN 0878339809.
   An updated volume, based on the original bestseller, containing all the original information (such as how to identify attention-deficit disorder, ways to master distraction, attention-deficit disorder's impact on the family) and the newest treatments available.

Treating the Unmanageable Adolescent: A Guide to Oppositional Defiant and Conduct Disorders by Neil I. Bernstein. Jason Aronson, 1997. ISBN 1568216300.
   An informative and helpful book based on chapter headings such as Understanding the Disruptive Behavior Disorders, Creating a Climate for Change: Diffusing Resistance, The Road to Self-Control, and Building Self-Esteem.

Conduct Disorder & Underachievement: Risk Factors, Assessment, Treatment, & Prevention by Harvey P. Mandel. John Wiley & Sons, 1997. ISBN 0471131474.

Explores the causes, assessment, treatment, and prevention of disruptive behavioral problems in underachieving children and adolescents, focusing on the relationship between poor grades and antisocial behavior.

Internet Sites

The National Attention Deficit Disorder Association
(at http://www.add.org/) "is an organization built around the needs of adults and young adults with ADD and ADHD. We seek to serve individuals with ADD, as well as those who love, live with, teach, counsel, and treat those who do."

Your Health Reference Center
(at http://yourhealth.com) provides general information about attention-deficit hyperactivity disorder children, signs and symptoms, and general guidelines about treatment and care.

The Research and Training Center on Family Support and Children's Mental Health at Portland State University
(at http://www.rtc.pdx.edu/resource/conduct.htm) offers a listing of resources about conduct disorder including a discussion of diagnosis and treatment and a listing of resources.

The School of Education at the University of Virginia
(at http://teis.virginia.edu/go/cise/ose/categories/add.html) lists hundreds of topics about attention-deficit hyperactivity disorder ranging from hyperactivity in adolescent African-American males to symptom checklists for children and adults.

The ADD/LD Resource Center
(at http://www4.interaccess.com/add) is an on-line guide to resources dealing with several different problems children have including attention-deficit hyperactivity disorder. It's sponsored by The Institute for ADD & Learning.

Where to Write

Learning Disabilities Association of America
4156 Library Road
Pittsburgh, PA 15234
412-341-1515

AACAP
3615 Wisconsin Avenue, N.W.
Washington, DC 20016
202-966-7300

Chapter 2

Eating Disorders

Anorexia Nervosa:
When Too Thin Is Not Really In

Nineteen-year-old Cindy is an attractive young woman who has had an uneventful childhood. She comes from a family with two other children. Upon graduation from high school she enters basic training in the Army with the hope of learning a skill she can apply once her enlistment is finished. College is not an option for Cindy since it is unaffordable, or at least her parents are not interested in paying for it or lending her the money. The weekend after she finishes her first 8-week course in telecommunications, her parents get a telephone call. A doctor at the Army base tells them that Cindy has an eating disorder called anorexia nervosa and that she is seriously ill. With the encouragement of relatives and the help of close friends, Cindy rallies and improves, but the eating disorder is still there. She is receiving help through individual therapy and seems to be making progress as judged by her slowly, but surely, increasing appetite and modest, but consistent, weight gain. Getting treatment fast and her relative youth have helped a great deal. She's beginning to think of her body and herself as more satisfactory. She knows, however, that she has a long way to go before food assumes an appropriate role in her life.

Q What is anorexia nervosa, and what are some of its symptoms?

Anorexia nervosa (or anorexia) is one of several eating disorders. It is characterized by such a severe reduction in food intake that the health and even the life of the person with the disorder is seriously threatened. Anorexia is by no means just a serious effort at dieting. Rather, the anorexic individual might eat a piece of fruit and a roll and call it a day's worth of calories. Anorexia can be an extraordinarily dangerous disorder with mortality rates between 10 and 15 percent.

Here are some characteristics of the person with anorexia, a disorder that primarily affects young females.

- Body weight that is at least 15 percent below the normal range expected in the absence of any physical illness that would explain such a low weight.
- Amenorrhea, or absent menstrual periods for females. The usual criterion used by mental health professionals as part of a diagnosis of anorexia is that three periods in a row have been missed.
- A distorted body view, such that the person with anorexia is always afraid of getting fat and always feels fat, regardless of her appearance or weight.
- Feelings of low self-esteem and feelings of low self-worth.
- A reduction in the amount of food eaten and denial of any feelings of hunger.
- Use of laxatives and diuretics, and excessive exercise.

Q I've heard that anorexia is a disorder that affects only women. Is this true?

For unknown reasons, anorexia almost exclusively strikes young women between adolescence and early adulthood and is rare in middle-aged adults of both sexes. Most cases of anorexia appear between 12 and 18 years of age.

About two in 1,000 women will have the disorder sometime in their lives, and about one-tenth that number of men (two in 10,000) are affected. The number of men is so small that men have rarely been used as subjects in research studies. Consequently, little is known about the disorder in men. The symptoms of the disorder in both men and women tend to be same.

Q What are some of the causes of anorexia?

No one really knows the cause of anorexia, in part because there has been little research into the factors that contribute to the disorder. However, several different predisposing factors increase the chances of developing the disorder.

These factors are low self-esteem (being uncomfortable with the impression one thinks others have of her), a need to maintain control over her life and her body (fueled by a feeling of powerlessness and being controlled by others such as an overly harsh parent), perfectionism (a need for everything to be perfect and taking measures to make it so when it is not), a fear of maturing (especially during adolescence when so many emotional and physical changes are occurring), and an obsession with weight.

Researchers speculate that an important contributing factor to the disorder is the social pressure young women experience when extreme body shapes and images are rewarded. A 1984 Glamour magazine article (of questionable scientific value, but interesting nonetheless) asked readers, "What would make you happiest?" Forty-two percent of the respondents, mostly women, placed weight loss at the top of their list. Even a cursory inspection of supermodels in the hottest fashion magazines reveal an emphasis on unhealthy and unnatural thinness. If thin is in, then really thin must be better, and it's not hard to imagine impressionable, young teenagers taking too seriously the value of losing weight and being thin. It wasn't too long ago when the emaciated look of "heroin chic" was the preferred image among fashion designers and models.

As readers of the local newspaper or fans of prime time television can attest, this "thin thing" always accompanies the promise of wealth, happiness, and success in thousands of commercial messages. Be thin and succeed. Be other than thin (fat or even normal), and you lose out. For some women, the social cost of even the perception of being overweight (regardless of whether they really are) is too much of a burden to bear.

There are other explanations for anorexia, such as food being a substitute for sex or a possible chemical imbalance in the brain, but little research supports either of these explanations.

Q What effects does anorexia have?

The most serious concerns of anorexia revolve around the physical health of the person with the disorder. Starvation, which is the most direct result of anorexia, is accompanied by several physical symptoms, some of them life threatening.

One of the most common physical effects of anorexia is an imbalance in the electrolytes needed by the nervous system to keep nerves and muscles functioning properly. Balanced levels of electrolytes such as sodium and potassium are essential for health and are affected first when the human body is starved.

Abnormally low heart rate and low blood pressure are often associated with anorexia, although not necessarily life threatening. However, irregular rhythms of the heart, also a potential consequence, are serious and often accompany the reduced work capacity the heart experiences when the body is starved of nutrients.

Some people with the disorder use laxatives or diuretics to lose the weight that is stored in the body as water. As the body responds to this loss, it works to retain water—hence the swelling known as edema.

Q Why is there such a big difference in the number of men and women who have the disorder?

No one knows why there is such a discrepancy, but it is thought to have to do with the types of social pressures we've discussed. In our culture, the most widely pictured female models are often very thin while the typical male models are muscular—a very different emphasis and influence for the impressionable young man or woman.

Q What approaches have been taken to treat anorexia?

Few systematic studies of treating anorexia have been completed under the controlled conditions necessary to reach a useful conclusion. Consequently, little information is available as to what treatments work best and which do not work. Several studies, however, examined the effectiveness of various treatments and how long the effects lasted.

The St. George's (London) study examined the effectiveness of three different treatment conditions. One group received inpatient and outpatient therapy consisting of weight restoration, dietary counseling, individual and family therapy, and even occupational therapy. A second group received outpatient individual and family psychotherapy, and the third group underwent only outpatient group psychotherapy. There was also a control group whose members did not receive any treatment.

The results? All three treatment groups benefited from their respective treatments. Average weight gains (the most important criterion for success in such studies) were higher among those who completed the treatment. Other important measures of success, such as level of sexual adjustment and social functioning, improved as well. Another really important outcome from this study was that the participants in the outpatient treatments (the second and third groups) showed as much improvement as did the patients who participated as inpatients. In addition, a follow-up study at 1 year showed that a significant portion of outpatients continued to maintain the weight they gained as a result of treatment.

The second set of studies was done in London at Maudsley Hospital.

In one of those studies, researchers examined the role the family might have in the treatment of anorexia. In this study, family therapy was compared with individual therapy. At the end of 1 year, family therapy was found to be the most effective treatment for the youngest patients and those who had the disorder for less than 3 years. For patients who were older or who had the disorder for a longer time, both treatments had poor outcomes. The younger the individual at the age of onset and the sooner the treatment begins, the better the expected outcomes of any treatment can be.

The other Maudsley study examined the value of outpatient treatment for older people with anorexia. This group of patients, ranging in age from 18 to 39 years (remember, for the vast majority of patients, the disorder begins in late adolescence) had a poor prognosis since the onset of the disorder was so late. One group received what was called educational behavioral treatment. Patients in this group monitored their daily eating behaviors, set weight goals, and discussed weight and body shape issues. The second treatment group underwent cognitive analytical therapy, which focuses on interpersonal issues. In both treatment groups, weight gains were within 15 percent of the targeted body weight set by the study's standards.

One serious limitation of the Maudsley studies was the lack of any non-treated control group. The lack of a control group makes it very difficult to attribute change to the treatment rather than some other related factor, such as the increased attention given to the patients in the treatment condition by the researchers.

One major outpatient study conducted in the United States compared the effectiveness of family therapy (called behavioral family systems therapy) and individual therapy (called ego-oriented individual therapy) in a group of girls who had developed anorexia during the previous 12 months. Behavioral family systems therapy includes parental control over eating, problem solving, and communications. Ego-oriented individual therapy encourages the development of insight and autonomy; parents, as well as patients, meet separately with therapists on a regular basis.

Both behavioral family systems therapy and ego-oriented individual therapy resulted in increases in body mass, which is a weight-to-height ratio used as a measure of change in studies of eating disorders. The behavioral treatment was more effective after 1 year had passed, and both treatment approaches produced significant reductions in negative communications and conflict between parents and children. Given that conditions of family conflict have been associated with the development of anorexia, this is good news and a potentially fruitful direction for future research.

Q What pharmacological treatments have been used in the treatment of anorexia?

Antipsychotic and antidepressant drugs have been used to treat anorexia, but studies consistently fail to show that medication works for anorexia. In one study, the use of fluoxetine (Prozac) resulted in significant weight gain and a reduction in depression and anxiety. This latter outcome should come as no surprise since fluoxetine has received enormous publicity as a treatment for depression. Less depressed people lead healthier lives in general and may be less prone to eating disorders.

Q In general, what would you recommend as the best treatment for anorexia?

Although there is not the body of well-controlled studies we would like, the results from the best conducted studies (of which there are few) provide some direction for making decisions.

First, outpatient treatment can be as effective as inpatient treatment. This is to the patient's advantage for several reasons. Treatment costs are greatly reduced, and the home generally provides a more friendly and accommodating setting than a hospital. Of course, if weight is dangerously low, hospitalization is required.

Second, while family members are important in the treatment process, they are not necessary for treatment to be effective. In other words, treating only the patient can be as effective as if she were treated as part of a more ambitious family-centered program.

Third, those cases with an early onset and relatively short duration have the best prognosis for treatment.

In sum, anorexia appears relatively infrequently, and there is not a lot of scientific knowledge about its causes or effective treatments. The informed consumer should be aware that any treatment program probably is not based on extensive clinical trials or the use of a control group. Trials and control groups are essential to prove any treatment that would be endorsed by most mental health professionals. We don't know much about this mental illness, but it is a serious condition that requires medical care.

Bulimia Nervosa: An Unending Cycle

Jill can't remember the last time a meal was just a normal part of her day. From outward appearances, she is a healthy, happy adolescent ready to start her last year of high school. That is what Jill wants her friends and family to believe. But, she actually suffers from bulimia nervosa, an eating disorder that is characterized by cycles of excessive eating and then forced vomiting. Even though she wants to stop, the cycle just perpetuates itself—one episode of overeating leading to another of self-induced vomiting, and then starts over again.

Once she started down this path, it did not take Jill long to learn how to excuse herself from the dinner table or even during a date to visit the bathroom, vomit what she had just eaten, and return as if nothing has happened. Jill was successful at hiding the disorder from others, but now she has developed symptoms that cannot be ignored. She needs immediate attention.

Q What is bulimia, and how does it differ from anorexia?

Anorexia and bulimia are both classified as eating disorders and have several things in common. They are both disorders that affect primarily young women. They both occur in about the same ratio of young women to young men (about ten to one). They are also both disorders that focus on issues of control and on an unhealthy relationship with food and what it represents. The four defining behaviors of bulimia are binge eating, purging, dietary restraint (or being very particular about what's eaten), and abnormal attitudes about body shape and weight.

The primary difference between the two disorders is that the bulimic individual is characterized by periods of uncontrolled binging where she eats as much food as possible at one sitting. This overeating is then followed by purging—self-induced vomiting or the use of laxatives or diuretics—to lose whatever weight would have been gained by the eating.

The practice repeats itself, not necessarily at every meal but often enough (at least twice a week) that binging and purging become a way of life. The percentage of young women with symptoms of bulimia is thought to be about 1 or 2 percent, almost 10 times the rate for anorexia, which might account for why this eating disorder has received more attention than anorexia in the scientific literature. Bulimia can also occur in middle-aged women.

This cycle of binging and purging usually results in no net weight gain, and the frequent weight fluctuations that accompany anorexia are not present. The lack of self-worth and constant need to evaluate body shape and image seem to be paramount issues facing the individual with bulimia.

Q There is a distinct set of symptoms that accompanies an eating disorder like anorexia. Are the symptoms similar to bulimia?

The symptoms that accompany bulimia are quite different from those that accompany anorexia, primarily because starvation is not present in bulimia, and the effects of purging (in the form of vomiting) and binge eating result in a different set of outcomes.

Here are some of the characteristics of the person with bulimia.

- Evidence that binge eating is taking place. Sometimes this pattern is observed directly, and sometimes the evidence is secondhand, as when large quantities of food are missing or stolen.
- Serious dental problems that result from frequent contact between dental enamel and highly acidic vomit. Also present for the same reason (the acidic vomit) are sore throat, mouth sores, and even irritation and tearing of the esophagus. Incidentally, frequent tooth brushing does not help once the dental problem starts.
- Evidence of vomiting or the use of laxatives or diuretics to lose whatever weight was gained.

As with anorexia, electrolyte imbalances and edema are common. Bulimia is also often accompanied by gastrointestinal problems such as abdominal distress, gas, and constipation. In some cases, the over-the-counter drug ipecac (used to induce vomiting in children who swallow poison) is used. This is a dangerous practice, since ipecac is a muscle poison which accumulates in the body and can lead to permanent damage to such vital organs as the heart.

Q What is the primary goal of treating bulimia?

The primary goal of treating bulimia is to establish a healthy eating pattern. This is done by removing both the overeating and the starving which forms the cycle of binging and purging. Once the overeating is dealt with successfully the cycle can be broken, and a more moderate approach toward food and eating can be established.

Q There's not a lot of information from good studies about the treatment of anorexia. Is this also the case with bulimia?

No. Several different types of treatments have been tested, and many studies of these treatments' effectiveness are of a high enough quality to produce trustworthy information. What appears to be most effective treatments are antidepressant drugs and a psychological therapy called cognitive-behavioral therapy.

Q What are some of the drugs that have been used in the treatment of bulimia, and how effective are they?

A number of different drugs have been used to treat bulimia, including appetite suppressants and antidepressants.

The use of an appetite suppressant makes perfect sense since excessive eating starts the cycle of binging and purging. If appetite can be dampened or moderated, overeating can be controlled. One appetite suppressant that has been investigated, but has been withdrawn from the market, is fenfluramine (Pondomin); sometimes taken in combination with phentermine in the combination popularly known as "fen-phen". However, recognition that these two drugs in combination may produce heart valve damage after prolonged use led to its withdrawal from the market. In one study, fenfluramine was found to reduce binge eating and vomiting but not to change the patient's attitude toward her shape and weight. Since a significant component of any eating disorder is the distorted body view the individual has, any treatment would ideally address such outcomes as self-worth and body image.

Antidepressants have been intensely studied and are the most commonly used type of drug to treat bulimia. The drugs that have been used include tricyclic antidepressants, monoamine oxidase inhibitors, selective serotonin reuptake inhibitors, and atypical antidepressants. Depression tends to appear in many people who suffer from eating disorders, so the availability of data concerning the effects of antidepressants on people who have bulimia and may also be depressed is easy to come by. The problem, of course, is how to separate the effects of the antidepressants on depression from the medication's effects on the eating disorder.

The best way to assess antidepressants' effectiveness in treating bulimia is to summarize the results of fourteen major studies conducted over the past 20 years. In these fourteen studies, twelve showed that antidepressant drugs worked better than a control or placebo treatment. This evidence clearly indicates the effectiveness of these medications. Since the same type of antidepressant was not used across the twelve studies, we can also conclude that different types of antidepressants appear to be effective although selective seritonin reuptake inhibitors are most commonly prescribed and one of them, fluoxetine (Prozac), has Food & Drug Administration approval for the specific treatment of bulimia. So if a patient, for whatever reason, does not respond to one class of antidepressants or can't tolerate a particular drug, another might be effective and tolerable.

Now to the interesting new directions. First, it's unclear how much antidepressant produces an effect on the symptoms of bulimia, or what is called the dose response factor. While some people might need very little medication to effect change, others may need more. The questions of how much medication should be prescribed and why (such as weight or severity of symptoms) have gone unstudied. Because the answers are unclear, the slightest bit more medication might be the turning point for a particular patient. Given the current knowledge, dosage seems to be idiosyncratic to the prescribing physician and patient.

Second, the long-term effects of using antidepressants in general have not been studied, nor have the side effects. And, finally, while there is plenty of speculation, it is unclear as to how these chemicals work to change the focus of control away from food. Even if a treatment works, knowing why is crucial, since it enables researchers and practitioners to consider the application of the treatment to other cases as well as other disorders.

Q OK, so antidepressants reduce overeating. What other forms of treatment have been used?

Cognitive-behavioral therapy is one of several types of psychological therapy used to treat bulimia. Cognitive-behavioral therapy emphasizes the critical role of how the individual thinks of herself in terms of body shape and body image. Cognitive-behavioral therapy also emphasizes how adaptive and healthy eating practices can replace unhealthy eating patterns.

It's fairly easy to understand how both the cognitive (or thinking) component and the behavioral (or learning) component of cognitive-behavioral therapy can be involved in the treatment of bulimia. It has long been known that people with bulimia have distorted perceptions of their appearance. Hence, the bulimic woman looks at herself in a mirror and sees someone who needs to lose weight. The cognitive interventions that accompany cognitive-behavioral therapy attempt to change those perceptions. Dysfunctional eating habits are behaviors that can be changed; healthy practices are taught and encouraged.

Q What are some of the important elements of cognitive-behavioral therapy?

The general model upon which cognitive-behavioral therapy is based places primary importance on the extreme personal value that is attached to an idealized (and often unrealistic) body shape and body weight. This distorted value usually results in a loss of control over eating, which in turn leads to the binge and purge cycle that characterizes the disorder.

There are many different types of cognitive-behavioral therapy that include some or all of the following elements. Reviewing these elements, which include many different aspects of everyday life, will give you some idea of how comprehensive the cognitive-behavioral therapy model is. This list of items in a cognitive-behavioral therapy program should also give you an idea of what to look for in such a program.

- The development of a trusting relationship with a therapist.
- The ability of the patient to self-monitor her behavior and to be aware of cues that might be associated with binge eating or purging.
- The development of patient awareness about cognitive-behavioral therapy, how it works, and the importance of change on both cognitive and behavioral levels.
- Regular weekly weighings so that progress can be directly observed and recorded.
- Information about how body weight can be regulated, the potentially adverse effects of dieting, and the medical and social consequences of purging.
- A well-designed program that includes a definite and regular pattern of eating, such as three meals a day.
- Strategies for self-control.
- Problem-solving techniques.
- Modification of unhealthy or inconsistent eating.
- Cognitive understanding and restructuring (creating new ways of thinking) of food and food-related experiences (such as Sunday dinner with family).

- Exposure methods where the patient becomes more comfortable with her weight and also the image she presents to others.
- Training to prevent any relapse of the symptoms.

Q How effective is cognitive-behavioral therapy?

Studies that have examined the effectiveness of treating bulimia with cognitive-behavioral therapy have shown it to be very effective. For example, a summary of ten studies showed a 79 percent reduction in purging with 57 percent of the patients showing signs of remission. A group of nine other studies showed a reduction in purging of close to 85 percent. With few qualifications, it seems that cognitive-behavioral therapy can be a successfully applied treatment.

In addition, a great deal of progress has been made in producing manuals to use as guides to administering cognitive-behavioral therapy. This means that a standardized treatment program is available. A trained mental health professional with the proper materials can successfully administer the program. Even effective self-help materials are available.

Q So, both medication and cognitive-behavioral therapy seem to work. Which is better?

The best way to compare alternative therapies is by examining each one within the same study. Here, we are interested in whether medication or cognitive-behavioral therapy (or a combination of the two) is more effective as a treatment for bulimia. We can turn to the results from a group of six studies to address the question.

First and most important, medication does work, but the outcomes of cognitive-behavioral therapy are superior. Long-term treatment outcomes also are better when cognitive-behavioral therapy is used alone compared with medication alone.

But what about their combined use? Adding medication to cognitive-behavioral therapy does make a significant difference. Cognitive-behavioral therapy works but the combination of both therapy and medication is superior to either alone.

Q What other psychological approaches have been used to treat bulimia?

Several different psychological techniques have been applied to the treatment of bulimia, among them supportive-expressive therapy, focal interpersonal therapy, self-help, and various other behavioral treatments.

In general, cognitive-behavioral therapy is superior to any one of these in treating the four specific features of bulimia—binge eating, purging, dietary restraint, and abnormal attitudes about body shape and weight. Some elements of the behavioral therapies worked equally well as elements of cognitive-behavioral therapy, but on the whole cognitive-behavioral therapy seems to be more effective.

Q Are there other eating disorders that we should know about?

The one other eating disorder commonly seen by mental health professionals is binge eating. This disorder is characterized by recurrent episodes of excessive eating without any excessive methods of weight control. There's no purging, over-exercising, or rigid dieting. You won't be surprised to learn that many people with binge eating are overweight, some so seriously that they are obese.

Q How does binge eating differ from bulimia?

Binge eating and bulimia have excessive eating in common. And like bulimia, binge eating is accompanied by concerns about shape and weight.

However, in the case of binge eating these concerns may be more understandable since the shape and weight of the individual with the binge eating disorder may indeed be something to be concerned about. Binge eating also tends to affect older individuals than does bulimia, with many patients in their forties. Finally, cases of males with binge eating disorder are not uncommon.

Q What treatments have been tried for binge eating, and how effective are they?

It is only reasonable that appetite suppressants should be tried as a treatment for binge eating, given that overeating is the most obvious symptom. The result of the one well-controlled study showed that the use of dexfenfluramine (known as Redux), was significantly more effective than the use of a placebo in reducing binge eating. No long-term follow-up has been conducted to see how effective this treatment is over time, a necessary feature of any successful treatment program.

Antidepressants have also been used as a treatment for binge eating. These drugs offer short-term effectiveness. With reductions in binge eating of up to 63 percent, considerably larger reductions than among the group that received a placebo, selective serotonin reuptake inhibitors such as fluoxetine (Prozac) have been used with some measure of success.

When discussing the effectiveness of medication for treating binge eating, there's one important caveat. In several studies (and keep in mind that not many have been done in the first place), the group that received a placebo improved to the same extent as the group that received the active medication.

Q *If cognitive-behavioral treatment works so well for bulimia, why shouldn't it work effectively well for binge eating?*

It does, and four controlled studies have been conducted that confirm its effectiveness. Some of these studies include other treatments such as exercise programs, but the reduction in binge eating can be dramatic, up to 94 percent. Also, special forms of cognitive-behavioral treatment—not the full-blown program but a self-managed alternative—have been shown to be effective as well, allowing for greater distribution of materials and assistance at a reduced cost.

Finally, behavioral weight control treatment shows the most promise for binge eating. Not only is it associated with a marked reduction in the frequency of binge eating, but weight loss may occur as well, at least in the short term.

Q *Where Can I Find More Information About Eating Disorders?*

Books

Bulimia: A Guide for Family and Friends by Roberta Trattner Sherman and Ron A. Thompson. Jossey-Bass, 1997. ISBN 0787903612.

Provides extensive information about bulimia both for the people who suffer this disorder and for those who care for them.

The Secret Language of Eating Disorders: The Revolutionary New Approach to Curing Anorexia and Bulimia by Peggy Claude-Pierre. Times Books, 1997. ISBN 0812928423.

Details of Claude-Pierre's program for eating disorders. This book describes a five-stage plan of treatment and offers patients' success stories.

The Deadly Diet: Recovering from Anorexia and Bulimia by Terence J. Sandbek. New Harbinger Publications, 1993. ISBN 1879237423.

Describes a step-by-step program for changing eating habits using a self-help approach.

Internet Sites

The Eating Disorders - Diagnosis and Treatment Web Site
(at http://home.planetinternet.be/~elombaer/ased/dia.htm#bulimia) is part of http://home.planetinternet.be/~elombaer/ased/index.html, a large support group for eating disorders. You can find information about different types of disorders, books available, and the location of organizations throughout the world. The eating disorders page also has instructions for computing a body mass index, a criterion often used to assess changes in body weight.

AABA - American Anorexia/Bulimia Association
(at http://www.social.com/health/nhic/data/hr0100/hr0123.html) has extensive educational and referral materials available.

Cath's Links to Eating Disorders on the Internet
(at http://www.stud.unit.no/studorg/ikstrh/ed/) offers extensive listings of resources including articles, books, support and discussion groups, and more.

Males & Eating Disorders
(at http://www.primenet.com/~danslos/males.html) contains information exclusively about the boys or men who have eating disorders. This site includes a large number of links to other resources, personal stories, and general information.

Several list servers are available such as listserv@maelstrom.stjohns.edu (find out about them at http://www.hiwaay.net/recovery/), the OASIS discussion group (find out about them at http://www.hiwaay.net/recovery/#OASIS), and the Eating Disorders Discussion Board (at http://www.eating-disorders.com/chatfrm.htm).

Where to Write

National Association of Anorexia Nervosa and Associated Disorders (ANAD)
P.O. Box 7
Highland Park, IL 60035
847-831-3438

National Eating Disorders Organization
6655 South Yale Ave.
Tulsa, OK 74136
918-481-4044 or 918-481-4076

Anorexia Nervosa and Related Eating Disorders, Inc.
P.O. 5102
Eugene, OR 97405
541-344-1144

Chapter 3

Sleep Disorders

Insomnia: Tossing and Turning

This is not the first and probably will not be the last time that Jeff will get up in the middle of the night, unable to fall back asleep. It is 4 A.M., and all he can think about is finishing that important report. He worries that he will nod off tomorrow afternoon with his head on his desk. It is just too hard to put in a full day's work on only four or five hours' sleep. More often than ever, Jeff has been having a tough time getting to sleep. He used to sleep like a baby; nothing could awaken him except the alarm. As he's gotten older, he has begun to have a more difficult time falling asleep and staying asleep.

A visit to the doctor is helpful, and Jeff is fortunate that his primary care physician has some knowledge of sleep disorders. After a few weeks of recording his sleep activities (when he goes to bed, when he gets up, and how well he sleeps), Jeff and his doctor arrange for a brief course of medication. Also, Jeff has to remember some dos and don'ts in preparation for sleep. These measures seem to work. Though he is not sleeping as he did when he was a young adult, Jeff is now sleeping enough that he can get through the day without letting his exhaustion overcome him.

Q What is insomnia, and how often does it occur?

Insomnia is having difficulty falling and staying asleep, but it is also defined as the perception or complaint of poor quality sleep. Insomnia might mean that one has difficulty falling asleep, frequently awakens during the night and is unable to fall back asleep, awakens too early in the morning, or experiences sleep that is unrefreshing.

The definition depends on the sleep needs of the individual and his or her level of satisfaction with sleep habits. Insomnia is not defined by how many hours someone sleeps each night or how long it takes to fall asleep. If someone finds sleep restful, no matter how many hours of sleep, he or she does not suffer insomnia. On the other hand, individuals who sleep 8 hours, but toss and turn and feel as if they've slept only an hour or two, might very well be classified as having this sleep disorder. Insomnia can also be classified on the basis of how long the condition lasts. Transient insomnia lasts for one night or a few weeks, intermittent insomnia occurs from time to time, and chronic insomnia is present on most nights and lasts for a month or more.

The highly idiosyncratic definition of insomnia presents major problems for mental health researchers. It is very difficult to standardize a definition of a disorder when the definition depends strongly upon the affected individuals' personal observations.

Insomnia is common in the general population, with more than one-third of all adults reporting occasional insomnia during a 1-year period. Up to 50 percent of adults report insomnia-type symptoms at least once in their lives. Of this relatively high percentage of adults who report insomnia, 1 in 10 considers the condition to be a serious problem. Despite insomnia's prevalence, a minority of sufferers is sufficiently motivated to visit their doctor for help. Instead, they use over-the-counter drugs to treat their sleeplessness.

The fact that so few people with sleep disorder choose to see their physician has some serious consequences. First, these people are not being adequately assisted in finding the cause for the insomnia and are managing (usually unsuccessfully) the disorder themselves. Second, the annual costs of this disorder are staggering, not only in terms of medications purchased but also in lost work time. In fact, the nearly 30 million people in the United States who suffer insomnia are more than twice as likely as the general population to be in an automobile accident or to get hurt while at work. The annual costs for managing insomnia in the United States are somewhere between $92.5 and $107 billion. A large part of these costs is in the purchase of non-prescription drugs.

Q Who is likely to have insomnia?

Certain demographic and psychological characteristics often accompany insomnia. The disorder tends to occur more frequently in people who are over 60 and more frequently in women. The problem seems to be worse in older people because the symptoms often tend to be dismissed by many physicians as just a naturally occurring part of the aging process. Physicians often expect older people to need less sleep, but that's not necessarily the case. Actually, older people just don't sleep as restfully. Also, insomnia is more difficult to treat among older adults compared with younger persons.

Divorced, widowed, and separated individuals are more prone to the disorder than are married individuals. Insomnia also is reported more often in lower socioeconomic groups than in groups with higher socioeconomic status.

The disorder is one that, unless treated, remains a trying part of one's life. Follow-up studies of young adult subjects over a 2- to 7-year period reveal that half of those people who had occasional episodes of insomnia had developed persistent insomnia. In another study, people diagnosed with chronic insomnia continued to suffer symptoms 5 years later. So, unless treated, it is unlikely that this disorder will "burn itself out" or spontaneously disappear.

Q How is insomnia diagnosed?

Insomnia is diagnosed through a complete medical history and a sleep diary maintained for about 2 weeks. The medical history helps determine if the insomnia has a basis in a medical condition. The sleep diary is completed by the patient and his or her bed partner (if there is one) and helps document the quantity and quality of the patient's sleep. While the diary can be an objective tool, remember that the definition of insomnia can be subjective since it is based on the patient's impressions of how good or bad sleep is.

At one point, sophisticated laboratory studies of insomnia were done, and the results of these studies were used as a diagnostic tool. Such sleep studies are now done only when a clearly discernible medical condition is thought to cause the disorder.

Q What are the different types of insomnia?

There are five different types of insomnia, each defined on the basis of its cause.

Primary insomnia is diagnosed when the individual complains of having difficulty getting to sleep, staying asleep, or having sleep that is not restful. In other words, the person wakes up tired. The difficulty and complaint lasts more than 1 month and is associated with difficulties at work, school, or home. This type of insomnia is distinctive in that it is not associated with any other sleep or mental disorder, nor is it due to exposure to a substance such as alcohol or any general medical condition.

Insomnia related to another mental disorder describes insomnia that is judged to be caused by another mental disorder, such as depression. Generally, mood disorders and anxiety disorders (see Chapters 7 and 8 for more about these disorders) are considered when evaluating symptoms of chronic insomnia.

Sleep disorder, secondary to a medical illness that may be producing pain, is the third type of insomnia. Substance induced sleep disorder results from the effects of substances including illicit drugs, medication, or toxins. Although this category includes abused drugs such as amphetamines, the category also covers such commonly available substances as nicotine, alcohol, and caffeine. This type of insomnia results from the direct physiological effects of these substances.

Finally, there is dyssomnia not otherwise specified which describes all other cases of insomnia.

Q What other conditions might appear along with insomnia?

While insomnia can occur by itself, it is often accompanied by other psychological or medical conditions. In general, people who suffer insomnia report high levels of distress, anxiety, and depression when compared with individuals who do not sleep poorly. Several different studies have found that people who have symptoms of insomnia are at an increased risk for developing psychiatric disorders within a 1-year period.

In addition, the lack of restful or adequate sleep can lead to such problems as deterioration of mood, low motivation, lack of attention, poor concentration, and low levels of energy. Once these symptoms reach into the workplace, they manifest themselves as poor job performance, increased irritability, and interpersonal problems. For example, in one study, poor sleepers in the Navy received fewer promotions, remained at lower pay grades, had higher rates of attrition, and had more frequent hospitalizations than good sleepers. Adequate sleep is critical to our rejuvenation and recovery, and the lack of sleep can clearly be debilitating.

It's easy to see how insomnia can become a vicious cycle: poor sleep leads to decreased personal effectiveness, which causes anxiety about job, family, and lack of sleep, which makes sleep all the more difficult. For many people with the disorder, worrying about insomnia worsens the insomnia! Part of the treatment for insomnia, as we discuss later, focuses on breaking this cycle through short-term use of medication.

Q How is insomnia treated?

Transient or intermittent insomnia, the kind that lasts for only a few days, often need not be treated at all. For example, insomnia caused by jet lag or the first few days in a new home will probably disappear in a few days given no other medical or psychological reasons for the restless sleep.

For longer lasting or chronic insomnia, there are two general methods of treatment. Several different medications have been used and have been shown to be moderately effective for relieving insomnia in the short run. To treat the symptoms with the hope of managing them over a longer period, behavioral treatments are used.

The general course of treatment follows four steps, although all four might not be necessary to obtain relief.

First, any underlying medical or psychological problem is diagnosed and treated. Since many cases of insomnia are caused by such factors, eliminating or treating them is an important first step.

Second, behaviors that might cause insomnia need to be identified and then reduced in frequency. Such behaviors can range from worrying at bedtime about tomorrow's meeting to consuming too much alcohol too late in the evening.

Third, medication (such as sleeping pills) is considered. However, the long-term use of medication, especially for chronic insomnia, is controversial. These drugs are usually prescribed at the lowest possible dosage and for the shortest period of time just to get over the initial lack of sleep. Rebound insomnia can occur after the abrupt stopping of medication, so the lowest possible dosage should be used, and patients taking medication for insomnia should be weaned off the medication gradually.

Finally, behavioral techniques should be used to encourage the patient to learn how to help sleep come naturally.

Q What medications are used to treat insomnia, and how effective are they?

A wide variety of medications have been used to treat insomnia. The medications used to treat insomnia have all been tested in well-designed studies where the important criteria of randomized and controlled trials are present. The most effective agents for treating insomnia are benzodiazepines such as lorazepam (Ativan), zolpidem (Ambien), temazepam (Restoril), and triazolom (Halcion). The least effective medications are antihistamines and tryptophan.

Benzodiazepines, as a class of drugs, have been studied for more than 20 years, so there is a good deal of information about their effectiveness. Although the different types of studies are often difficult to compare, more than 90 percent of them report the usefulness of this class of drugs in treating insomnia. Clearly, benzodiazepines work in reducing the symptoms of chronic insomnia in a large number of different patients.

The use of zolpidem (Ambien), which is relatively new to the market, has been studied more recently. Since it is a newer drug, many of these studies have used new and more reliable techniques to determine the drug's effectiveness. As one might expect, zolpidem has been compared to benzodiazepines, to placebos, and to no treatment. In almost all cases, the response to zolpidem has been positive. Like benzodiazepines, zolpidem is an effective and safe medication for reducing the symptoms of insomnia.

As far as over-the-counter drugs, there are simply not enough well-controlled studies to reach any conclusion as to the effectiveness of these preparations.

There's one other substance that deserves mentioning, especially since it is a naturally occurring hormone. Melatonin is available over the counter and affects the biological rhythms that tell our bodies when to awake and when to sleep. The few controlled studies that have examined the effects of melatonin provide results that appear somewhat contradictory; while total sleep time diminished, quality of sleep improved. It is also important to note that merely being a naturally occurring substance does not imply a drug's safety or effectiveness.

Q What are some of the possible side effects of benzodiazepines and zolpidem?

The basic concerns with the use of benzodiazepines and zolpidem are tiredness during the day, memory problems, possible effects on physical coordination, dependence on the medication and very rarely, seizures when the drug is withdrawn. Zolpidem (Ambien) appears less likely to be associated with these problems.

Q What behavioral treatments have been used?

Five different types of behavioral therapy have been used to treat insomnia. Each is based on the idea that at least some symptoms of the disorder are learned and under the control of the individual. Specific strategies can be taught to deal with those symptoms and their consequences.

Stimulus control therapy consists of a set of lesson-like procedures that are designed to alleviate behaviors that are not compatible with restful sleep. Using this therapy, the patient tries to create an environment where different events act as cues for sleeping and not for anything else. Stimulus control therapy is also referred to as reconditioning, since the person learns to respond to certain cues that are associated with sleeping. The more control one has over where, when, and how one sleeps, the more likely the person is (with good instruction) to create a successful sleep space. Consistent with this idea, the patient is generally advised to follow five rules or procedures.

1. The patient should go to bed only when sleepy. Lying in bed and not being able to sleep helps perpetuate a pattern of restlessness and insomnia.

2. The bedroom should be used only for sleeping and sex. It should not be used as a place for watching television, reading, eating, or working, regardless of the time of day.
3. If the patient goes to bed and is unable to sleep, he or she is encouraged to change the environment by going to another room for 15 to 20 minutes and then returning to bed to try again to sleep. The "other room" should not be a bedroom. This step is repeated as often as necessary to achieve sleep. The idea is to break down the association between the bedroom and the accompanying insomnia.
4. No matter how much sleep the patient gets, he or she should get up at the same time every morning.
5. Finally, no naps allowed. Naps help form a pattern that sleeping is acceptable anywhere and at any time, and that pattern is to be discouraged.

Sleep restriction therapy also prescribes a very clear set of do's and don'ts. Here, the amount of bed time, literally, is tightly controlled at first. Many people with insomnia spend far too much time in bed trying to sleep and being unsuccessful. With sleep restriction therapy, a specific time during which sleep is allowed is determined. The idea is that the individual will make best use of that time and sleep efficiently. This amount of time is usually set through reviewing a sleep diary, as we mentioned earlier. As the patient's sleep becomes more restful, the time allowed in bed is increased. The hope is that the amount of sleep time will be increased as the sleeping becomes more restful and efficient.

Relaxation therapies are designed to reduce the amount of thinking or body movement that might keep someone awake. The techniques focus on muscle relaxation and biofeedback. Restlessness certainly does not promote sleep, and these relaxation techniques are aimed at allowing the person to sleep without interference from troubling thoughts, "racing" minds, or physical restlessness.

Sleep hygiene education focuses on health practices associated with sleep such as diet, exercise, and substance use and abuse. For example, it's fairly clear that sleep difficulties can be related to drinking coffee or other caffeinated substances before bedtime. On the other hand, a light snack (not containing any stimulants) may promote sleep. The sleep hygiene method also focuses on environmental causes of insomnia such as a sleeping space that is too hot or noisy.

Finally, cognitive-behavioral treatment focuses on thoughts and ideas that perpetuate insomnia.

Q How effective are the behavioral treatments of insomnia?

At least thirty-three studies of behavioral intervention for insomnia have been conducted. The subjective symptoms of insomnia (such as patients' dissatisfaction) and the more objective indicators of poor quality sleep (such as irritability and restlessness) seem to respond very well to behavioral treatments.

Of these treatments, stimulus control, sleep restriction, relaxation, and cognitive-behavioral therapy have been effective in the management of insomnia. Using a behavioral strategy, patients seem to fall asleep 15 to 30 minutes sooner and wake up 1 to 3 times less often during the night. Total sleep time increases 15 to 45 minutes. While medication is more reliable in the short term, behavioral strategies tend to produce more sustained effects.

Q What about the combination of behavioral strategies plus medication to treat insomnia?

Too few studies have examined the question of whether a combination of behavioral and pharmacological approaches is better than one method alone although this is a fairly common clinical practice. However, given the fast-acting nature of medication and the long-term effectiveness of the behavioral approach, combined treatment seems like an excellent direction for future research.

Q Where Can I Find More Information About Insomnia?

Books

67 Ways to Good Sleep by Charles B. Inlander and Cynthia K. Moran. Walker & Company, 1995. ISBN 0802713068.

Discusses solutions to specific sleep disorders ranging from jet lag to snoring and includes steps you can take to address them. Those steps include eating right, reducing anxiety and stress, and ways to handle changes in bedtime schedule and environment.

Get a Good Night's Sleep by Katherine A. Albert. Simon & Schuster, 1996. ISBN 068480428X.

Recommends alternative therapies as well as traditional medicines to help deal with different types of sleep problems. One unique thing about this comprehensive book is the diagnostic quiz that readers can use to analyze their sleeping patterns and to determine both the physical and psychological factors affecting their sleep. The quiz also provides a guide to combating sleeplessness.

Goodbye Insomnia, Hello Sleep by Samuel Dunkell. Dell Publishing Company, 1996. ISBN 0440222273.

Focuses solely on insomnia and is based on the earlier successful hardback edition. It discusses advances in sleep medicine and how dramatically the person with the insomnia disorder has been helped.

The Sleep Rx: 75 Proven Ways to Get a Good Night's Sleep by Norman Ford. Prentice Hall, 1994. ISBN 0131439189.

Another paperback version of a previously successful hardcover. Teaches consumers to become their own "sleep doctor" and to overcome insomnia using the most successful, all-natural, holistic techniques taught at the nation's leading sleep disorder centers. The 75 sleep prescriptions address behavioral, environmental, psychological, and nutritional causes of insomnia.

Internet Sites

The American Sleep Disorders Association

(at http://www.asda.org/sitelnks.html) lists extensive resources for sleep-related topics including Sleepnet, information on children's sleep problems, the SleepWell, and pointers to national centers where research on sleep disorders is being done.

The Sleep Insomnia Program

(at http://www.proaxis.com/~iris/sleep.html) features the home page of Sara Richards, a mental health counselor, and contains information about insomnia-related programs. It also includes an annotated book list (some of which are described above), a list of other Web resources, and ideas for helping the person who suffers this disorder.

The Sleep Home Page at UCLA

(at http://bisleep.medsch.ucla.edu/) offers hundreds of links including a directory of centers and individuals doing research on sleep disorders.

Healthy Sleep

(at http://www.pacificcoast.com/healthy/healthy.html) might be commercial, but it does provide some basic information about many different facets of sleep including the stages of sleep, the stress-sleep connection, sleep troubles, myths about sleep, and much more. This is a great resource for general information about sleep and sleep disorders.

The Sleep Disorder Center of Central Texas

(at http://www.sleepdoctor.com) for anyone who wants information about sleep disorders such as snoring, seizures, insomnia, nightmares, restless legs, and many others. A good source of basic information including a description of sleep stages in the normal adult.

Where to Write

American Sleep Disorders Association
1610 14th Street N.W., Suite 300
Rochester, MN 55901
507-287-6006

National Center on Sleep Disorders Research
National Heart, Lung, and Blood Institute
31 Center Drive, Room 4A11 MSC 2490
Bethesda, MD 20892-2490
301-496-7443

Chapter 4

Sexual Disorders

Sexual Dysfunction: When Sex Doesn't Work Right

It doesn't matter how hard Bob tries to concentrate when making love to his wife, he just cannot get or maintain an erection. An otherwise healthy young man, he is feeling desperate and inadequate, even though Helen is understanding and patient. It has gotten to the point where both partners are frustrated, and arguments over what to do have started to affect their relationship.

Bob's first visit to the doctor rules out factors such as poor circulation and complications of his prescription drugs. The doctor also establishes that Bob sometimes awakens with an erection, a normal occurrence for males, but that knowledge does not make the problem any easier to treat. Visits to a psychiatrist are useful in exploring Bob's feelings about intimacy and about women, but everyone seems to be at a loss about what to do to fix the problem. Working together, Bob, Helen, and the mental health professionals they consult agree that the best approach is to use a medication that helps increase the flow of blood to the penis and results in an erection. While other choices are available, this option best fits their style of intimacy and sounds the easiest treatment for Bob to accept.

After a few visits to the doctor's office and some instruction (and emotional support), Bob now regularly achieves an erection and participates fully in this important part of a committed relationship.

Q What are sexual disorders and how often do they occur?

Sexual disorders or sexual dysfunctions encompass the broad category of disorders that have to do with sex. While sexual disorders can have their origins in either the physical or psychological realm, the consequences are surely the province of the mental health professional. For many people, few things are more emotionally and psychologically disturbing than not being able to successfully participate in sexual activities.

Few studies of the frequency of sexual disorders have results that can be applied to the general population. This is because the surveys that do exist used different methodologies and even different criteria in the diagnosis of the disorders. Comparisons among these different studies are difficult to make and are of questionable value. However, based on the information that is available, here are some general estimates. Current evidence suggests the following percentages of adults experience one of these disorders:

- female orgasmic disorder   5 to 10 percent
- male erectile dysfunction   4 to 10 percent
- male orgasmic disorder   4 to 10 percent
- premature ejaculation   36 to 38 percent

There's not enough information to make even an informed estimate regarding the frequency of such disorders as female arousal disorder, vaginismus, dyspareunia, and hypoactive sexual desire disorder.

Some studies indicate that male erectile problems increase with age (especially after age 50). But such findings, as is true with many others, are related to the methods used to obtain the information. For example, in one study, 4 percent of the 51-year-old male subjects indicated on a questionnaire that they had a sexual disorder. But when questioned face to face, the portion increased to 26 percent.

Q What kinds of sexual disorders are there?

There are 11 different types of sexual disorders. Here is a brief description of each one.

- Hypoactive sexual desire disorder: the individual has a persistent and recurring absent or very low desire for sexual activity.
- Sexual aversion disorder: sexual contact with a partner is avoided.
- Female sexual arousal disorder: the female cannot maintain adequate lubrication or a level of sexual excitement.

- Male erectile dysfunction: an adequate erection cannot be obtained or maintained for the completion of intercourse.
- Female (or male) orgasmic disorder: there is an absence of an orgasm.
- Premature ejaculation: a man ejaculates with minimal stimulation upon penetration and before he wishes to.
- Dyspareunia: genital pain associated with sexual intercourse, mostly due to lack of lubrication or vaginismus.
- Vaginismus: muscle spasms in the vagina interfere with sexual intercourse.
- Sexual dysfunction: due to medical conditions such as poor circulation.
- Substance-induced sexual dysfunction: sexual dysfunction is explained by intoxication or the recurrent use of medications.

Q In general, what factors are thought to cause sexual disorders?

Once physical explanations are ruled out, most clinicians believe that sexual disorders are caused by anxiety about performance, previous negative experiences with sex, and self-defeating thoughts. Much of the therapy targeted at these disorders is aimed at addressing these probable causes.

Q What are some problems involved in doing research in the area of sexual disorders?

Studies that examine the effectiveness of treatments for certain sexual disorders have particular problems that make it difficult to reach a conclusion about what treatments work. The problems fall in six general areas:
- The use of very small groups of people, making it difficult to generalize to larger groups.
- The lack of comparison groups such as controls groups.
- The lack of random assignment to treatments, which decreases the likelihood of knowing for sure that the treatment, and not other factors, is what works.
- Poor definitions and diagnostic criteria, which decrease the likelihood that experiments can be accurately replicated.
- Few measures of long-term outcomes.
- Poor descriptions of the therapies used.

Such shortcomings make it very difficult to meet the high standards of research necessary for the mental health professional and the patient to resolve the disorder. In addition to these concerns, another issue is especially pertinent to this category of disorders.

As when studying any other mental disorder, scientists studying sexual disorders hope to conduct well-controlled investigations. With sexual disorders, however, researchers have to pay special attention to the complexity of the issues, since sex is such a fundamental part of the human condition.

For example, what criteria, other than directly asking the participants, might one use to judge whether intercourse is satisfactory? Is the number of times one has an orgasm as important, more important, or not as important as the level of satisfaction obtained? The dynamics of sex and sexual relationships are so complex that it is very difficult to draw conclusions that apply to groups rather than to one individual.

Q If there are so many problems with research, what characterizes a successful or effective treatment for a sexual disorder?

A set of five factors is associated with the successful treatment of sexual disorders. There is no research on the particular weight that any one factor or any combination might carry. The factors:

- The couple's having a good overall relationship, an important predictor of success.
- A high degree of motivation by the partners to see that the therapy works.
- The absence of any serious psychiatric or mental disorder in either partner.
- The dual attraction of both partners to each other.
- Both partners' following the treatment program from the earliest possible time and performing whatever tasks are assigned. In other words, they need to do their homework.

These five characteristics don't guarantee success, but they certainly increase the odds of a positive outcome.

Q How have sexual disorders been treated in the past?

Prior to 1970, psychoanalytic techniques were used to assist the clinician in understanding and treating sexual problems. The general thinking among mental health professionals was that sexual problems were linked to unconscious and unresolved conflicts during childhood. Because the focus was so much on the individual, clients were rarely treated together as a couple. The focus on dream analysis, intrapsychic conflict, and the interpretation of underlying motives led to rich and interesting anecdotes and case studies, but not much information that could be applied to any other individual than the one being treated.

Behavioral therapy, which focuses on unlearning undesirable habits, started gaining attention in the early 1950s. These techniques directly addressed specific sexual disorders and assumed that a sexual disorder is the result of a learned, anxiety-producing response. The job of the mental health professional was to extinguish the response or help the client "unlearn" the anxiety that interfered with normal sexual functioning. Systematic desensitization, the primary tool used in this type of therapy, would pair anxiety-eliciting events with neutral ones, thereby gradually reducing what was thought to interfere with successful sexual behavior.

A major shift in the way sexual dysfunctions are treated resulted from the pioneering work of Virginia Masters and William Johnson and their 1970 survey of almost 800 cases of sexual dysfunction. Their treatment included residential care and individual and couple psychotherapy under the supervision of a sex therapy team. Masters and Johnson based their treatment program on three fundamental assumptions. The first assumption was that sexual experiences are based on a sequence of physical and psychological arousal. Second, past experiences (or habits) and anxiety are very important in understanding the origin and maintenance of sexual disorders. Third, therapy for sexual disorders has to be specifically focused. By far, the most important contribution that Masters and Johnson made was to point out how the fear of future failure based on previous failures is the most potent and universal experience in sexual disorders.

The next general treatment trend, neo-Masters and Johnson, was characterized by the integration of the Masters and Johnson approach with behavioral and psychoanalytic interventions. For example, couples were treated by addressing both partners' individual status (such as age or health) and interpersonal contributions (the origin and maintenance of the dysfunction).

As new medications became more effective in the treatment of mental disorders in general, this treatment option was applied to sexual disorders, especially male sexual dysfunction. As you will read later, such therapies as intracavernosal (a part of the penis) injection and oral medications for erectile dysfunction and the use of selective serotonin reuptake inhibitors for premature ejaculation have influenced the entire field of treatment. Unfortunately, few gains have been made in the use of medication in treating female dysfunction.

Q How are hypoactive sexual desire disorders treated, and how effective is the treatment?

Treatment of this disorder through individual psychotherapy seems to be effective in that 50 to 70 percent of both men and women show immediate gains following therapy. Unfortunately, these gains are not maintained over the long term (defined as 3 years or more) by at least half of the participants. Although, sexual desire (the main symptom of this one disorder) seemed to decrease over these 3 years, the level of sexual satisfaction was improved and maintained.

While psychotherapy has been shown to be effective in the short run, there's no record of such success in the pharmacological treatment of desire disorders. Some evidence indicates that the hormone androgen is necessary as a component of sexual desire, but there's no evidence that such a drug increases desire in men or women with the disorder.

Q What is erectile dysfunction? Is it the same as impotence?

Erectile dysfunction is the inability to achieve or maintain an erect penis sufficient for sexual intercourse. According to some experts, erectile dysfunction may be the most untreated condition in the world. Only 5 percent of those affected ever receive treatment, even though treatment is effective 95 percent of the time.

An erection occurs when the nerves surrounding the two side-by-side cylinders in the penis called the corpora cavernosa are stimulated, resulting in an expanding of arterial blood vessels. The blood flows into these erection chambers, and an erection results.

The inability to get and maintain an erection used to be referred to as impotence, but currently the phrase *erectile dysfunction* is used. That term is more precise, since it refers only to problems with erections and not to general sexual disorders.

Q What are some of the causes of erectile dysfunction, and how is the cause diagnosed?

The most frequent physical cause of erectile dysfunction is vascular or blood vessel disease, such as hardening of the arteries. Other diseases such as multiple sclerosis, diabetes, and alcoholism can cause erectile dysfunction. Injuries to the pelvis and the penile arteries can also be causes. Non-physical causes of erectile dysfunction include stress and anxiety.

The first step in diagnosis for the male is a complete physical examination, where neurological and other tests are performed. The exam can help identify or rule out any physical cause of erectile dysfunction. The doctor may examine the prostate gland and general vascular function. Blood and urine tests may also be performed.

One of the most important tests, however, is the *nocturnal penile tumescence and rigidity* (NPTR) test. This test is used to determine if the condition is due to physical or non-physical causes. The NPTR test is done by attaching a special gauge to the man's penis before going to bed for the night. Since all healthy men have erections as a part of normal sleep, the lack of an erection during sleep indicates that the cause is physical. If there are erections during sleep, but none upon stimulation or during normal sexual activity, the cause is most likely psychological.

Q How is erectile dysfunction treated?

In general, erectile dysfunction is treated by a urologist unless the cause is determined to be psychological. Then, mental health professionals are best suited to treat the disorder.

Psychological treatments include behavioral, cognitive, and interpersonal interventions. The less entrenched the set of behaviors (such as performance and anxiety problems), the easier the habits and learned behaviors leading to dysfunction are to change.

The pharmacological treatment of erectile dysfunction consists of oral medication or the injection of or insertion of medication into the shaft of the penis to help relax the smooth muscle in the penis and increase the flow of blood.

A new and extraordinarily popular treatment is the oral drug sildenafil (Viagra) which takes about 1 hour to be effective. The drug works by stimulating the production of the chemical responsible for blood flow to the penis. Viagra has been very successful in the treatment of erectile dysfunction, and the drug appears to be well-tolerated and quite safe, although there have been some reports of side effects including vision and sleeping problems and a handful of deaths in patients who also had heart disease and were taking certain specific heart medications. Another drug taken orally, apomorphine, is also being tested in clinical trials.

Drugs such as yohimbine (or Yocon) and trazodone (Desyrel) have shown some success but have side effects as well. Yohimbine can produce some uncomfortable side effects such as nervousness and increased blood pressure. There have been case reports of trazodone being associated with abnormally long-lasting erections (priapism) and spontaneous orgasms.

Injection directly into the penis provides consistent and well-documented results, but there is little information about any psychological side effects of this treatment. While many men shy away from injecting themselves, the use of a very small needle under antiseptic conditions is relatively unpainful and safe.

Common agents injected to induce erections include phentolamine and papaverine (Pigitine) and prostaglandin (the active ingredient in Caverject) administered either individually or in combination. Which specific drug is used depends upon the doctor's diagnosis as to the cause of the dysfunction. For example, the combination drugs seem best suited for erectile dysfunction that results from severe arterial disease (where circulation is restricted).

Another recently developed treatment is MUSE, or medicated urethral system for erection. This method uses a suppository inserted into the tip of the penis. The suppository delivers a dose of alprostadil, a drug that causes the arteries in the penis to relax, increasing the blood flow and allowing an erection to occur. Pilot studies show that up to 65 percent of men with erectile dysfunction using this treatment had intercourse at least once in the 3-month treatment period while only 19 percent of the placebo group did.

Q How effective are these treatments?

A high percentage of men with a years-long history of erectile dysfunction and those who more recently developed the disorder achieve both immediate and long-term gains through the various therapies just discussed. The treatments are less effective with men who have had the condition for a longer period than with those who recently developed the dysfunction. The most complete and well-designed studies show that two-thirds of the men who undergo comprehensive treatment for this disorder are satisfied at their improvement at follow-ups that range from 6 weeks to 2 years.

Relapses do occur occasionally. An interesting issue for the client and mental health professional is how to deal with such situations. Couples who talk about the relapse and who have accepted that difficulties were likely to recur appeared to have adjusted well. Couples who stopped having sex and who pretended that nothing was wrong did not fare as well.

So much for psychological and pharmacological treatment of erectile dysfunction. Are there other treatments for this condition available?

One popular alternative treatment is a vacuum device, often called a vacuum tumescence device. With a vacuum device, a cylinder is placed around the penis and air is pumped out, with the resulting negative pressure forcing blood to flow into the penis and resulting in an erection. To maintain the erection, a rubber tension ring is placed at the base of the penis to restrict the outflow of blood. This is a nice alternative for the man who can't bear the thought of injecting himself in his penis or for whom other therapies are unsuccessful. Side effects are minimal, and success ranges from 70 to 100 percent.

Another technique, the penile implant, requires surgery. Penile implants have been successfully used since 1960 to treat more than 100,000 impotent men. Implants should be the course of last resort. While many different types of implants are available, the three-piece models (two cylinders, reservoir, and pump) generally produce the best results. When they work well, they can provide a very successful and satisfying erection. Side effects such as mechanical failure (about 5 percent), infection (about 2 percent), and pain can be formidable obstacles to their continued use.

Q How is premature ejaculation treated?

Premature ejaculation is defined as ejaculation that occurs before the individual or his partner is ready. It is primarily a non-physical disorder, the origin of which is not very well understood. It is most common among young men, in part because their sexual needs are most intense. The disorder is treated most successfully using one of two behavioral methods or with medication.

The first is called stop-start. First, the penis is stimulated until highly aroused. This is the start phase of the treatment. The stimulation is then stopped before ejaculation, and the stimulation and stoppage procedure is then repeated. The hope is that the time between stimulation and ejaculation is increased, thus permitting arousal without ejaculation and resulting in satisfying intercourse.

The start-squeeze method is similar to the start-stop method, except that as arousal increases, the individual or his partner squeezes the end of the penis to reduce arousal and minimize the chances of early ejaculation.

Pharmacological treatment of premature ejaculation has seen some success as well. Drugs such as sertraline (Zoloft), paroxetine (Paxil), and clomipramine (Anafranil) have been successful in the treatment of premature ejaculation. Clomipramine may be the preferred drug since it can be taken on an as-needed basis (up to 6 hours before attempted intercourse). While few side effects are recorded for any of these drugs, the pharmacological treatment of premature ejaculation may become a lifelong process.

Q How is female orgasmic disorder treated, and how successful is the treatment?

This type of disorder, in which a woman cannot reach an orgasm or can do so alone but not with a partner, typifies some of the difficulties in conducting research in treating sexual disorders. For example, measuring success is problematic. Should we measure success based on orgasm reached through intercourse or orgasm alone or orgasm through some subjective rating of intimate interactions? Adding to this confusion is the fact that society hypes the idea that women can easily and regularly achieve multiple orgasms and that any woman who doesn't is abnormal.

The most successful treatment of female orgasmic disorders is by training women to achieve an orgasm through masturbation. Treated individually, in couples, or in groups, success rates can be as high as 90 percent, and the long-term gains seem to be maintained for all but about 15 percent of participants.

Over time women demonstrate an increased capacity to achieve orgasm anyway, regardless of treatment. Why? Researchers think that the longer one has the dysfunction, the more opportunity there is for practice and to be reinforced for success. Also, inhibitions tend to decrease over time.

Q How is male orgasmic disorder treated and with what degree of success?

Male orgasmic disorder is also known as retarded ejaculation, delayed ejaculation, or incompetent ejaculation and is found in about 3 to 8 percent of men.

There are no large-scale, well-designed studies of this dysfunction, which is thought to be almost totally psychological in origin. The cause of this problem is thought to be insufficient stimulation to achieve an orgasm, and the prescribed treatment is vigorous and intense stimulation such as through the use of a vibrator. In smaller studies, this treatment has been successful in up to 80 percent of the men who participated. Another perspective is that this disorder is actually a desire disorder of the type we discussed earlier. Here, the recommended course of treatment is to work with the partner to reduce anxiety.

Q What are vaginismus and dyspareunia, and how are they treated?

Vaginismus is persistent and recurrent involuntary spasms of the musculature of the outer third of the vagina. It can affect a woman at any age. As one might expect, it can cause significant distress, embarrassment, and difficulty in maintaining an intimate relationship.

The cause is thought to revolve around the woman's concerns about intimacy or the man's insensitivity to his partner. Interestingly, about 10 to 30 percent of the partners of women with vaginismus report erectile or ejaculatory dysfunction (difficulty ejaculating). It's not clear whether the male's problem follows or precedes the female's. Vaginismus can be treated in a variety of ways, including exercises to gain control over the muscles and graduated self-insertion of dilators of increasing size.

Dyspareunia is painful intercourse which primarily affects woman but can also affect men. It occurs in 10 to 15 percent of women. There are no estimates of its occurrence in men. The cause of dyspareunia can be physical (such as pelvic inflammatory disease or vaginismus) or psychological in nature, resulting, for example, from prior sexual abuse or discord in a relationship. Treatment involves the use of lubrication or even surgery when necessary to treat conditions that may not be amenable to self-dilation. Other treatments are marital sexual therapy including an emphasis on communication skills, psychological intervention, and patient education.

Q Most of the sexual disorders that have been covered have to do with physical or psychological difficulties. Are there other causes of sexual disorders, such as drugs?

Most definitely. Substance-induced sexual disorders refer to sexual disorders associated with drug intoxication and the use of prescribed medicines. Most information that we have about this type of dysfunction focuses on substance abuse and the use of antihypertensive and psychiatric drugs in males. Sexual dysfunction has long been associated with the chronic abuse of alcohol, especially as it relates to male erectile dysfunction. In general, it's unclear what effect alcohol and drugs have on female sexual behavior.

The information available on the effects of drug abuse on sexual functioning is fairly clear, but once again more so for males, probably because the dysfunction is so much more easily diagnosed. Several studies on the use of narcotics indicate that they diminish desire but that a normal level of sexual desire returns during drug-free episodes. Drugs such as cocaine and amphetamine also reduce level of desire. Finally, almost all classes of antihypertensive drugs such as reserpine (Ser-Ap-Es), or propanolol (Inderal) and psychiatric drugs such as lorazepam (Ativan), or alprazolam (Xanax) have been reported to interfere with normal sexual functioning. The major problem with the reports on the effects of these drugs is that most of them are anecdotal and not based on well-designed studies in which control groups have been used.

Of the psychiatric drugs, the most has been written about the effects of antidepressants on sexual performance. They have also been noted to cause sexual problems including loss of libido or desire, erectile dysfunction, and orgasm delay. These findings are more reliable and trustworthy since they are based on well-designed studies employing control groups.

Q In terms of the treatment of sexual disorders, what can we expect to see in the future?

Normal sexual functioning is a complex interaction of biological, emotional, and psychological events. Any disruption in these spheres can cause a problem. That's one reason it is so difficult to establish effective treatments for such dysfunctions.

However, advances, especially in pharmacology, are playing an increasingly important role in the treatment of such disorders. Neurochemical studies of both animals and humans have revealed important chemical agents that act on different areas of the brain and their effect on sexual behavior.

Advances are also being made in the way sexual disorders are identified and diagnosed. Where the *Diagnostic and Statistical Manual* system is regularly used to assist mental health professionals in the diagnosis of mental disorders, the use of this diagnostic tool historically has been only an afterthought for diagnosis and treatment of sexual disorders. Now that the *Diagnostic and Statistical Manual* system focuses more on the varieties of sexual disorders than it has in the past, the use of the system will probably allow for more complete and reliable diagnoses.

Finally, while many disorders in this part of the chapter, such as erectile dysfunction and lack of orgasm in women, can be treated successfully, the real challenge is to design programs that maintain those gains.

Paraphilias: Strange Attractions

Ever since adolescence, Richard, could not control the urge to expose himself to young women. Now, as a young adult, he has taken to hiding behind buildings during the early evenings, then rushing out, opening his fly, and taking out his penis in front of women leaving work for home. He finds this activity more arousing than any other sexual activity he has experienced. Although not as often, Richard also masturbates in view of others, especially in his car, waiting for anyone to look in and acknowledge what he is doing.

This behavior continued into middle adulthood, stopping only when Richard is caught by the police and charged with exhibitionism. His family is horrified and Richard is placed in a treatment program and on probation.

The primary treatment consists of teaching Richard how to control inappropriate thoughts and urges while encouraging him to focus on appropriate sexual behaviors for a man his age. After several years of therapy, he no longer feels the same sense of urgency to expose himself, but the fear that he will slip is still there. He finds it a constant battle to control his insistent sexual urges.

Q What are paraphilias, and how do they differ from other sexual disorders?

All paraphilias (and we'll list them shortly) have four things in common. First, they are characterized by recurrent, intense, and sexually arousing fantasies, urges, or behaviors that involve inappropriate objects. Second, these urges and fantasies continue for more than 6 months. Third, these fantasies and urges cause considerable distress or impair day-to-day functioning. Finally, a paraphilia may involve non-human objects, children, or non-consenting adults, or humiliating oneself or one's partner. Paraphilias also occur almost exclusively in men.

The defining difference between normal and abnormal sexual fantasies is the appropriateness of the focus. For example, constant thoughts or behaviors about having sex with a child meet these criteria for a paraphilia, but constant thoughts or behaviors about having sex with a spouse would not. Everyone has momentary and fleeting thoughts of sexual fantasies. When they become preoccupations that overwhelm behavior constraints, serious consequences can occur.

The eight generally recognized types of paraphilias all involve fantasies, urges, or behaviors.

- Exhibitionism is the exposure of one's genitals to a stranger.
- Fetishism is the use of objects to gain sexual satisfaction.
- Frotteurism is touching or rubbing against a non-consenting person.
- Pedophilia is sexual activity with a prepubescent child.
- Sexual masochism is enjoying or craving sexual activity that causes one's self humiliation or pain.
- Sexual sadism is sexual excitement through activity that causes another person pain or humiliation.
- Transvestic fetishism is sexual activity by heterosexual males involved in cross-dressing.
- Voyeurism is the observing of unsuspecting persons who are nude, disrobing, or involved in sexual activity.

While any one of these paraphilias can be a serious mental disorder, it is not uncommon for several of them to occur together, creating a difficult diagnostic and treatment situation for the mental health professional. Not all the disorders mentioned above are covered in the following sections of the chapter.

Q How often do paraphilias occur?

The incidence or prevalence of paraphalias in the general population is not known due to the very private nature of the activity. Consequently, most studies have examined those disorders that may result in crimes, since information on the incidence and prevalence of paraphilias is usually available only in offenders' and victims' memories. In fact, many researchers believe that 90 percent of paraphilic acts go undetected and unreported.

The little epidemiological data available are isolated to certain groups. For example, between 30 and 70 percent of college-age females have been victimized in some fashion. The majority of these events occurred before they were 16 years old. Studies have shown that 50 percent of women report being victims of exhibitionism.

Q What are some of the causes of paraphilias?

Far more effort has been spent theorizing about paraphilias' origins than their treatments. Several models have been suggested for the origin of paraphilias. Unfortunately, most of these are very difficult to test empirically. Without scientific tests, it is almost impossible to extend these models into the area of treatment. However, it is useful to examine the general categories so the consumer can at least be informed.

Behavioral learning models are some of the earliest and most influential explanations of paraphilias. These models are based on the assumption that sexual deviations develop as the result of early conditioning, a type of learning. Social learning models extend the behavioral learning model by including the social context within which the deviant behavior occurs. For example, a child who is the victim or observer of inappropriate sexual behaviors (such as incest) imitates that behavior and is reinforced for that behavior as an adult.

Compensation models propose that offenders are deprived of normal social sexual contacts such as meaningful sexual relationships and consequently seek gratification through deviant means.

The physiological models are gaining more respect as our understanding grows of how hormones affect behavior and how the central nervous system operates. Because many sexual offenders combine elements of aggression with sexual behavior, a search for a relationship between aggression and male sexual hormones has been of interest to researchers for many years. Unfortunately, there has been little corroborating evidence to support this model. Damage to the central nervous system has been thought to be a possible cause as well, but similarly little empirical data exists to confirm this possibility.

Q What are some difficulties in diagnosing paraphilias?

Problems in assessing paraphilias fall into three general categories. First is the generally private nature of sexual activity in our society. Second, many therapists are untrained to treat such disorders and hesitate to inquire about sexual behavior. And finally, many offenders are reluctant to divulge the critical information necessary to identify different types of paraphilias and, therefore, design successful treatments.

The definitive diagnosis of paraphilias may be one of the most difficult for even the well-trained mental health professional. That is because of the complexities of sexual behaviors and the strong societal preference to keep discussions of such issues out of sight and mind. Difficulties in reaching an assessment also mean that definitive treatment methods have not been developed because it is unclear how to measure a treatment's success.

For most mental disorders, such as phobias, the therapist and the client join together to defeat the illness. They both have a common goal—helping the client get better. That's not always the case with a sexual offender—usually the most visible example of someone with this type of disorder since others keep it private. In those cases, the behavior itself is often highly rewarding and satisfying, regardless of its degree of deviance or the harm it might cause others. In fact, many offenders, when faced with the irrefutable evidence that they have committed deviant acts, will not accept responsibility, or minimize their involvement. In fact, overcoming denial is often thought to be the first and most important step in effective treatments.

Any assessment procedure of a paraphilia involves the collection of large and varied amounts of information about the offender and the behavior committed. This information can involve police reports, a presentence investigation (since many offenders are required to receive treatment as a condition of sentencing), psychological and psychiatric evaluations, child protection agency reports, depositions, and any testimony recorded. Since offenders often distort information (such as saying, "She asked for it"), the therapist should obtain as much information as early as possible, even before the first clinical interview.

Q *I've heard about a machine, where something is attached to the offender's penis, that can be used along with other information to help assess paraphilias. What is this, and how does it work?*

The penile plethysmograph (or PPG test) is a machine that measures changes in the circumference of the penis and is the most widely used measure of sexual arousal. It is the standard for the assessment of the sexual offender and is often a requirement or condition of parole. The polygraph, or lie detector, is another machine used.

The penile plethysmograph works something like this. A thin rubber band, which is actually a mercury strain gauge, is placed on the patient's penis (in private and usually by the patient) on the midshaft of the penis. The client is then asked to view explicit material, such as slides or movies and to create his own descriptions of sexual activity. Penile circumference is recorded in conjunction with the type of material shown, and a measure of arousal is obtained.

Interestingly, despite the great pressure to appear "normal," the majority of offenders demonstrate arousal to deviant sexual stimuli. For example, pedophiles show increases in penile circumference in reaction to images that depict sexual scenes involving children. This tool is frequently used for evaluation and assessment and for treatment purposes as well.

However, the penile plethysmograph does have serious reliability problems associated with it. For example, just over 30 percent of pedophiles and incest offenders don't become more aroused than average when viewing child pornography. Also, cheating is possible (the offender might not pay attention to the stimulus), the use of the instrument has not been standardized (the materials used to arouse subjects differ), the testing situation is very intrusive, the equipment is expensive (about $8,000) as is its administration, and the use of the test results in court as evidence is questionable. Perhaps most important is that arousal to certain types of sexual material is not necessarily predictive of an associated crime. It's not a crime to be aroused, and being aroused does not necessarily lead to a deviant act. In spite of these serious reservations, the penile plethysmograph is still one of the few tools that can assist the clinician in the assessment of a paraphilia.

The polygraph is fraught with even more problems. During questioning about his or her behavior, an offender's pulse, blood pressure, skin response, and heart activity are measured. Questioning occurs in a setting where the offender knows his honesty is being challenged. The polygraph's use certainly can't help establish the rapport necessary for a trustful and successful therapist-client relationship, which is so often essential given the nature of sexual disorders. Also, some offenders fail the polygraph test and then admit their crimes, but others can lie and pass.

Q What general approaches have been taken in the treatment of paraphilias, and how effective have they been?

Again, very little is actually known. It's hard to draw conclusions even where good measures of a treatment's effectiveness exist. That's because those treatments may be applied to more than one paraphilia and the results are grouped together. Also, treatments may take place in different settings, such as institutions versus community settings, and be applied to groups or individuals. These factors make it impossible to establish even a preliminary judgment of whether a treatment in itself, or some other factor, caused a specific outcome. In addition, the lack of control groups, small test groups, and the lack of follow-up leave therapists and consumers wondering what is best.

Anecdotal evidence leads us to believe that the most important factor in the success of a treatment is the development of a trusting relationship between a client and therapist. This is not easy since many clients are in treatment involuntarily (being forced by a court). Also, the nature of the disorder is very private, and few men want to reveal their thoughts.

However, some treatment approaches have shown some positive results, and many mental health professionals are hopeful about their use in the future. Cognitive-behavioral therapies have resulted in the most effective outcomes to date. Some cognitive-behavioral treatments emphasize the behavioral end of the continuum and focus on how inappropriate behaviors can be unlearned. Other approaches within this perspective focus on the offender's mental processes and how those can be changed and related to appropriate or non-offending behavior.

Medication is the other primary treatment of these disorders, especially hormonal treatments and medications such as antidepressants. These medications have shown some degree of success.

Q *Many different cognitive-behavioral treatments are available. What are some of them, and how effective are they?*

The more behavioral of these approaches to treating paraphilias include aversive conditioning, positive conditioning, and reconditioning. Each of these is based on the premise that paraphilias are learned behaviors and, given the correct contingencies, can be unlearned.

Aversive conditioning is based on the traditional classical conditioning paradigm where deviant responses are paired with an unpleasant stimulus. For example, one form of aversive conditioning called *covert sensitization* first trains the patient to relax and then has him visualize scenes of deviant behaviors followed by a negative event. For example, a patient who typically exposes himself to schoolchildren might be asked to imagine himself outside a school, calling girls to his car, and them exposing himself. Next, he is asked to imagine his penis getting caught in the zipper of his pants and experiencing great pain. He then is encouraged to imagine getting his penis back in his pants, driving away, and breathing easier.

If a client is especially difficult to treat, the degree of unpleasantness might be increased, and the aversive stimulus might take the form of a foul odor being introduced via an open bottle or a special pump. This is called *assisted aversive conditioning*. Here, the hope is that the foul odor, which usually brings on a feeling of nausea, will be paired with the deviant behavior, and the behavior itself takes on the quality of being unpleasant.

There are three stages in aversive conditioning:
1. An increase in deviant sexual arousal.
2. The presentation of an aversive consequence.
3. An escape from the aversion associated with the arousal—hence a new pattern to escape the behavior as well as the aversive consequence.

Another aversive conditioning technique is called *aversive behavior reversal*, known for its efficacy as well as its apparent simplicity of administration. This technique has been referred to as shame therapy since the offender is literally shamed into stopping the deviant behavior. For example, the graduate student who is caught exposing himself to women on campus is required to expose himself to hospital staff for 3 minutes on three separate occasions. The staff is instructed not to respond at all but to just watch silently. The rationale behind this treatment is that the forced exposure is sufficiently aversive and that it is unlikely to be repeated. A slight variation of this theme is when offenders are videotaped committing their crime and then forced to watch themselves. For many, the offense they committed is so distasteful that the experience of watching the tape has a profound impact.

Finally, vicarious sensitization has offenders view a series of videotapes showing deviant behaviors and their consequences. It's a kind of shock therapy, with the offender watching a victim describing the revenge she would like to extract from her offender while on screen, or watching actual scenes of a surgical castration and phallectomy (removal of the penis).

The positive conditioning techniques use positive reinforcement, mostly to reinforce appropriate arousal and appropriate social behaviors. Social skills training and alternative behavior completion try to get the offender to begin thinking about positive sexual behaviors and how successful avoidance of deviant behavior can be beneficial. For example, one such treatment scenario might have the offender imagining he is riding home one night and sees an attractive young woman in the car next to him. He gets aroused by the thought of following her and then exposing himself to her. He fights the urge, succeeds, and instead spends time congratulating himself for refusing to give in.

Finally, reconditioning techniques deal mostly with providing feedback to the offender so his behavior can be changed as soon as possible. For example, the plethysmograph (in plethysmographic biofeedback) can be connected to an external light, and the client works to keep the light within a particular range of color while being exposed to sexually stimulating material. Here, the effort is to "disconnect" the level of arousal from the stimulus that acts to reinforce it. Or, masturbation techniques can be used to teach the offender not to associate the pleasure in masturbation and climax with deviant behaviors.

The more cognitively based approaches, such as restructuring cognitive distortions and empathy training, emphasize the other end of the cognitive-behavioral continuum.

Restructuring cognitive distortions is based on the premises that errors of thinking can lead to errors in behavior and that the way one thinks about things in part determines their behavior. For example, the pedophile seeing a young girl in shorts might incorrectly think that "she wants me," or the exhibitionist might think, "she is a slut anyway." First, the inaccuracy of these thoughts needs to be pointed out and then thoughts need to be restructured to be more appropriate and more closely tied to reality.

Finally, empathy training attempts to get the offender to understand the victim's point of view. Usually, such therapy consists of identification of the victim, identification of the victimizing act, identification of the harm that has been done, role reversal ("How would you like it if you were touched in places you don't want to be touched?"), and the development of empathy.

Both the behavioral and cognitive approaches (under the general rubric of cognitive-behavioral) have seen some success. The accumulation of knowledge from several well-controlled studies does not exist, however, preventing us from reaching any general conclusion.

Q Does medication work in the treatment of paraphilias?

The use of several medications has demonstrated that sex drive can be reduced. More important, however, is the fact that sex drive is not consistently related to paraphiliacs' behavior, making the possible link between sex drive and behavior a weak one.

As far as hormones go, both medroxyprogesterone acetate (Depo-Provera) and cyproterone acetate have been shown to be effective in the treatment of sexual offenders. These medications decrease the level of circulating testosterone, the hormone thought to be responsible for sex drive. Both hormones reduce sex drive and aggression. They also result in a reduction in the frequency of erections, self-initiated sexual behaviors, and sexual fantasies as well as the frequency of masturbation and intercourse. As further proof of their effectiveness, offenders, who have taken the medication and then stop, rebound to previous levels of these undesired behaviors. It is important to point out, however, that high levels of circulating testosterone do not mean that a male is predisposed to a sexual disorder. These hormones are usually used in conjunction with behavioral and cognitive therapies.

Other types of medication that have been used in the management of paraphilias are antidepressants such as fluoxetine (Prozac), also used to treat depression and obsessive compulsive disorders. It appears that such treatment reduces sex drive but does not sufficiently target sexual fantasies.

Q The fact that there are no well-documented studies of the effectiveness of treatments for paraphilias leaves the consumer (and therapist) at somewhat of a loss as to what to do. Isn't there anything that's worked in a setting with reliable scientific controls and procedures?

Yes. Three institutional programs have reported sufficiently controlled studies, the results of which can be regarded as useful.

The first such program tested offenders incarcerated in a penitentiary. Here, a program combining cognitive and behavioral treatment for 101 child molesters and rapists was much more successful than traditional psychotherapy. After an average 9-year follow-up, those who participated in the treatment condition offended only 15 percent of the time compared to 50 percent of those who were not treated.

The two other programs, also based on the cognitive-behavioral model, treated child molesters, pedophiles, and rapists. These programs also found participants' recidivism rate to be far lower than that of the controls.

In addition to these three institutionalized programs, six outpatient programs have shown positive results, once again using cognitive-behavioral methodologies. In the largest of these, the recidivism records of some 4,000 offenders were examined 9 years after the treatment. The recidivism rate ranged from only 4 percent for exhibitionists to a high of 25 percent for rapists, still well below the level of 50 percent for those who did not receive any therapy.

The above studies provide some data for the consumer to conclude that a cognitive-behavioral approach does reduce paraphiliac behaviors.

Q What does the future hold for treating paraphilias, and what issues will continue to make evaluation and treatment difficult?

What's needed in the future are epidemiological studies that would allow an accurate estimate of how big a problem paraphilias actually are and how often the various paraphilias occur along with other disorders. Attention also needs to be given to other populations of offenders (such as females) and the development of treatment programs for adolescent offenders.

The problems of high drop-out rates (up to almost 70 percent for some aversion therapies), treatment expense, ease of access, and inadequate assessment techniques leave clinicians and researchers in this field with plenty of challenges. For the consumer, he or she needs to be aware of the shortcomings afforded by such treatments as described here but also of the potential for success that some of the treatment programs have shown.

Q Where Can I Find More Information About Sexual Disorders?

Books

Handbook of Sexual Dysfunctions: Assessment and Treatment edited by William O'Donohue and James H. Geer. Allyn & Bacon, 1993. ISBN 0205147879.

Brings together the best available information on diverse sexual problems and describes the future research agenda. Each chapter contains the psychopathology, assessment, and treatment of a specific disorder.

Questions & Answers About Sex in Later Life edited by Margot Tallmer. Charles Press, 1995. ISBN 0914783750.

A question-and-answer format discussing sex and old age on a variety of subjects. This presentation is informative and unintimidating. Questions include: Does interest in sex wane or disappear as people get older? What constitutes a good sexual experience for older women? How do older people feel about masturbation? Do older people have extramarital affairs?

The New Injection Treatment for Impotence: Medical and Psychological Aspects by Gorm Wagner and Helen Singer Kaplan. Brunner/Mazel, 1993. ISBN 087630689X.

A two-volume work on sexual disorders, describing a safe and effective treatment of male impotence.

Of Simultaneous Orgasms and Other Popular Myths: A Realistic Look at Relationships by Haresh Shah. Azad Publications, 1997. ISBN 096544290X.

Offers a discussion of the multi-faceted and complicated aspects of relationships between men and women.

Incestuous Families: An Ecological Approach to Understanding and Treatment by James W. Maddock and Noel R. Larson. W. W. Norton & Company, 1995. ISBN 039370193X.

Presents an approach to managing incest that focuses on both individual and systemic dynamics. It seeks to rebalance the relationships within the family and restructure certain aspects of individual family members' sexuality and personality.

Internet Sites

Erectile Dysfunction Information and Resources
(at http://www.pslgroup.com/erectile.htm) is part of the Doctor's Guide to the Internet and is an informative and comprehensive guide to everything involving this disorder. It includes medical news, related Internet sites, discussion groups, and basic information. The medical news section is especially current.

The Diagnostic Center for Men
(at http://www.for-men.com/impotent.html) contains information on treatment options for erectile dysfunction, oral medications, hormone replacement, injection therapy, and vacuum constriction devices. It also has basic information about the disorder.

Online Sexual Disorders Screening for Women
(at http://www.med.nyu.edu/Psych/screens/sdsf.html) at New York University's Department of Psychiatry provides a brief and simple multiple-choice exam for

women to learn the general likelihood that they have a sexual disorder. This test is not diagnostic but rather informs the woman as to relevant issues. The site provides referrals to the American Psychiatric Association where centers for evaluation and treatment can be found.

Continuing Medical Education—Sexual Disorders

(at http://mhsource.com/disorders/sexual.html) lists hundreds of questions asked about sexual disorders and the answers from experts at this Internet-based educational association.

Sexual Offense Recovery Online

(at http://www.sexualoffenserecovery.com/) is an on-line service providing information and consultation assistance to victims of sexual abuse.

Chapter 5

Substance Use Disorders: Dangerous Addictions

Pat and Mary had it all, or so they thought. The two professionals had a family of three attractive young sons and even a pedigree dog to run about in the backyard of their large house on a tree-lined street. Mary had met Pat during her freshman year in college. While she knew then that he liked to drink, she didn't realize he had a problem with alcohol until years later, when Pat started missing important work appointments, becoming verbally abusive to her and their oldest son, and spending more and more time recovering from drinking bouts. In due course, he lost his job. The marriage, like so many others where alcohol is involved, ended. While there were other troublesome issues in the marriage, the alcohol dependency that Pat had developed overshadowed them all.

Distraught and isolated, Pat has little choice but to get help. He goes through a detoxification program at the local substance abuse clinic and is then given medication to reduce his craving and help avoid a relapse. Nothing is for sure, and Pat's initial expression of concern about "falling off the wagon" prompts him to share his fears at his first of many weekly Alcoholics Anonymous meetings. He makes friends there, and works hard, but takes nothing for granted.

Q *What is a substance use disorder, and how common are they?*

A substance use disorder is characterized by the compulsive use of a substance which interferes with normal activities and has an adverse effect upon the user's health or quality of life. A substance disorder also has one (or more) of the following four characteristics, all occurring within 1 year.

- Use of substances in a setting where it is physically hazardous such as drinking and driving.
- Social or interpersonal problems such as marital conflicts or parenting concerns.
- Work or school problems related to substance abuse such as absences, suspensions, and incompletion of work.
- Illegal activity tied to substance abuse such as drug dealing and underage drinking.

Substance use disorders affect almost every segment of our society and, as a group, are among the most common of all mental disorders. Surveys of households have found a lifetime prevalence rate (at any time during the person's life) of 15 to 18 percent and 6-month prevalence rate (during the last six months) of between 6 and 7 percent. These rates don't include addiction to nicotine, one of the most common and difficult disorders to treat. Nicotine addictions are especially common—1 out of 5 adults smoke.

Q It seems as if substance use disorders are extremely common. They must take quite a toll on those around the individual as well as the person who has the disorder. How costly are they?

Very. Substance use disorders cost billions of dollars each year in everything from lost time at work to the cost of drug testing, screening, and rehabilitation programs. In a recent *New York Times* survey of 250 employers, 52 percent indicated that drug and alcohol addiction are significant problems in their businesses and 30 percent said that employees would be immediately dismissed if drug- or alcohol-related behavior was displayed on the job. The good news is that 80 percent of these companies offer employee assistance programs and 79 percent believe that such assistance is an effective (but expensive) method for returning employees to the workplace.

As far as medical expenses, the direct medical costs associated with smoking totaled $50 billion in 1996—all of which are avoidable. And, smoking-related illnesses are responsible for about 7 percent of total health care costs in the United States.

Q What substances are abused, and what are the general definitions and goals of a successful treatment program?

The substances that we will deal with in this chapter are the ones you hear most about in the news and read about in your daily newspaper: nicotine, alcohol (a depressant), cocaine (a stimulant), and opioids or heroin (a narcotic).

Successful treatment of substance abuse results in the ability to function according to one's societal role with total abstinence being the accepted treatment goal. Total abstinence is often not achieved, but a significant reduction in use such that the individual can assume a functional role is some evidence of success. So, for the individual who smoked two packs of cigarettes a day (forty cigarettes) and cuts down to ten cigarettes with the help of counseling and medication, the outcome could be considered a success. Or, for the person addicted to heroin, a transfer to a methadone (which satisfies the craving without the euphoria associated with heroin) maintenance program, while still addicted to a substance (methadone rather than heroin), would be indicative of successful treatment.

Q In general, what approaches are taken in the treatment of substance use disorders?

While all mental disorders cost society in one way or another, substance use disorders hold a somewhat unique position since they involve either excess consumption or possession of substances that are illegal. Many of these substance use disorders are disorders of excess.

Many of the addictions discussed in this chapter involve complex chemical and biological processes, hence, the development of specialized medications to treat the different types of substance disorders.

However, even though medication is sometimes the choice for treatment, the social and psychological processes associated with addictions are also very important to identify and treat. Almost every study of addiction to any substance shows that psychosocial treatments such as support groups, the involvement of family and friends, groups such as Alcoholics Anonymous, and cognitive-behavioral therapy are all of value. In fact, programs such as Alcoholics Anonymous are probably as, if not more, effective than any medication for the treatment of alcohol abuse.

Q *Isn't it somewhat of a contradiction to treat a drug problem using another drug?*

Yes—but it's not as simple as a one word answer. As you will see, there are many good studies (approaching the high standard that we talked about in the Introduction), that show medication to be highly effective in the treatment of various types of substance use disorders. Therefore, at the most basic level of our concern, people can be helped to overcome their addiction. While there used to be an "all addicts are alike" approach, current thinking leads us to be more aware of the patient-treatment match. Here, different types of programs and different medications are matched with particular types of disorders which hold the key to more treatment success than was once thought possible.

Q *If smoking is such a serious problem, what are the ways that nicotine dependence is treated, and how effective are they?*

Nicotine dependence is a powerful addiction and an extremely difficult one to treat. Those who begin smoking prior to age 21 have even more difficulty succeeding. Withdrawal from nicotine can be characterized by irritability, impatience, hostility, anxiety, a depressed mood, difficulty concentrating, restlessness, and weight gain. Part of the reason it is so difficult to stop smoking is that, even in times of less tolerance for smoking in general, it is still a socially acceptable behavior with few prohibitions and social condemnations associated with it. In addition, there is a powerful psychological link created and reinforced thousands of times between smoking and pleasant social experiences such as eating and being with friends.

The symptoms of withdrawal can be blocked however, through the use of two popular treatment techniques, and a third that has just been introduced to the market. The first is through the absorption of nicotine in chewing gum through the mucous membranes, and the second is directly through the skin (using a nicotine patch). The third approach, and newest alternative, is through the use of a pill. However, neither of these techniques yield the levels of nicotine delivery accomplished through smoking, which sends the drug directly into the bloodstream through the lungs. While chewing gum and the patch have shown to be effective and have enabled many smokers to reduce their nicotine dependence over several days to several weeks, the craving for the psychoactive effects of the drug continues. The results of several studies show that abstinence rates can vary from 9 to 40 percent 6 months after treatment has ceased. These are not very high numbers considering the magnitude of serious damage that smoking does to one's health and how many people are chronically ill because of it.

The latest effort at treating this addiction focuses on the use of a nicotine-free pill containing bupropion (Zyban) that is taken for 7 to 12 weeks. At least one study has shown it to be more effective than the nicotine patch. Since this is a medicine with the potential to cause some side effects (including seizures in a very small group of people who tested the drug) the use of the medication has to be closely monitored by a physician.

Research is also being conducted on the combination of a nicotine patch and a nicotine antagonist, macamylamine. Other medications such as clonidine (Catapres) and naltrexone (ReVia) have also been used, but the results are so far inconclusive. Since smoking and depression have been associated, antidepressants such as fluoxetine (Prozac) have also been used in conjunction with nicotine replacement therapy. Preliminary studies have shown that the use of antidepressants in non-depressed smokers significantly improved abstinence rates.

While gum and patches and medication such as bupropion do provide some success, the more recent practice has been to combine the use of these medications with behavioral therapy.

Q What kind of medications have been used for alcohol dependency, and how effective are they?

The treatment of symptoms of alcohol withdrawal, after detoxification, usually consists of chlordiazepoxide (Librium) or diazepam (Valium) and a multivitamin. These medications are prescribed to control the anxiety and restlessness that are characteristic of the early stages of withdrawal. As far as treatment of alcohol dependency, four types of medications have been used including antidipsotropics, serotonergic antidepressants, antianxiety anxiolytics, and medications that block the reinforcing effects of alcohol use, called opiate antagonists.

Antidipsotropic medications produce an unpleasant reaction when alcohol is consumed, thereby acting as a deterrent to drinking. Disulfiram (Antabuse or Temposil) inhibits the formation of certain chemicals which allow alcohol to be metabolized and can be administered either orally or implanted. So when a drink is taken, a toxic reaction occurs. The patient's skin turns color (to a purplish hue), and the patient becomes severely ill, often including vomiting, for 30 to 60 minutes. In treatment, this drug should be administered at least 24 hours after the last drink, and there are several precautions that the patient needs to be aware of. For example, the ingestion of certain types of foods, including mouthwashes, wine sauces, or vinegars (which contain alcohol), can trigger a reaction, as can inhalation of vapors from certain after-shave lotions (because of their high alcohol content). While the use of disulfiram is indicated for some patients, such as those who are highly motivated to stop smoking, there's not a great deal of evidence that it is effective over an extended period of time. In fact, in several studies disulfiram has been found to be no more effective than placebos.

Serotonergic antidepressants play an important role in mood regulation and may influence the development and maintenance of alcohol use disorders. In addition, some studies have shown that up to 30 percent of alcohol-dependent patients suffer major depression after the detoxification period. The use of antidepressants such as fluoxetine (Prozac) and the antianxiety medication buspirone (BuSpar) lead to a short term reduction in alcoholic consumption in heavy drinkers. Other types of antidepressants including tricyclic antidepressants such as amatriptyline (Elavil), may also be effective, especially with heavy drinkers.

Drugs like acamprosate (Campral) work to reduce the anxiety associated with withdrawal and maintenance, especially during relapses once detoxification has occurred. Several studies have shown positive effects.

Finally, opioid antagonists such as naltrexone (ReVia) now approved for use by the FDA, partially block the pleasurable effect of alcohol and reduce the craving associated with withdrawal.

Q What are some of the psychological treatments that have been used for alcohol dependence, and how effective are they?

There is an extensive body of studies that have explored the psychological treatment of alcohol dependency. This may in part be true because alcohol abuse and dependency is a widespread problem. More than 18 million people in the United States are considered to be alcohol dependent, and about 20 percent of all people have had a drinking problem at one time or anther. While most of these patients are men, the number of women with alcohol dependency has increased over the past 30 years, probably because of changing social standards and more equality in the social status of men and women. Alcohol dependency results in about 200,000 deaths a year that can be attributed either directly or indirectly to alcohol abuse and even higher levels of accidents and injuries. And, the cost of such abuse is upwards of $135 billion per year—in lost wages, illness, accompanying medical expenses, and treatment—enough to warrant extensive investigation into expenditures on research programs.

Among the most promising types of psychological therapies available for alcohol substance disorder is cognitive-behavioral therapy. This is broadly defined to include social skills training, community reinforcement, and behavioral marital therapy. Cognitive-behavioral therapies focus primarily on enhancing patients' skills in coping with everyday life circumstances (including a possible relapse) and on improving the match between patients' skills and environmental demands.

Alcoholics Anonymous has been widely successful as a program for treating alcoholism, as "a fellowship of men and women who share their experience, strength and hope with each other that they may solve their common problem and help others to recover from alcoholism.". It is the best known of all self-help groups. While not designed on any documented set of data or theoretical approaches, its practices (such as group support, autonomy, and self-governance) contain elements most experts consider important and useful. The effectiveness of Alcoholics Anonymous has been self-assessed every three years since 1968 with increasing rates of success.

Q Of these cognitive-behavioral techniques, which have been found to be most effective?

Especially effective in the treatment of alcohol dependence have been social skills training and community reinforcement. Both of these treatments have shown consistently positive results.

Social skills training focuses on developing assertiveness and communication skills. Patients, with the guidance of professionals, learn how to initiate social interactions, express their thoughts and feelings, and respond appropriately to criticism from others. In short, the program tries to teach patients how to effectively deal with the trials of everyday life found in home, school, and the workplace.

The Community Reinforcement Approach at first consisted of interventions to help the family and assist with job-related and legal problems. It also included meeting places where patients could enjoy each other in an alcohol-free environment. Later in its development, the club idea was dropped and a buddy system instituted along with group counseling. Other additions (such as the use of medications) have occurred over the years, but the central tenet of the program is its many forms of support for the patient from the community, both following detoxification and during the long and sometimes difficult road back to "normal."

Behavioral marital therapy is a psychosocial approach that has also been shown to be effective. After the patient's drinking behavior and marital relationship have been assessed, interventions are implemented that focus on improving the relationship and resolving conflicts and problems.

Q What other factors contribute to the success of psychological treatments of alcohol dependency?

Several factors have been identified as being important to the success of alcohol abuse treatment programs.

The characteristics of the therapist have a profound effect on the outcomes of the treatment, and there's some evidence that substantial differences exist for different therapists. In general, therapists who are more interpersonally skilled, less confrontational, and more empathetic have better outcomes than those therapists who are not. While such qualities as interpersonal skills are not easy to objectively judge, it's not hard for a patient to reach some conclusion about a therapist's general approach and whether he or she seems attuned to the needs of a patient.

Another factor is the length of treatment. Any treatment has been found to be better than none, but it also appears that a brief treatment can be as effective as extended treatment. In fact, the evidence for the effectiveness of low-cost brief treatment is very strong. The acronym FRAMES summarizes the six ingredients of effective treatments including Feedback about personal risk, the importance of personal Responsibility, clear Advice on how to change, a Menu of alternatives to consider for change, Empathy on the part of the therapist or treatment team, and Self-efficacy or optimism.

Finally, in addition to the characteristics we just noted, follow-up care after inpatient care has been associated with better results.

Q What kind of medications have been used for cocaine dependency, and how effective are they?

The major efforts at developing medications that would treat patients with cocaine use disorders have focused on blocking the reinforcing effects of cocaine and altering the neurochemical action of cocaine on an individual's behavior. Up to now, no medication has been identified that reliably does either. There are studies using antidepressants and agents that act on the dopamine pathways in the brain that have shown some success, however.

Antidepressants may have a role in the treatment of cocaine dependence because many users report feelings of depression following a reduction in cocaine use. The use of antidepressants such as desipramine (Norpramine) was thought at one time to reduce cocaine use in some patients, but this finding has failed to be substantiated in more recent studies.

Dopaminergic agents, such as amantadine (Symmetrel), bromocriptine (or Parlodel), and methylphenidate (Ritalin) work to counter the pleasurable effects that drugs such as cocaine produce when the chemical dopamine is produced and flows into the bloodstream. Studies with animals have shown these medications significantly reduce the craving for the drug, but an insufficient number and type of studies have been done with humans to draw conclusions. Thus, at present, no medications are known to be effective for the treatment of cocaine use. Psychosocial therapies are more beneficial.

Q What kind of medications have been used for heroin dependency, and how effective are they?

Addiction to opiates such as heroin goes back more than 100 years in the United States and thousands of years in other cultures. The primary response to its use in Western countries has been based on legal, and not medical standards. Historically, physicians have been restricted in the medical management of this substance disorder, but the development of medications over the past 20 years has shown that medical management can be superior to incarceration regarding abuse and recidivism.

There are two general approaches to the medical treatment of heroin addiction. The first is detoxification and then treatment for withdrawal symptoms (as with other substance addictions). The second is the use of a long-acting medication such as methadone. Very few treatments for any substance disorder have been more effective in the long-term than the use of methadone.

Even with intensive therapy, the majority of opiate users who have been detoxified experience a relapse. Methadone, developed during World War II as a synthetic substitute for other pain-killing opiates, was discovered as a viable alternative to heroin in the early 1960s. Its use transfers the patient from heroin (a short-acting drug that lasts only a few hours) to a drug (methadone) that can be taken once a day by mouth. The advantage of methadone is not only its ease of use, which appeals to patients, but also its oral delivery system reducing the potential of HIV transmitted illness through shared needles.

Methadone has been shown to be an extraordinarily effective synthetic drug in its ability to reduce the effects of heroin such that the patient decreases levels of heroin use and eventually stops. Methadone is effective in improving all areas of functioning. When coupled with psychosocial interventions such as cognitive-behavioral therapy, improvement is seen by reductions in illicit drug use, reduced symptoms and family problems, and increased employment. Most methadone treatment facilities (funded through public resources) allow 6 months for treatment, upon which time the patient is expected to pursue other types of therapy to assist in his or her maintenance program. Many mental health professionals feel, however, that the length of the treatment should be determined by the patient's needs rather than some arbitrary time limit.

A third alternative heroin treatment is the use of naltrexone (ReVia), a narcotic antagonist. Narcotic antagonists block the euphoric effects of heroin. Naltrexone is taken by mouth once daily or every other day, and has minimal side effects. It is not addicting and has very little potential for abuse. However, since patient non-compliance with this treatment is a common problem, a favorable treatment outcome requires a positive therapeutic relationship and careful monitoring of medication compliance.

Q How many people take methadone, and what are the qualities of a good methadone program?

Approximately 120,000 patients in the United States receive methadone as a treatment for heroin addiction on any given day.

A good program is one that has an adequate counseling staff, uses adequate doses of methadone, and has a success rate of about 60 to 70 percent as defined by improvement in functional status such as at work, in interpersonal relationships, and at school. However, there are not many complete treatment programs as just described due to underfunding. And even when there is a program available, the services that are offered might simply be inadequate. Many programs just dispense methadone without offering the accompanying counseling that is thought to be an essential factor in helping patients stabilize and improve their lives.

Q I've heard lots of controversy surrounds the use of methadone. What are some of the issues?

It's widely accepted that methadone is an excellent treatment for heroin addiction, but it is not a cure. Rather than being dependent upon heroin, the patient is, instead, dependent upon a synthetic substance. For many people, the issue is one of dependency and abuse—of any substance. So, replacing a dependence on heroin with methadone is not progress in that view. The availability of increasingly pure heroin has also created a problem for methadone maintenance programs, requiring higher dosages of methadone to prevent withdrawal effects.

Q Where Can I Find More Information About Substance Use Disorders?

Books

The Betty Ford Center Book of Answers: Help for Those Struggling with Substance Abuse and for the People Who Love Them by James W. West. Pocket Books, 1997. ISBN 0671001825.

Answers the most basic questions about addiction, from one of the world's most famous treatment centers for addiction.

Substance Abuse Sourcebook: Basic Health-Related Information About the Abuse of Legal and Illegal Substances Such As Alcohol, Tobacco, Prescription Drugs edited by Karen Bellenir. Omnigraphics, Inc., 1996. ISBN 0780800389.

A collection of articles originally published for a lay audience and organized into separate sections on general information, statistics, alcohol and other illicit substances of abuse, substance abuse during pregnancy, prevention, and intervention, treatment, and recovery.

The Enlightened Smoker's Guide to Quitting by B. Jack Gebhardt. Element, 1998. ISBN 1862041849.

A seven-step program presented in a non-judgmental and humorous manner that has been shown to be successful in seminars conducted by the author.

Smack by Melvin Burgess. Henry Holt & Company, Inc., 1998. ISBN 080505801X.

A highly believable book about adolescents and drug abuse.

Internet Sites

NOAH: New York Online Access to Health Care
(http://www.noah.cuny.edu:8080/) has well-written and informative discussions on an extensive listing of substance-abuse related topics and includes a list of service providers. Another nice feature is that the site can be seen in English or Spanish.

Mental Health Net Resources on Substance Abuse and Alcoholism
(http://www.cmhc.com/guide/substnce.htm) has the largest listing of, and links to, Web resources plus links to news groups such as alt.recovery, alt.recover.aa (alcohol), alt.recovery.na (narcotics), and alt.recovery.nictotine (smoking), a link to nine mailing lists and pages of related resources. This is a treasure chest of information.

Indiana Prevention Resource Center
(http://www.drugs.indiana.edu/) offers information on prevention, updated statistics, resources, and an extensive library of book and article summaries. Even though a good deal of information deals with issues pertaining to the state of Indiana, there is more than enough general information to serve as a valuable resource.

Online Intergroup of Alcoholics Anonymous
(http://www.aa-intergroup.org/index.html) is the on-line site that serves all the on-line A.A. groups. Here you can find out about on-line meetings, convention

schedules, and information about A.A. (also at http://www.alcoholics-anonymous.org/).

The National Clearing House for Alcohol and Drug Information
(http://www.health.org/aboutn.htm) is the information service of the Center for Substance Abuse Prevention of the Substance Abuse and Mental Health Services Administration in the U.S. Department of Health & Human Services. It's the world's largest resource for current information and materials concerning substance abuse and is a great rescue for professionals and patients alike.

Where to Write

Center for Substance Abuse Prevention
5600 Fishers Lane
Rockville, MD 20857
301-443-0365

Alcoholics Anonymous
P.O. Box 459
Grand Central Station
New York, NY 10163
212-870-3400

American Academy of Addiction Psychiatry
7301 Mission Road, Suite 252
Prairie Village, KS 66208
913-262-6161

National Association of Alcoholism and Drug Abuse Counselors
1911 N. Fort Myer Dr., Suite 900
Arlington, VA 22209
800-548-0497

National Coalition of Hispanic Health and Human Services Organizations (COSSMHO)
1501 Sixteenth Street, N.W.
Washington, DC 20036
202-387-5000

Chapter 6

Somatoform and Dissociative Disorders

Somatoform Disorders: When Physical Symptoms Have No Apparent Cause

Jean's mother died suddenly from a brain aneurysm. Every time Jean gets the smallest of headaches, she worries that she, too, has some incurable brain abnormality, probably a brain tumor. Her first stop is her family doctor. The doctor examines Jean and assures her that everything is fine but agrees to refer her to a neurologist after her insistence that there really is something wrong. The neurologist listens carefully to Jean's concerns and decides to do some testing, including an MRI. The results are negative. Jean, though relieved, is not convinced.

In the following few weeks, Jean calls and visits her family doctor repeatedly with the same complaint but without any apparent physical cause. Eventually, her doctor realizes that Jean could be suffering from a particular type of somatoform disorder, called hypochondriasis. Such individuals are preoccupied with fears of having a serious disease in the absence of underlying medical conditions to warrant such fears. Jean thinks she is physically sick, but she is not. Jean's doctor refers her to a therapist who specializes in somatoform disorders. Although there is no magic cure for this type of mental disorder, a good patient–therapist relationship and cognitive therapy help Jean to understand that her fears are real to her but not an accurate assessment of her physical condition.

Q What is a somatoform disorder, and how often does one occur?

A somatoform disorder is characterized by complaints of physical symptoms such as headaches or backaches but without an identifiable cause. Somatoform disorder symptoms might also take the form of an unreasonable fear of having a disease or placing a disproportionate importance on simple symptoms. For example, a person might have a headache and think he must have a brain tumor or some other serious neurological disease.

Community surveys by mental health professionals have found that about 0.5 to 1 percent of the general adult population has such a disorder. The rates are probably much higher, perhaps because several physicians are the ones who first see such disorders. (After all, if one thinks he or she is physically ill, why would one go to a psychiatrist or a psychologist?)

Q Are there different types of somatoform disorders?

Somatoform disorders are of five general types. All are characterized as chronic problems that probably need lifelong attention, and most people who have any of these disorders have been symptomatic for an extended period of time. Categories of the disorder are based on the presentation of symptoms ("My back hurts so much I can hardly walk") or on circumstances or situations that lead up to the disorder (such as anxiety about work or a relationship that results in a painful headache).

- Somatization: the individual complains of many different physical (sometimes called somatic) disorders that have no medical explanation, and these symptoms are reported as being present over an extended period of time. These complaints about general health don't have an excessive impact upon the individual, in that work and school can continue, but this type of somatoform disorder is often accompanied by depression and anxiety.
- Conversion: the individual suffers an abnormality or a deficit in a motor or sensory system for which no physical explanation can be found. An example of a conversion disorder is blindness with no physical or medical reason detectable. This type of somatoform disorder is thought to have its origins in some type of stress or environmental event. The symptoms are not voluntarily produced by the individual.
- Somatoform pain: a somatoform disorder characterized by persistent pain that is distressing, disabling, or both. Also, when there is an identifiable reason for the discomfort, the individual's report of pain exceeds what would normally be expected. The pain is often located in more than one site (such as head, back, and abdomen).

- Hypochondriasis: an unremitting or unrealistic fear or preoccupation that one is seriously ill. Regardless of any medical assurances, examination, or treatments, the condition continues. Hypochondria is different from somatization, in which the concern is about general state of health. In hypochondria, the concern is about a specific illness.
- Body dysmorphic disorder: a distressing preoccupation with an imagined physical defect or physical characteristic.

Q How is somatization treated, and how effective are the treatments?

Somatization is characterized by multiple physical complaints without any medical explanation. The criteria most often used are the presence of four pain symptoms (such as, "My head and back ache"), two gastrointestinal symptoms (such as vomiting), one sexual symptom (such as lack of interest), and one neurological symptom (such as tingling fingers). Somatization generally begins in early adolescence or early adulthood and is a chronic condition that needs to be managed throughout one's adult life.

The general treatment for somatization stresses many of the qualities of any good treatment program. These include an emphasis on regular contact with a physician, acceptance by a therapist of the patient's somatic symptoms as being real, avoiding unnecessary diagnostic testing, minimal use of new (to the patient) therapies, and a stable level of contact with the treating professional. Such a treatment plan should lead to improved tolerance of discomfort and less unnecessary medical care. Much of treating somatization (and all the somatoform disorders for that matter) involves finding the balance between providing the appropriate level of care while not overindulging or unduly reinforcing attention-getting behavior.

Does this approach work? The results of at least one study seem to indicate yes. Patients with somatization participated in the treatment described above and showed marked decreases in the use of health care services, a primary indicator of success. The comparison groups of patients who did not participate showed no such decrease.

To date, no strategies for the treatment of somatization through drugs has been shown effective.

Q How is conversion disorder diagnosed and treated, and how effective is the treatment?

A diagnosis of conversion disorder can be made after an extensive medical or neurological examination that finds no physical explanation for a patient's abnormal or deficient motor functioning (such as not being able to see or walk). The other important criterion is the onset of symptoms after some identifiable psychological conflict or source of stress. The popular media have reported cases of Vietnamese women who have gone blind after witnessing atrocities during the Vietnam conflict. Such an occurrence could be an example of a conversion disorder.

No data resulting from any controlled studies are available regarding the efficacy of treating conversion disorder. In general, mental health professionals know that patients who have the symptoms for a long time and along with other mental disorders such as anxiety or depression require more intensive treatment and have less positive outcomes.

In the studies that have been done, about one-half of conversion disorders respond to various supportive treatments:

- Emotional support regarding the events that may have precipitated the disorder.
- Explanations that not all physical symptoms have corresponding physical causes.
- A lowering of expectations that symptoms will resolve rapidly.
- A constant effort to reinforce any improvement.

Even those who are not helped by these treatments may be helped by the use of antianxiety or antidepressant medications.

When the conversion disorder is chronic and complicated by other factors, intensive behavioral therapy, including the use of reinforcement and use of unpleasant or aversive stimuli, has been somewhat effective, especially in an inpatient setting.

Q How is somatoform pain treated, and how effective is the treatment?

Psychological factors seem to contribute significantly to the onset, severity, exacerbation, and maintenance of pain that is the focus of this somatoform disorder. Cognitive-behavioral approaches have resulted in significant treatment success, with the goal of reducing pain-related stress. In treatment the pain is certainly acknowledged, and often the best measure of success is a reduction in discomfort. Different types of group therapies have been found to be superior to no-treatment control conditions for patients with chronic lower back pain and temporomandibular (or jaw) pain. With young children, cognitive-behavioral therapy has been found to be superior in treating stomach pains than standard pediatric care.

Antidepressants can be of some assistance with pain, as they are with some other somatoform disorders, such as conversion disorders. Such medication does generally reduce the intensity of pain, but the effect is somewhat delayed, and the doses are lower than for treating depression. Interestingly, the benefits of antidepressants may not be uniform across pain conditions, indicating that their effectiveness is largely dependent on the characteristics of each individual case.

Q How is hypochondria treated, and how effective is the treatment?

Hypochondria is a relatively common type of somatoform disorder, with 4 to 9 percent of the general population being affected. The disorder usually begins in early adulthood and can be chronic or recurring.

As with conversion disorder, hypochondriasis has been the subject of too few controlled studies to say definitively what works and what does not. However, there have been several case studies and uncontrolled studies that support the use of cognitive-behavioral programs for treatment of hypochondriasis. The essential features of this approach seem like common sense. These features include correcting misinformation and exaggerated beliefs, as well as pointing out how one's thinking can work to maintain the fear that accompanies certain diseases.

Unlike some other somatoform disorders, this form of the disorder seems to respond to medication. Antidepressants have been shown to have a positive effect. Their helpfulness suggests there may be a similarity, both in clinical symptoms and in the effectiveness of the treatment, between the person who has hypochondriasis and one who has an obsessive-compulsive disorder (see Chapter 9). The drugs that have been used with some success are clomipramine (Anafranil), fluoxetine (Prozac), and imipramine (Tofranil).

Q What is body dysmorphic disorder and how is it treated?

Body dysmorphic disorder is also known as dysmorphobia. It is a preoccupation with body parts and images, such as excessive concern about a birthmark or being flat-chested. It can start in adolescence and is usually chronic. Interestingly, medical or surgical interventions (even when physically successful) are usually unsuccessful in appeasing the individual's concerns. In fact such steps may even intensify the symptoms, perhaps because the physical focus of the disorder is gone, but the psychological disorder still remains. Thus, anyone considering cosmetic surgery to accomplish what he or she believes will be a radical change should also consult a mental health professional to help determine the reason for the perceived need to change. Depression, delusions, obsessive-compulsive disorder, or eating disorders often accompany this somatoform disorder.

The available evidence suggests that cognitive-behavioral therapy, often in group sessions, is an effective treatment for body dysmorphic disorder. Here, the focus can be on identifying and challenging distorted body perceptions, interrupting self-critical thoughts, dealing with situations that provoke anxiety about the perceived defect, and refraining from self-inspection and too much introspection. As with hypochondriasis, clomipramine and other antidepressants have had some success in treating this type of somatoform disorder.

Q I've heard of people faking an illness that they don't really have. Is that a type of factitious disorder?

Yes. When a person fakes symptoms or an illness in an attempt to maintain the role of a sick person, this practice is referred to as a factitious disorder. People with these disorders may go to very elaborate ends to falsify and fabricate medical histories and even intentionally produce physical symptoms (such as by taking excessive amounts of medication).

Munchausen's disorder, in which an individual experiences a self-produced illness, is a prototypical factitious disorder first described in 1951. The individual intentionally produces physical symptoms or signs of a disorder but the disorder can also include self-inflicted wounds and the exaggeration of already existing conditions. Munchausen's syndrome by proxy is defined as the fabrication of an illness in a child by a parent (most often the mother). In one study, about half of the mothers involved in Munchausen's syndrome by proxy had either smothered or poisoned their child as part of the fabrication, and seventeen of the forty-seven mothers had a personality disorder of some kind. Another study revealed that 20 percent of the patients with Munchausen's by proxy themselves had mothers who were diagnosed as having Munchausen's syndrome.

Dissociative Disorders: A Disruption of Awareness

Jane can't remember much about the evening; she left her job at the regular time with the office mate she was taking home, locked the side door of the building, and went to her car in the north parking lot. Her last memory is of opening the door to her car. The next thing she knows, she is looking up at a doctor and several nurses in the hospital emergency room, who tell her she was in an auto accident in which her passenger was seriously injured and is now on the critical list. The physical damage Jane experienced has yet to be fully determined, but the psychological insult is clear: Even weeks later, there are gaps in her memory of the event. For a time immediately following the accident, she even had trouble remembering details of her personal life, like where she lives and details about her work.

Jane is suffering a type of dissociative disorder called dissociative amnesia, in which she cannot recall important recent events, like the car accident. She also experiences distress from the sight, smell, and even the presence of almost any car similar to hers. The memory is alive and obviously not forgotten—it's just not conscious. Her therapist provides her a safe environment where she can talk about the experiences. He uses simple hypnosis and has her talk freely about what happened that night. After a few sessions, she begins to remember and relive the frightening accident that took place. Once she understands the reason for her anxiety, her feelings of not being in control and her heightened anxiety subside significantly.

Q In general, what is a dissociative disorder, and what types of dissociative disorders are there?

A dissociative disorder is a disconnection between a person and the most fundamental dimensions of his or her personality, such as who he is, what his personal history is, and even where he is. Dissociation can occur normally, as when you become so lost in a book that you lose track of time or are mesmerized by a particular visual experience or find yourself daydreaming. Even being a little "spaced out" is a normal dissociative experience. While a dissociative disorder is basically similar, it is much more extreme in that the disorder seriously interferes with, and prevents, normal everyday functioning. Estimates of the prevalence of dissociative disorders in the general population are about 1 percent.

The reader should keep in mind that there is more controversy over the diagnosis and treatment (and even the existence) of dissociative disorders than virtually any other mental disorder. For years, arguments for and against the existence of this general class of disorders have continued and they will likely not abate in the future. The informed consumer should read widely and carefully when making decisions about the treatment options that we discuss for these conditions.

Q What is dissociative amnesia, and what are some of its characteristics and causes?

Dissociative amnesia (also called psychogenic amnesia) is the inability to recall important personal information, and this lapse cannot be explained by ordinary forgetfulness. For example, it's normal to forget a phone number but not where you were yesterday. The incidence of dissociative amnesia, unsurprisingly, increases during war and during natural and manmade disasters. Remembering terrible things that happen in these situations is too painful to recall.

Dissociative amnesia is the most common of all dissociative disorders. Besides being a disorder itself, it is also a symptom of other dissociative and anxiety disorders (see Chapter 8). In fact, some amnesia occasionally accompanies post-traumatic stress disorder (see Chapter 10) and somatization disorders (see our earlier discussion). It also is common in dissociative fugue and dissociative identity disorder (discussed later in this chapter).

In diagnosing dissociative amnesia, several physical and psychological disorders need to be ruled out. Among them are medical and neurological disorders such as epilepsy, brain tumors, head trauma, certain medications, drug and alcohol abuse, and cardiovascular abnormalities.

Most cases of dissociative amnesia can be divided into two categories, depending on the timing of the trauma that precipitated the amnesia. Acute dissociative amnesia is usually associated with more recent trauma, whereas chronic dissociative amnesia involves patients who experienced a traumatic event years prior to their developing memory loss.

Q How is dissociative amnesia treated, and how effective is the treatment?

Since so many cases of dissociative amnesia have occurred during wartime, the development of most treatments has occurred during wars. The first step is to remove the soldier from the front line, or, similarly, to remove the patient from the source of stress, be it physical abuse or something else. When the patient is removed from the stress and placed in an environment perceived to be safe, symptoms often disappear spontaneously without further treatment. In such a setting, the therapist and patient can work on recalling the past experiences necessary to help the patient's recall. When such recall does not come freely, hypnosis and drug-assisted treatments sometimes are used to relax the patient and help recall. While many different types of barbiturates have been used, the most popular are sodium pentobarbital and sodium amorbarbital. Sometimes, these drugs need to be administered continuously during a session to ensure that the patient remains relaxed.

There are many anecdotal reports of successful hypnosis, but, as with the use of medication, there are no well-designed and well-conducted studies that provide information to allow a judgment as to the effectiveness of hypnosis.

Q What is dissociative fugue, and what are some of its characteristics and causes?

Dissociative fugue (also called psychogenic fugue), which occurs in about .2 percent of the general population, is characterized by unexpected movement or flight with an impaired ability to remember one's past. The travel may last for hours or for days. In some cases, patients cannot remember their identity, or they establish a completely new one. The difference between dissociative fugue and dissociative amnesia is that in the latter, patients are aware of their loss of memory. In dissociative fugue, patients don't realize they cannot remember—instead, the new identity conveys new memories as well. Once this new identity is established, there is no switching between the old and the new. The new identity is the one the person has, and rarely does this new identity appear anything other than normal.

A whole list of factors predisposes one to dissociative fugue, including extreme psychological distress such as from war or disaster, personal or financial losses, heavy alcohol use, or intense and overwhelming stress such as experienced in an assault or rape. Some episodes of dissociative fugue occur during sleep or are associated with sleep deprivation, although this phenomenon is not understood. Dissociative fugue is the least understood dissociative disorder, one that many mental health professionals do not believe even exists.

Q How is dissociative fugue treated, and how effective is the treatment?

The treatment of dissociative fugue follows the same guidelines as for dissociative amnesia, but, once again, there's very little information about the effectiveness of any of these treatments. However, there is a significant collection of information from therapists about what the goals of treatment should be. These are the assurance of safety, the development of a trusting therapeutic relationship, the recovery of personal identity, a review of factors that may trigger future fugues, the reintegration of the traumatic memories into the patient's personal history, and a returning of the patient to his or her previous life.

No medication has been associated with treatment of the disorder, although medication (as described for dissociative amnesia) has been used to assist in the reintegration of memories.

Q What is dissociative identity disorder, and what are some of its characteristics?

Dissociative identity disorder has long received a great deal of attention in the popular media, perhaps accounting for its popularity both as a criminal defense and as the focal point of many repressed memory incidents. Also known as multiple personality disorder, dissociative identity disorder is defined as the presence of two or more distinct personalities or personality states that alternate in taking control of a person's behavior. The disorder occurs in perhaps 0.01 percent of the general population, although some estimates have been as high as 1 percent. These altered states are sometimes called alters and can have different names, ages, sexes, and other personal characteristics. The patient can switch very quickly from one personality to another without any obvious precipitating factor. There is no more controversial psychiatric disorder. In fact, it's fair to say that many of America's psychiatrists and psychologists question whether such a mental disorder occurs.

Usually, a person with the disorder has two to four different personalities (but up to fifteen have been discovered) at the time of diagnosis and has a primary or host personality that carries the patient's given name. It is usually this host that seeks treatment, and it is not uncommon for the host not to be aware of the alters. The average age at diagnosis is 29 to 35 years, and the disorder is more common in women than men (about 6 women to 1 man). Women typically present more personalities than men do.

The general criteria for diagnosis of dissociative identity disorder includes dissociative amnesia and a lack of physiological causal factors such as blackouts from alcoholism. These symptoms are typical in addition to having two or more distinct personalities including a host personality.

Q How is dissociative identity disorder treated, and how effective is the treatment?

It is easy in some ways to think about how patients with dissociative identity disorder were treated before modern psychiatry: as being possessed. Perhaps because the disorder is so disturbing, it has received much press, such as the detailed descriptions of cases known as Estelle and Janice, Leonie and Lucie, and the many faces of Eve.

The treatment of dissociative identity disorder generally involves many of the steps we described earlier for all dissociative disorders. These are the development of a therapeutic relationship based on safety and trust, negotiation with the patient about treatment options, development of a contract against self-harm and harm to others, history taking, a discussion of the trauma that may have played a role in the development of dissociative identity disorder, negotiating conflicts among different personalities, and helping the patient deal with the potential conflicts between the multiple personalities. It's generally accepted that the therapist also will try to work with the patient to develop a social network and a support system, perhaps including the current family as well as the family of origin. Even when things go well, however, the treatment of dissociative identity disorder can be a long and difficult process.

In one of the first reported studies evaluating the outcomes of therapy for dissociative identity disorder, 67 percent of the participants were successful following treatment. Success is defined here as reaching "fusion" or, in more practical terms, three stable months of continuity of memory, no signs of multiple personalities, a subjective sense of unity, absence of other personalities during hypnosis, and an awareness of what were previous attitudes and emotions of the other personalities, now integrated into one. And of these 67 percent, 33 (or 27 percent of the entire group of participants) showed no signs of disassociation during the follow-up 27 months later.

The results from this study also found that individuals with fewer personalities required shorter periods of treatment and were less likely to relapse. Also, male patients had fewer personalities and briefer treatments than females.

Q What other treatments of dissociative identity disorder have been tried?

Very little empirical evidence allows us to recommend any one treatment for dissociative identity disorder as more effective than another. There is a wealth of information available about other attempts at treatments, and these results are anecdotal. Still, the studies do provide a look at what is being done and what is being tried. The following treatment techniques are among those.

- Group therapy presents an opportunity for dissociative identity disorder patients to deal with humans in a social context. The group therapy enhances individual therapy, which is the mainstay of treatment.
- Family treatments are recommended since the disorder is usually the result of family dysfunction. If the disorder has been precipitated by a family member, identifying the abuser and terminating the abuse cycle can be helpful in treatment.
- Hypnosis allows for the recovery and reproduction of important information.
- Medications such as antidepressants, neuroleptics, benzodiazepines, anticonvulsants, beta blockers, and mood stabilizers have all been tried in the treatment of dissociative identity disorder. There are no systematic reports of their success or lack thereof.
- Electroconvulsive shock has decreased depression in patients who have dissociative identity disorder and are depressed, but the treatment has not changed the dissociative identity disorder symptoms.

Q What is depersonalization disorder, and what are some of its characteristics and causes?

Depersonalization disorder is characterized by feelings of detachment from one's self. It is like an "out-of-body experience," in which a person feels as if he or she can observe his or her behavior from a distance. Some psychiatric disorders associated with depersonalization disorder are panic disorder (Chapter 8), agoraphobia (Chapter 8), post-traumatic stress (Chapter 10), schizophrenia (Chapter 11), drug intoxication and withdrawal (Chapter 5), and mood disorders (Chapter 7). Depersonalization disorder has also been associated with neurological disorders including epilepsy, sleep deprivation, Meniere's disease, and sensory deprivation.

While the incidence of depersonalization disorder is not known, it is thought to be the third most common psychiatric symptom following depression and anxiety. Also, it is believed that under stress, up to 50 percent of all adults have experienced at least one brief episode of depersonalization disorder. Likewise, 12 to 14 percent of normal college students, 30 percent of individuals exposed to life-threatening danger, and 40 percent of hospitalized psychiatric patients have experienced such an episode.

While there's little information as to what might cause depersonalization disorder, there are suggestions that anatomical abnormalities in the brain, similar to those that cause epilepsy, might be responsible.

Q How is depersonalization disorder treated, and how effective is the treatment?

As with other dissociative disorders, few, if any, controlled studies have been done. Also, the anecdotal information about treatment of this disorder is not as complete as with other dissociative disorders. It seems that a little bit of everything has been tried. Among such treatments are antidepressant medications, electroconvulsive shock therapy, education, dynamic therapy, and the use of psychostimulants. The necessary information to make any judgment about effective treatments of this disorder is just not available.

Q Where Can I Find More Information About Image Disorders?

Books

Dissociative Identity Disorder: Theoretical and Treatment Controversies edited by Lewis M. Cohen, Joan N. Berzoff, and Mark R. Elin. Jason Aronson, 1995. ISBN 1568213808.

A thoughtful and informative work focusing on the various points of view surrounding issues raised by the diagnosis and treatment of dissociative identity disorder.

Mind-Body Problems: Psychotherapy With Psychosomatic Disorders edited by Janet Schumacher Finell. Jason Aronson, 1997. ISBN 1568216548.

Focuses on the theoretical bases as well as the clinical realities of examining the mind-body relationship as it relates to image disorders.

Broken Images, Broken Selves: Dissociative Narratives in Clinical Practice edited by Stanley Krippner and Susan Marie Powers. Brunner/Mazel, 1997. ISBN 0876308515.

A collection of personal accounts by individuals who have experienced dissociative disorders.

The Three Faces of Eve by Corbett H. Thigpen and Hervey M. Cleckley. Three Faces of Eve, 1992. ISBN 0911238514.

Accounts of dissociative identity disorder, based on the experiences of Chris Sizemore.

Internet Sites

Mothers Against Munchausen's Syndrome by Proxy Allegations
(at http://www.msbp.com/) was created to respond to the number of false allegations about mothers causing their children to be ill.

The International Society for the Study of Dissociation
(at http://www.issd.org/) is a huge source of information about dissociation and the society, including information about its yearly meeting, membership, awards, and the society's journal.

Sidran Foundation and Press
(at http://www.sidran.org/) is a national non-profit organization devoted to education, advocacy, and research related to trauma-related stress in children and adults.

The Wounded Healer Journal
(at http://idealist.com/wounded_healer/index.shtml) is a collection of books, ideas, chat group, forums, and features about abuse and survivors.

Chapter 7

Depressive and Bipolar Disorders

Major Depressive Disorder: More Than Just "Down In the Dumps"

One problem with depression is that the depressed person can all too easily conclude that he or she is just "in a slump" or "a bit blue" and should be able just to snap out of it. Linda thinks precisely this way after her second child is born. Despite having every reason in the world to be happy—including a good marriage and a healthy baby— she describes her life as if it were an unbearable weight weight on her shoulders. Usually an energetic and focused young woman, Linda now considers it a major accomplishment to get through the day meeting her new infant's needs without breaking down in tears and calling her husband for help. These feelings continue for months; ultimately, Linda accepts her depression as part of her everyday existence, not knowing this disorder is common and highly treatable.

Finally, in despair, Linda visits a psychiatrist who prescribes a commonly used medication for treating depression along with therapy. While it usually takes 4 to 6 weeks to see any response to the antidepressant, Linda begins to feel better in days and, along with the therapy, she comes to better understand and deal with her disorder. The dreary Midwest winter and the her toddler's incessant curiosity no longer overwhelm her. Her feelings of isolation and loneliness come and go, but don't have the profound effect on her life that they once did. Linda may have to take the medication for at least 6 months, but she is blessedly freed from the terrible depression that paralyzed her.

Q *What is major depressive disorder, and how often does it occur?*

Major depressive disorder (sometimes referred to as unipolar depression)is an emotional disorder in which the individual feels unmotivated, sad, listless, and emotionally drained. It has many accompanying characteristics, which can interfere with work, play, eating, and sleeping—practically every facet of everyday living. Depression is an important disorder for mental health professionals to understand because it is the most commonly diagnosed psychiatric disorder among adults.

The lifetime risk for a major depressive disorder is 10 to 25 percent for women and 5 to 12 percent for men. At any point, between 5 and 9 percent of all women and between 2 and 3 percent of men suffer depression. As important, is the fact that up to 15 percent of patients with severe major depressive disorder die by suicide. As people with depression get older, the likelihood of death by suicide increases.

Q *What are some symptoms of the person with a major depressive disorder?*

The person with a major depressive disorder has persistent sadness that may be accompanied by physical symptoms. The emotional symptoms include a loss of interest in everyday and even special activities, increased irritability, a lack of motivation, an absence of pleasure, and strong pessimism. Physical symptoms include weight loss, absence of appetite, profound fatigue, difficulty sleeping or great difficulty in getting out of bed, and a decreased ability to concentrate. Other mental disorders often occur along with or are precipitated by major depressive disorder. These disorders include anxiety, eating disorders, psychosis, substance abuse, and serious medical illnesses including heart disease.

Q *What's the difference between depression and just feeling bad?*

The symptoms of depression are much more intense and persistent. For example, the loss of a loved one would certainly sadden an individual, but the associated grief and sadness subsides over time. With depression, the sadness remains and becomes pervasive, affecting every aspect of the individual's daily functioning.

Q In general, how effective are antidepressants in the treatment of depression?

The treatment of major depression with antidepressants is a milestone in psychiatry because of their high rate of success. In fact, the success rate of antidepressants is so high that it is comparable to the treatment success of major medical disorders including some types of heart disease, hypertension, and diabetes. While there are differences in the effectiveness of the various classes of antidepressants, they clearly work much better than no treatment at all and better than a placebo as well. Before effective antidepressants were developed, other medications including barbiturates and amphetamines, were used to treat depression. These were in time, found to be ineffective and in many cases, addictive.

The classes of antidepressants vary in their chemical actions on the brain, side effects, and safety. Tricyclic antidepressants, for years (beginning around 1960) were the treatment of choice. Modern-day preparations are almost uniformly safe as long as other medical conditions are taken into consideration.

No mental disorder has received as much scrutiny as depression, perhaps because such a large number of people suffer the disorder. Also, no other disorder has been the focus of so many studies involving thousands of patients at levels where there are sufficient safeguards against contamination of the results by uncontrolled sources of differences. In other words, consumers can have a great deal of confidence in the tests of these drugs' effectiveness in treating major depressive or unipolar depression disorder.

Q What role do tricyclic antidepressants play in the treatment of depression, and what are some of the advantages and disadvantages?

Tricyclic antidepressants were the treatment of choice for major depression for many years. First introduced into the United States in the 1960s, the following seven tricyclic antidepressants have been approved for use: imipramine (Tofranil), desipramine (Norpramine), amitriptyline (Elavil), nortriptyline (Pamelor or Aventyl), doxepin (Sinequan), trimipramine (Surmontil), clomipramine (Anafranil—only approved in the United States for obsessive-compuslive disorder), maprotiline (Ludiomil), and amoxapine (Asendin), though not technically tricyclics, are often grouped with them.

Randomized studies have shown tricyclic antidepressants to be much more effective than a placebo and comparably effective to medications such as the newer selective serotonin reuptake inhibitors. The side effects of the tricyclics, however, can make them difficult to tolerate and even dangerous for some patients. Side effects include dry mouth, blurred vision, constipation, urinary hesitancy, difficulty remembering, increased heart rate, weight gain, and sleepiness. For some patients with physical illness such as heart problems, an overdose can be deadly. In fact, tricyclic antidepressants are the number one cause of overdose death among prescription drugs in the United States.

On the other hand, some therapists believe that tricyclic antidepressants are the treatment of choice for severe depression and are far somewhat more effective than alternatives, yet this is controversial.

Q What role do monoamine oxidase inhibitors play in the treatment of depression, and what are some of the advantages and disadvantages?

How monoamine oxidase inhibitors came to treat depression is fascinating. During the early years of this century when tuberculosis was rampant, an antitubercular drug, iproniazid, was observed to produce mood elevation in many patients. This observation led to the two MAO inhibitors currently used in this country. They are phenelzine (Nardil) and tranylcypromine (Parnate).

Some of the disadvantages of monoamine oxidase inhibitors include the need for multiple dosages during the day (an inconvenience providing a chance to forget) and restrictions of certain foods such as aged meats, cheeses, and red wine to avoid a drug interaction that can cause death. Other side effects include dizziness, sexual dysfunction, insomnia, palpitations, and edema or swelling. Monoamine oxidase inhibitors are not the first line of medications used to treat depression because of these side effects.

Q What role do selective serotonin reuptake inhibitors play in the treatment of depression, and what are some of the advantages and disadvantages?

Selective serotonin reuptake inhibitors have become the most commonly prescribed medications for treating depression. They are hugely popular, with more than 25 million patients having been treated with one. The first of these popular medications, fluoxetine (or Prozac), was introduced in the United States in 1988. Since then, four other selective serotonin reuptake inhibitors have been introduced: sertraline (Zoloft), paroxetine (Paxil), fluvoxamine (Luvox), and citalopram (Celexa). These are effective drugs and desirable, primarily because the side effects are neither dangerous nor difficult to live with. Among them are nausea, diarrhea, insomnia, nervousness, and sexual dysfunction. Conservative dosing can control all of these but sexual dysfunction. Sexual dysfunction (from which about 30 percent of the users suffer) seems to be less dose-related and is seen at even low doses.

Q What other medications are used to treat depression, and what are some of their advantages and disadvantages?

Other medications have been used to treat depression. Among them are venlafaxine (Effexor), bupropion (Wellbutrin), trazodone (Desyrel), nefazodone (Serzone), and mirtazapine (Remeron). As with any medication, these too have advantages and disadvantages.

Q How do I know when an antidepressant is not working, and how long a trial period is necessary?

Antidepressants are not working if the patient does not experience any relief. In other words, the person stays depressed and the symptoms listed earlier in the chapter do not subside. While it can be difficult to wait 8 weeks, that is the recommended period to determine if an antidepressant is working. If there is no relief after this 2-month period, then another antidepressant should be tried.

One of the important things about antidepressants is that if one drug is not effective, or has intolerable or unpleasant side effects, another drug from the same class of drugs or from another class might indeed work. A physician should decide on the medication to be tried.

Q Even though antidepressants have been very effective in treating depression, what are some issues in judging which antidepressant might be best?

First, there's the basic definition of what constitutes a satisfactory response to a drug. A 50 percent decline in severity of depression symptoms is generally accepted as the measure of success in clinical studies. Second, as we discussed in the introduction, the role of the placebo in testing the effectiveness of a medication is always an issue. Remember that a placebo condition is not the same as receiving no treatment at all. Even though the patients in the placebo condition do not receive the drug being tested, professionals (in evaluation, diagnosis, and "treatment") still provide them a considerable amount of attention. This attention can sometimes have a profoundly positive effect on symptoms.

Third, how quickly a patient responds to an antidepressant is a major consideration. It generally takes 4 to 6 weeks before the therapeutic benefits of antidepressants become clinically evident. While there are great individual differences in response time, with some patients improving within days, there is always a preference for medications that work faster for all. In the most extreme cases, professionals want the depression lifted as soon as possible to reduce the likelihood of suicide or some other dramatic action.

Fourth, factors such as sex, age, and other medical or psychological disorders need to be taken into account when finding the best medication. For example, there is very little information regarding the use of antidepressants with children and adolescents. Also, women of childbearing age have been excluded from some clinical trials because of fears of potentially seriously harmful effects should they become pregnant. Unfortunately, this situation results in inadequate knowledge about the group (young women) at greatest risk of unipolar depression.

Finally, the particular pattern of comorbidity—or occurrence of depression along with other disorders—is a focus of current research. Prevalence rates of unipolar depression in patients with medical disorders such as cancer, diabetes, heart attacks, Parkinson's disease, multiple sclerosis, and Alzheimer's disease are between 25 and 50 percent. Since so many of these patients are taking medications for other disorders, it is of paramount importance for antidepressants to be safe in combination with those other medications.

Q *Medication has been very effective as a treatment for depression, but what other therapies are considered when a treatment decision is made?*

Behavior therapy, cognitive-behavior therapy, and interpersonal psychotherapy, especially in conjunction with medication, have been used effectively to treat depression. On the following pages, we will look at each of these therapies and evidence of their usefulness as alternatives or as co-treatments with antidepressants.

Q *How is behavior therapy used in the treatment of depression, and how effective is it?*

Behavior therapy focuses largely on improving social and communication skills and on decreasing unpleasant or negative life experiences. A behavior therapy program uses procedures designed to change overt behaviors and monitor daily activities. Such a program also assesses the level of mastery of these activities, assigns increasingly difficult activities to the patient, and helps identify behavioral solutions to counterproductive patterns of behaviors. Interestingly, this same model of therapy has been applied to depressed patients who are having marital difficulties. In fact, marital disputes are the most frequently discussed topic among depressed patients participating in therapy.

In general, well-designed and adequately controlled studies have found behavior therapy to be effective for treating depression. However, behavior therapy sometimes does not receive the recognition it deserves as an effective treatment tool. This may be because of the controversy that surrounds any therapeutic technique based on behavioral methods and the implication that behavior is being controlled.

Q How is cognitive-behavioral therapy used in the treatment of depression, and how effective is it?

The most extensively evaluated psychological treatment for depression is cognitive-behavioral therapy, sometimes referred to simply as cognitive therapy. In practice, cognitive-behavioral therapy consists of sixteen to twenty sessions over a period of 12 to 16 weeks. The focus of the therapy is on changing the depressed patient's negative view of the self, the world, and the future. The hope is to change the negative view of virtually everything in the person's frame of reference.

Throughout the therapy, the patient is encouraged to monitor his or her own behavior and associated thoughts and feelings. The idea is to help the patient understand the connection between these thoughts and feelings and overt behaviors. The patient and therapist examine beliefs underlying positive and negative thoughts, and the goal is to change the negative thoughts that resulted in depression in the first place. The focus on the therapy eventually shifts to maintaining positive thoughts and dealing with negative ones as they relate to behaviors that characterize depression. In sum, when the way a patient thinks about his or her behavior is radically changed, so the associated negative behaviors can be changed as well.

In general, cognitive-behavioral therapy is an effective treatment for depression as confirmed by many studies in many different settings. However, for the more depressed patient, antidepressant medication alone or in combination with cognitive-bchavioral therapy be the best treatment.

Perhaps the most important thing to remember about cognitive-behavioral therapy is that its effectiveness depends on how well trained the therapist is. Cognitive-behavioral therapy is much more than just "the power of positive thinking" (as many popular psychology books would lead you to believe). Any therapist using this technique must be competently trained for the technique to work.

Q How is interpersonal psychotherapy used in the treatment of depression, and how effective is it?

Interpersonal psychotherapy is based on the assumption that a patient's interpersonal relations play a significant role in both the onset and maintenance of depression. As you might expect, the therapy's focus is on the identification and amelioration of difficulties in interpersonal functioning such as fulfilling roles, dealing with unresolved grief, and social isolation.

Only two large studies have provided evidence as to the efficacy of interpersonal psychotherapy for the treatment of depression. In general, the findings are that interpersonal psychotherapy both as a treatment alone, as well as in conjunction with antidepressants, is a very successful strategy in treating depression.

Q Electroconvulsive therapy to treat depression sounds like something out of the dark ages. Is it still being used, and is it effective as a treatment for depression?

Electroconvulsive therapy is still being used (more than 10,000 times each day), and in some cases works very well in the treatment of depression. It is used after patients have not responded to, or can't tolerate the side effects of, antidepressants, and after patients don't improve with other therapies. A special use of electroconvulsive therapy is when depression is severe and needs immediate attention. Such a case would be when a patient is severely depressed and perhaps suicidal, and it is too risky to wait for an antidepressant or some other therapy to work.

In general, electroconvulsive therapy is a very effective treatment for depression with short-term memory constituting the most common adverse effect.

The use of electroconvulsive therapy is effective but primarily in the treatment of depression that is thought to be the result of physiological causes such as an imbalance in brain chemistry. Does it work better than antidepressants? It's difficult to say, since electroconvulsive therapy is terminated when depression lifts, but medication is continued for maintenance reasons.

Q How does electroconvulsive therapy work?

Electroconvulsive therapy was developed based on the observation of patients with depression who had epileptic-like seizures. Following a seizure, the symptoms of the disorder seemed to abate. Since a seizure occurs when electrical activity is the brain in disorganized, the thought was that artificially creating a seizure through electrical shock could produce a remission of symptoms in depressed patients.

Electroconvulsive therapy is straightforward. After a complete physical examination, the patient undergoes six to twelve treatments. During treatment, the patent is medicated to induce sleep and relax the muscles in the body. The electric stimulus is then delivered through electrodes attached to the head. The procedure takes no more than 15 minutes, and the only recorded side effect is slight amnesia that eventually disappears.

Q *There is another type of depressive disorder I have heard about called dysthymic disorder. How does it differ from major depressive disorder, and how is it treated?*

Although dysthymic disorder is a form of depression that is less disabling than a major depressive disorder, by definition, it can last for at least 2 years or more. Dysthymic disorder has many of the same symptoms of major depression, occurs more frequently in women than men, and about 3 percent of the general population will suffer dysthymic disorder at one time during their lives.

The generally milder nature of dysthymic disorder can be misleading in that it can be a serious disorder. Initial symptoms might be withdrawal or shyness during childhood and poor school performance, as is common in children of parents with major depression. Many people who suffer dysthymic disorder will also experience a major depressive disorder later in their lives. Fortunately, dysthymic disorder responds to the same types of pharmacological agents used in the treatment of the major depressive disorder.

Bipolar (Manic Depressive) Disorder: Very Happy and Very Sad

Jane knows that her mother had problems, but she does not relate them to her own difficulties managing her work and parenting responsibilities. Her mother was hospitalized often during Jane's childhood, when Jane and her sisters were told, "Mom needs time to rest—she's exhausted." It wasn't until the early years of Jane's marriage that she learned her mother was treated repeatedly for bipolar disorder, in which her mother would swing with little warning from normal mood to the deepest of depressions to wild excitement and unrestrained enthusiasm, and then back again. Treatment seemed to help, but there were always relapses, more swings and more hospitalizations.

Jane knows that there is an unusually high co-occurrence of such bipolar disorder in parents and their children. As a result, she becomes concerned when she notices herself becoming irritable and unusually focused on the smallest of tasks at work. Passing these symptoms off to fatigue and waiting for them to disappear doesn't work. The little irritations become big ones, and her unusually high level of energy becomes so extreme that she needs little sleep and disrupts everyone else's schedule in the family. Then the next thing she knows, she's so far "down in the dumps" that she can barely get out of bed and make it to work. When a sister recalls their mother's experience, Jane thinks she could be suffering some of the symptoms of the same type of mental disorder. A visit with a psychiatrist and extensive discussions lead to medication and family therapy. The result? Jane's behavior comes under control as long as she takes her medication. But she's continues to worry about the stress that each day brings and how it might precipitate another one of her "crazy" (her husband's word) up-and-down swings.

Q *What is bipolar disorder, and how often does it occur?*

Bipolar disorder is a major mood disorder, characterized by moderate or severe depression that alternates with extremely high levels of elation, physical activity, and unbounded (and unrealistic) cheerfulness and optimism most of the time. Bipolar disorder has both the characteristics of depression and characteristics of mania (such as excitability and thoughts of grandiosity).

Bipolar disorder is a severe, recurrent psychiatric disorder that occurs in 1 to 1.6 percent of all adults over their lifetime and in 1.2 percent of all children and adolescents. At least 80 percent of the patients who have an initial episode of mania will have one or more subsequent episodes. This illness is a serious public health problem because of its chronic and disruptive nature. For example, long-term outcomes seldom include complete recovery, and the recurrence rate can be as high as 50 percent even with treatment. The higher the number of manic episodes prior to treatment, the more unlikely that treatment will be successful.

The social costs of bipolar disorder are even more staggering. A large public health study showed that a woman experiencing the onset of bipolar disorder at age 25 can expect a 9-year reduction in life expectancy, 14 years of loss in productivity, and 12 years of overt illness—all very expensive from both a human and a financial cost. In addition, approximately 1 in 3 patients shows deficits in work functioning 2 years after hospitalization, and only 20 percent work at expected levels of employment during the 6 months after an episode.

Even though bipolar disorder is a serious mental disorder affecting millions of people, less than one-third of bipolar individuals ever receive any treatment, the lowest percentage of any psychiatric disorder.

Q *What are some symptoms of a bipolar disorder?*

The person with a bipolar disorder in the manic phase can have an inflated sense of self-esteem and an excessive level of grandiosity. He or she is easily distracted, needs little sleep, is almost frantically active, and is highly focused on work to be done (be it school, home, or business). He or she can also become excessively involved in otherwise pleasurable activities that have a high potential for serious consequences. For example, a person with the disorder may become overly sexually active or make foolish investments due to unrealistic optimism. Even more seriously, at least 25 percent of patients in the depressed phase attempt suicide, and up to 50 percent of patients are suicidal when treatment begins.

Perhaps the strongest case for any genetically inheritable psychiatric disorder has been made for bipolar disorder. Bipolar disorder is a highly inheritable illness with concordance rates (a measure of how likely it is that a disease is shared) between 60 and 70 percent for identical twins. In family studies, the risk for bipolar disorders (and major depressive disorder as well) among first-degree relatives (such as parents and children) is much higher than those not as directly related.

Q Lithium was one of the first drugs used to treat any mental disorder. How effective has it been in the treatment of bipolar disorder, and what are its side effects?

Lithium was the first modern anti-manic medication and has been the cornerstone of treatment for patients with bipolar disorder in the United States. It was approved for use in 1970, and five studies have demonstrated that it is superior to a placebo in the treatment of bipolar disorder. These studies span 40 years (from 1954 to 1994), and the criteria used to diagnose bipolar disorder have changed considerably during this time (primarily because of new research findings and changes in political and social climates), making it difficult to generalize these findings to new groups of patients. However, lithium has substantially helped patients with this mental disorder and it is a well-tolerated medication. It has been likened to penicillin as a "miracle drug" in the treatment of this mental disorder.

Some possible side effects of lithium are gastrointestinal discomfort, kidney dysfunction (accompanied by thirst and excessive urination), an increase in white blood cell count, difficulty with motor coordination and concentration, and an increase in acne in adolescents. Approximately 20 to 40 percent of patients who take lithium either cannot tolerate the drug or do not find it effective. In addition, the difference between a therapeutic dose and a toxic dose of lithium is quite small, so any regimen including lithium as a treatment requires that the patient's blood levels of lithium be closely monitored.

Q What other medications have been used to treat bipolar disorder, and how effective are they?

Several other medications have been used to treat bipolar disorder. The anticonvulsant divalproex (Depakote) and carbamazepine (Tegretol) have been used with some degree of success in the treatment of bipolar disorder.

The use of divalproex has resulted in a success rate of up to 80 percent of people with bipolar disorder and a reduction in the severity of manic and depressive episodes in the remaining patients. Depakote, the brand name of divalproex, is the first mood stabilizer to be approved by the Food and Drug Administration in 25 years.

Carbamazepine has also been effective for treating bipolar disorder, but several studies that reported this finding also used antipsychotics or lithium as part of the treatment. It is not clear whether carbamazepine acting alone would have produced the same result. Side effects of divalproex and carbamazepine can include nausea, indigestion, weight gain, and muscle tremors.

Q *What about the effectiveness of antipsychotic medications? Do they have any role in the treatment of bipolar disorder?*

Before lithium was introduced, antipsychotic medication was one of the few available classes of pharmacological agents used for the long-term reduction in bipolar symptoms. Today, these drugs are used to bolster the effects of lithium, divalproex, and carbamazepine, but there is little information about their effectiveness when used in such combinations. Antipsychotic medications may be useful in the initial management of bipolar disorder, but should not be used over a long period if possible because of potentially serious motor side effects.

Q *In general, how effective have drugs been in the treatment of bipolar disorder?*

Evidence from well-conducted and well-controlled studies indicate that drugs such as lithium and divalproex are effective in the treatment of acute mania. However, some patients only have a partial response to these medications, and some even respond poorly to all three. Other studies clearly show that lithium and divalproex (Depakote) are effective as a prophylaxis against future manic and depressive episodes.

Continued research into alternative pharmacological treatments is definitely needed. Possible areas of research include the efficacy of combining these three drugs with one another, or combining an antipsychotic with one of these three drugs. However, none of these directions has been pursued in controlled studies to determine their effectiveness.

In addition, the three medications may be well-suited for treating symptoms of mania, but less effective for treating the symptoms of depression, hence the possible need for an antidepressant in addition to the mood stabilizer.

Q *It's clear that the use of medication is an effective*
way to treat bipolar disorder. What about
psychosocial treatments?

A leading view of the bipolar disorder is that it is caused by major imbalance in the neurochemistry of the brain as well as a possible genetic component. Negative family environments and stressful life events are thought to exacerbate these imbalances.

Because of the biological nature of the disorder, pharmacological treatments are clearly the primary treatment approach. Psychosocial treatments of bipolar disorders pick up where pharmacological treatments leave off. Psychosocial treatments' main focus is emphasizing adherence to medication regimens, decreasing hospitalization and relapses, improving the quality of life, and helping teach and improve mechanisms for coping with stress. A major report on bipolar disorders from the National Institutes of Mental Health concluded that the most understudied area in the treatment of this disorder is in the use of psychosocial therapy as a supplement to pharmacological therapy.

The major components of a psychosocial treatment program for bipolar disorder can include education about the disorder, adherence to medication, individual psychotherapy, and marital or family therapy.

Q *How effective is education in helping individuals*
with bipolar disorder adhere to his or her
medication routine?

Patients with bipolar disorder frequently express concern about how little they know about their disorder or the medications they are taking. Of the few studies that have been done, however, there is an important and positive relationship between what patients and their families know and adherence to a medication regime.

The primary focus of any educational program should be information about the nature of the bipolar disorder and how it can be successfully treated. Again, the issue of medication adherence is particularly important. Despite the high risk of relapse due to non-adherence, 18 to 53 percent of patients on long-term maintenance medication do not adhere to their prescribed regimen. In one study, adolescents whose bipolar disorder had been stabilized with medication had a relapse rate of 92 percent compared with a rate of 38 percent for those who continued their medication without interruption. If medication is resumed once it has been discontinued, there is a danger of the manic episodes being more extreme than they were before the medication was discontinued.

Educating patients about their condition and medication has been shown to be a powerful intervention. In one program, patients in an experimental group were given nine lectures about the nature of their disorder and its pharmacological management. Those who received the lectures adhered better to medication regimes at the outpatient follow-up 5 months later than did patients who didn't receive the lectures. Patients who received the lecture were also less fearful of the side effects of medication. In another study, the briefest of education programs (a 12-minute video) resulted in patients' increased knowledge about medication, more favorable attitudes about the medication, and increased adherence. This education proved a true ounce of prevention resulting in far more than a pound of cure, given the social and human capital costs incurred when patients stop taking their medication and experience a relapse.

Q Does educating family members about the disease help?

It helps those family members better understand the disorder and the course of treatment, but it does not help the patient adhere to the medication regime.

Q Is cognitive-behavioral intervention effective in the treatment of bipolar disorder?

Only one well-designed and controlled study has been conducted of the effectiveness of cognitive-behavioral therapy on bipolar disorder as an adjunct to pharmacological therapy. In this study, a group of patients being treated with lithium was compared with another group being treated with lithium and receiving cognitive-behavioral therapy. The cognitive-behavioral therapy was designed to alter specific thoughts and behaviors that possibly interfere with adherence to medication.

The 1-hour daily therapy sessions over a 6-week period led to significantly better medication adherence. In addition, the group that received the treatment had significantly fewer hospitalizations over the next 6 months and fewer mood swings. There was no difference between the two groups in the number of relapses that occurred.

Q *If someone within a troubled family suffers bipolar disorder, trying family or marital therapy would seem to make sense. Has that been tested?*

Yes, several different types of programs are being studied as to their effectiveness in treating bipolar disorder. Current information about their usefulness is limited, but results are available on one such program, inpatient family intervention.

Inpatient family intervention is a brief program focused on helping participants (who are hospitalized patients and family members) to cope with the hospital experience and make plans for after hospitalization. Patients and family members are encouraged to accept the disorder as real and probably chronic. They also are asked to identify stressors both within and outside the family that precipitate bipolar disorder episodes. In addition, participants are encouraged to learn ways to modify these precipitating patterns and cope with future stressors. Inpatient family intervention has been shown to result in better post-hospitalization adjustment, including improvements in general attitudes toward the family by the patient.

Q *What other psychosocial treatments are being investigated?*

Interpersonal and social rhythm therapy is an individual, outpatient therapy program that is an alternative to a group or family setting. Although the social context of a bipolar disorder is important, many bipolar patients either live alone or prefer to be treated alone. The two goals of interpersonal and social rhythm therapy are to help patients understand and negotiate the social context associated with their mood swings and to encourage patients to recognize the impact of interpersonal events on their everyday social lives. Interpersonal and social rhythm therapy involves taking a thorough history of the patient's disorder, conducting an inventory of the number and quality of relationships in the patient's social and familial networks, and identifying problem areas such as grief over losses, interpersonal disputes, and role transitions (such as from work to home).

Family-focused treatment, meanwhile, is designed for patients who have been recently hospitalized or treated on an outpatient basis for a manic or depressive episode. This treatment consists of five stages. First, the program is explained to the patient and his or her family members. Second, a series of evaluations of the family members' attitudes toward one another is conducted. Third, educational activities take place where the family and patient are familiarized with the nature and symptoms of the bipolar disorder. This educational component focuses on adherence to medication and on how non-adherence and relapse are often tied to family dynamics. Fourth, basic communication skills are taught and practiced. Finally, participants learn problem-solving techniques including solving core family conflicts that are usually related to the disorder. In one pilot study, only one out of nine (11 percent) patients in family-focused treatment program had a relapse, whereas fourteen out of twenty-three (or 61 percent) of those who did not participate in family-focused treatment (but who also received medication) had a relapse.

Q Where Can I Find More Information About Mood Disorders?

Books

A Brilliant Madness: Living with Manic Depressive Illness by Patty Duke and Gloria Hochman. Bantam Books, 1992. ISBN 0553072560.
    A recounting by actress Patty Duke of her struggle with manic depression, including more clinical aspects of manic depression written by Hochman.

Lie Down in Darkness by William Styron. Vintage Books, 1992. ISBN 0679735976.
    A vivid description of a Southern family's encounter with depression.

The Depression Workbook: A Guide for Living With Depression and Manic Depression by Mary Ellen Copeland and Wayne London. New Harbinger Publishers, 1992. ISBN 1879237326.
    Lots of valuable information including history, causes, and treatment of mood disorders. The book also includes several self-help tools.

Listening To Prozac by Peter D. Kramer. Viking, 1993. ISBN 0670841838.
    The controversial bestseller that focuses on the implications of using antidepressants to treat mood disorders.

Touched with Fire: Manic-Depressive Illness and the Artistic Temperament by Kay Redfield Jamison. Free Press, 1993. ISBN 068483183X.
    A fascinating book that discusses the lives of nineteenth-century poets, writers, and composers who suffered bipolar disorder.

The Essential Guide to Mental Health: The Most Comprehensive Guide to the Psychiatry for Popular Family Use by Jack M. Gorman. Griffin Trade Paperback, 1998. ISBN 0312187157.
    A layman's guide to the latest information about the treatment of mental disorders through the use of medication.

Internet Sites

Dr. Ivan's Page

(at http://www.psycom.net/depression.central.html) is an extensive clearinghouse with hundreds of links including discussion group links to resources on major depression, manic depression (bipolar disorder), cyclothymia, dysthymia, and other mood disorders. Almost every possible question about mood disorders is answered here or at one of this site's links.

Mood Disorders

(at http://www.psych.helsinki.fi/~janne/mood/mood.html) presents a general set of references and links to pages that deal with mood disorders, including depression and bipolar disorder. Users can even initiate a search of archives containing thousands of articles form the medical literature (at Medline) from here.

Depression FAQ

(at http://www.psych.helsinki.fi/~janne/asdfaq/) is a simple set of questions and answers about depression.

The New York Times Women's Health

(at http://www.nytimes.com/specials/women/whome/depression.html) offers information, resources, and facts about depression in general and, because of the high incidence, among women in particular.

Depression.com

(at http://depression.com/) sponsored by Bristol-Meyers Squibb, contains information on depression and weight gain, suicide, sex, sleep, and anxiety as well as information about the use of antidepressants, living with a depressed person, and the latest findings regarding the treatment of this disorder.

Discussion groups can be found at alt.support.depression, alt.support.depression.manic, and alt.support.depression.seasonal.

Where to Write

The National Depressive and Manic-Depressive Association
730 North Franklin, Suite 501
Chicago, IL 60610
1-800-82-NDMDA

The National Alliance for the Mentally Ill
200 North Glebe Road, Suite 1015
Arlington, VA 22203-3754
1-800-950-6264

The National Foundation for Depressive Illness
P. O. Box 2257
New York, NY 10116
1-800-248-4344

Chapter 8

Anxiety and Phobic Disorders

Generalized Anxiety Disorder: That Uncomfortable Feeling

This is Jane's senior year at a large Midwestern university, and she continues to have that chronic, always present anxiety about a large part of her everyday activities. It's not just that she's worried about the next class or whether her date will be fun on Friday evening. Rather, she always feels anxious, yet cannot really pinpoint what it is that she is anxious about. When she tries to identify the source of her uncomfortable feelings, she finds herself giving up, since nothing specific seems to fit. Besides her set of worries, she's also restless, often irritable around friends, and even has difficulty sleeping. Jane has what is called generalized anxiety disorder, and she knows that it is having a major impact on her well being.

The psychiatrist at the student health center has seen many young men and women with this anxiety disorder, since it is a common one, and she knows that one method of treatment for such pervading anxious feelings is through medication. She prescribes what she thinks will work best for Jane and keeps a close watch on her progress over the next four to six weeks. She also arranges for Jane to participate in behavior therapy designed to teach her how to control her anxiety through relaxation exercises and related techniques. With this combined treatment, Jane is definitely better able to work through the everyday trials and tribulations of being a college student with far less intrusive worries and concerns.

Q What is generalized anxiety disorder, and how common is it?

Generalized anxiety disorder occurs when an individual feels anxious all the time and when there's no obvious reason for concern. For example, excessive worrying about health or money or family, when no apparent threat exists to any of these, might be symptoms of a generalized anxiety disorder. In most cases, this exaggerated concern occurs regardless of the setting or the situation. It is often called free-floating anxiety and occurs in about 5 percent of the general population over the course of a lifetime. It most often strikes people in childhood or adolescence and is twice as common in women as in men. Generalized anxiety disorder is especially important, as it is often considered the "basic" anxiety disorder that is a consistent component of other anxiety disorders. Also, up to 60 percent of patients with generalized anxiety disorder have a history of at least one other mental disorder. Yet, surprisingly, generalized anxiety disorder has received relatively little attention.

What's the difference between simple anxiety and a generalized anxiety disorder? Anxiety is not an inappropriate reaction to many situations. Anyone who has experienced a major life event—such as marriage, an important entrance examination, or a crucial interview—is aware of the normal, anxious feelings that can accompany such an event. The difference between that kind of anxiety and generalized anxiety disorder is that the disorder leaves the individual debilitated by the anxiety. Anxiety reaches such a high level that normal functioning is no longer possible.

Q What are the symptoms of a person with generalized anxiety disorder?

The person with a generalized anxiety disorder is excessively and uncontrollably anxious and worried, and this state occurs over an extended period. For diagnostic purposes, the period is 6 months. It is as if the worries find their way into every aspect of the person's daily activities.

In addition, three or more of the following six symptoms are present:
- restlessness or feeling on edge
- becoming easily fatigued
- being irritable
- having difficulty concentrating on work
- being tense
- not being able to fall asleep or having trouble staying asleep and sleeping soundly

Generalized anxiety disorder is not caused by any physiological factor such as substance abuse, medication, or a medical condition. On the other hand, a generalized anxiety disorder can result in physical symptoms including trembling, twitching, muscle tension, headaches, sweating, and hot flashes.

Q In general, what's the most effective psychosocial treatment for generalized anxiety disorder?

Evidence is limited about the effectiveness of psychosocial treatments for generalized anxiety disorder. Just the same, several studies have shown positive results. For example, one early study lacking in control and methodological sophistication found that a generalized anxiety disorder treatment program consisting of biofeedback, relaxation training, and cognitive treatment resulted in a generalized improvement at the end of the treatment as well as 3 months later.

In another early but more controlled clinical trial, the effects of anxiety management as a treatment were tested. Anxiety management is a multicomponent treatment package using a self-help booklet and therapist-conducted treatment sessions. The treatment components in the study included education about anxiety, relaxation exercises, distraction, cognitive restructuring, and exposure to possibly anxiety-producing stimuli. Patients receiving the anxiety management program improved significantly on every measure of anxiety at the end of treatment, and these gains were maintained or improved at a 6-month follow-up.

In another set of studies, progressive muscle relaxation along with cognitive therapy was compared to progressive muscle relaxation with non-directive (or unstructured) therapy. All patients showed improvement at the end of the study as well as during a follow-up, but the relaxation and cognitive therapy group was superior.

Finally, in the most rigorous set of studies conducted to date, two treatments known to be effective were compared with each another. Patients were assigned to one of three groups: cognitive-behavioral treatment, behavior therapy, or a wait list. The behavior therapy consisted of progressive muscle relaxation, graduated exposure, and rebuilding confidence. The cognitive-behavioral treatment consisted of the traditional cognitive-behavioral therapy where patients are taught to organize and use their thoughts in relation to a specific goal they may set as part of their therapy. The wait list group received neither treatment.

The results showed that cognitive-behavioral therapy was superior to behavior therapy, the same result found in several other studies. The superiority might be the result of the additional power that the cognitive component has when added to already effective behavioral therapy.

Q What should we look for in the future regarding psychosocial treatment of generalized anxiety disorder?

At this time, the most successful way to treat generalized anxiety disorder is through cognitive-behavioral therapy with the goal of bringing the worry process under the patient's control. Substantial progress has been made in the past few decades, and most studies have found that highly structured cognitive therapy is more effective than nondirective or unstructured therapy, such as psychodynamic therapy. There is little evidence, however, that one cognitive-behavioral approach is better than any other.

Continued research in the area of generalized anxiety disorder is essential. The earlier reported figures of a 5 percent lifetime prevalence rate represents between 30 and 40 million of the general population who may experience anxiety that is sufficiently severe to warrant some type of clinical intervention.

Q What types of medications are used to treat generalized anxiety disorder, and how effective are they?

As with other mental disorders, generalized anxiety disorder can be treated with several different types of medication. Following is brief description of each type, what we know about its effectiveness in reducing the symptoms of the disorder, and known side effects.

- Benzodiazepines, such as diazepam (Valium), have been used in well-controlled studies for over 30 years, and the results have been mixed regarding their effectiveness in treating generalized anxiety disorder. Abundant data and clinical experience attest to their usefulness in treating anxiety, although in some studies they have not outperformed the placebo. These latter studies are difficult to interpret because definitions of generalized anxiety disorder have changed, as have recommendations for dosage rates and maintenance therapies. The side effects of benzodiazepines include sleepiness, motor skills impairment, and amnesia. These drugs can also be difficult to discontinue and "withdrawal syndrome" is often a problem. The major public health concern about using benzodiazepines focuses on their potential for abuse, although the abuse of these drugs rarely occurs in patients who are not already being treated for alcohol or substance abuse.

- Azapirones, such as buspirone (BuSpar), have been effective in treating the symptoms of generalized anxiety disorder, yielding 30 to 50 percent reductions in anxiety symptoms. This class of drugs takes longer to work than the benzodiazepines and does not cause drowsiness. Side effects are generally very mild and may include nausea, dizziness, and headaches.
- Antidepressants, such as imipramine (Tofranil), paroxetine (Paxil), and venlafaxine (Effexor) have been effective. More information about dosage and other important factors related to treatment are now being gathered and it is likely that antidepressants will eventually be considered the best medication for generalized anxiety disorder.

In addition to benzodiazepines, azapirones, and antidepressants, some other medications, such as beta blockers, have been tried as treatments for generalized anxiety disorder. There is too little information to reach any conclusion as to their effectiveness.

Q *What does the future hold for treating generalized anxiety disorder with medication?*

While there is a good deal of information about the medical treatment of generalized anxiety disorder, less information is available regarding the long-term efficacy or the optimal duration of treatment. For example, few studies have examined the long-term usefulness of medications such as benzodiazepines. They're very effective for about 6 weeks. It's questionable whether they are necessary thereafter, especially if the patient can learn how to deal with the anxiety through some of the psychosocial techniques we mentioned earlier. However, regardless of what medication is used, many patients relapse after medication is withdrawn (with no supplemental psychosocial treatment), leading to the conclusion that generalized anxiety disorder for some individuals may be a chronic illness and require long-term care.

Panic Disorder: When Anxiety Is Out of Control

Michael is a young and intelligent tax lawyer who is becoming increasingly isolated from his friends. They in turn have become increasingly worried about him. Michael spends more and more time at home and even has difficulty getting to work each day, even though his profession has always been very imporant to him. He has no idea why, but he incrasingly finds himself in situations in which he experiences all the elements of a panic attack, the primary component of panic disorder. His breathing becomes labored, his heart races, he sweats, and he feels as if the world is closing in on him. These attacks have been going on for some time. The only way he can avoid the embarrassment and anxiety of having attacks in public is to stay home. The attacks are not predictable, but at least he can choose the place where he has them.

When his job is ultimately threatened because of his increasing reluctance to travel to interview clients, he takes the important step of seeking professional help. Some very effective treatments are available for this disorder, and Michael finds a private psychiatrist who is able to see him. After an introduction and friendly chat, then more serious discussion about Michael's fears, the doctor tells Michael he can learn to anticipate his panic and to use his reasoning skills to master the anxious feelings. Michael also begins taking medication to help ensure that the panic attacks do not occur again. A year later, although some of the feelings still arise, at least Michael has come to feel they are under his control.

Q What is a panic disorder, and how common is it?

Panic disorder is an anxiety disorder characterized mostly by panic attacks. A panic attack is a frightening experience of feeling totally out of control, and it is often accompanied by very unpleasant physical symptoms. The lifetime prevalence rate is about 3.5 percent, and about three to six million Americans suffer the disorder. Twice as many women as men have it, and panic disorder is often accompanied by other conditions such as depression or substance abuse. Panic disorder often leads to phobias. (See the discussion about phobias later in this chapter.) The disorder usually starts in young adults, with the peak age of onset during the late teens and early twenties. About half the people with the disorder develop it before they are 24 years old.

Although everyone gets anxious, a person with a panic disorder often avoids any activity (even going out of the house) that might provoke a panic attack. Since a panic attack can come on without warning, an individual with the disorder finds himself or herself always on guard for another attack. Because the individual never knows when such an attack will occur, avoiding any possibility of one seems like the best strategy. That strategy is clearly not the best for dealing with work, school, friends, and family.

Q What are the characteristics of a panic attack?

People with panic disorder experience frequent and unprovoked panic attacks that are characterized by some or all of the following symptoms:

- palpitations or a pounding heart
- sweating
- shaking
- shortness of breath
- feelings of choking
- chest pain
- nausea
- dizziness
- fear of losing control
- fear of dying
- numbness or tingling sensations
- chills or hot flashes
- feelings of unreality

Panic attacks are frightening since the individual has no control over when and where they will occur. In the beginning, panic attacks occur without warning and without any way to stop them. The person's level of fear is unrelated to the actual situation, and panic attacks usually last only a few minutes because the body cannot maintain the intense level of emotional and physical involvement for long.

Q In general, what psychosocial treatments are available for panic disorder, and how effective are they?

Most psychosocial treatments for panic attack have been cognitive-behavioral in nature, and the various approaches share many similarities. The methods tend to include education about the nature of anxiety and panic, cognitive therapy, some form of exposure to a panic-inducing experience, and development of the skills necessary to cope with the panicky feelings. Here is a description of some approaches and how effective they are.

- Panic control treatment is one of the most often used treatments. It includes exposing the patient to sensations similar to those experienced during a panic attack. The program includes a cognitive restructuring component, directed at correcting misconceptions about anxiety and panic as well as correcting cognitions that overestimate the threat of danger associated with a panic attack.
- Breathing retraining, part of a relaxation effort, is also incorporated into panic control treatment. This step helps control the hyperventilating that often accompanies a panic attack. In several studies, panic control therapy has been found to be more effective than a control condition. In one study 81 percent of patients were panic-free 2 years after treatment.
- Cognitive therapy has been shown to be an effective treatment for panic attack. In one well-controlled study, after 8 weeks of treatment, 71 percent of the patients who received cognitive therapy were panic-free as compared with 25 percent of the patients who did not receive any supportive therapy. Even more impressive was the finding that at a 1-year follow-up, 87 percent of the patients remained panic-free.

Finally, alternative psychosocial treatments also have been used to treat panic attacks. A promising approach called emotion-focused therapy focuses on interpersonal triggers for panic attacks.

In addition, some attention has been devoted to the delivery of treatments for panic attacks without the intense and costly regular supervision of an on-scene therapist. In one study, patients received cognitive-behavioral treatment with either a standard amount of therapist contact (such as weekly hour-long sessions) or reduced hours of contact with a therapist plus telephone contacts. Both ways of treating panic disorders were equally effective, although at present most clinicians recommend face to face therapies.

Another more cost-efficient approach is through bibliotherapy, in which a manual is used as the basis for treatment. One study found the provision of such a manual to be as effective as cognitive-behavioral therapy. Patients maintained their panic-free status at the 3- and 6-month follow-ups. Perhaps most importantly, the attrition rate from the bibliotherapy and cognitive behavioral groups was zero, suggesting that these are desirable and not at all aversive ways of treating people who experience panic attacks.

Q What types of pharmacological treatments are available for panic disorder, and how effective are they?

The main pharmacological treatments of panic disorders have been antidepressants and monoamine oxidase inhibitors in the 1960s and 1970s, benzodiazepines in the 1980s, and, most recently, selective serotonin reuptake inhibitors.

- Selective serotonin reuptake inhibitors, such as paroxetine (Paxil) and sertraline (Zoloft) have been effective in the treatment of panic disorder with few side effects, leading to a high number of patients completing the treatment. They are the first line of defense and the pharmacological agent of choice.

- Tricyclic antidepressants such as imiprimine (Tofranil) offer the benefit of once-a-day dosing and have been used with great success in panic disorder. Tricyclic antidepressants are often not well-tolerated, which is why clinical trials of these drugs can have dropout rates upwards of 50 percent. The most common reasons for dropping out are jitteriness and weight gain.

- Benzodiazepines such as alprazolam (Xanax) and clonazepam (Klonopin) have worked for panic disorder with 55 to 75 percent of patients free of attacks at the end of one study. One advantage of alprazolam over other treatments for panic disorder is its quick action, with symptoms being reduced in the first week or two of treatment. Another advantage is its generally superior tolerability, but it does have some side effects such as drowsiness and slight memory impairment in a small percentage of patients who use the medication. A more serious concern is the possible development of dependency associated with difficult withdrawal.

- Monoamine oxidase inhibitors such as phenelzine (Nardil) have been shown to be effective against panic disorder. These medications are potent but produce many side effects, including weight gain, insomnia, sexual dysfunction, and dizziness. They also require that the patient rigidly avoid certain food and medications. These medications are only used when other treatments fail. They are not well tolerated and can be very dangerous in combination with foods containing tyramine such as certain cheeses, wines, and even avocados.

Q How effective is a combination of both medication and behavior therapy?

There have not been many well controlled studies that provide information that can be used to answer this question. A recent multicenter study failed to find an advantage of the combination over either treatment, although other treatments have found the combination to be superior.

Phobias: Irrational Fears of People, Places, or Things

Jim is afraid of anywhere that even hints of his being enclosed in a small space. That includes elevators, airplanes, and even small cars where his head bumps against the roof. He feels uncomfortable, even trapped. The thought of being in a crowded lobby without easy access to the outside world makes him so anxious that he sometimes can't function. Jim suffers a specific phobia called claustrophobia. The best treatment for him is called desensitization. Here, Jim is gradually exposed to the objects or situations he fears so much. By showing great courage, he learns to master the frightening situation, rather than having the situation master him.

Jim finds the help he needs in a program designed just for people who fear being in confined spaces. His first step is to talk with his psychiatrist and support group about his fear. Over an extended period, he is placed in situations that gradually approach the small spaces he fears. The first situation is just a few people in a wide-open office space. Then it is the same number of people in a smaller space, but still one large enough that Jim can easily see the outside. Then it is an office with a closed door and no people. Then he is placed with people in the office, then eventually standing near an elevator during quiet times of day. Jim's graduation takes place the day he rides a crowded elevator up to the 14th floor, gets off, crosses the hall, and takes another car down.

Q What is a phobia, and what different forms can it take?

A phobia is a marked and persistent fear that is caused by the presence of an object or a situation. Aquaphobia, a fear of water; claustrophobia, a fear of small places; or acrophobia, a fear of heights, are all examples. Agoraphobia, the fear of leaving home, is a common phobia. Phobias are irrational in that the fear caused by them is not associated with a real danger. Looking over the railing of the 1,500-foot-high Empire State Building would be expected to produce some anxiety, and a person experiencing it would not be labeled as phobic. When a fear interferes with an individual's daily functioning, however, there is cause for concern. A person who has a phobia is overwhelmed by anxiety and avoids the feared object or situation as well as people and events associated with the source of fear.

There are three categories of phobias: agoraphobia, specific phobias, and social phobias.

Agoraphobia is the fear of being alone in any place or situation from which the person thinks that escape is impossible or difficult. An extreme example of agoraphobia is the person who is afraid to leave the safety of his or her home (where he or she is in control), even for such simple tasks as food shopping or mailing a letter. A less extreme example is the person who will avoid a crowded movie theater or a bus that only has standing room. Agoraphobia is usually a complication of panic disorder, described in the preceding section of this chapter. The panic disorder patient may associate specific places with having a panic attack or fear such situations in which if an attack occurs, help is not immediately available.

Specific phobias are those directed at specific objects or situations, such as claustrophobia or acrophobia. Specific phobias used to be called simple phobias, and there are five subtypes of specific phobias:

- animal, such as fear of dogs or spiders
- natural-environmental, such as the fear of open spaces
- blood-injection, such as the fear of getting an injection
- situational, such as the fear of riding in a car
- other, including any (such as fear of vomiting or choking) that does not fit into the previous four categories

Social phobia (also called social anxiety disorder) is the fear of being in a situation where others are watching the individual, with the result being embarrassment or humiliation. Because of this fear, people with this type of phobia find the most mundane of tasks, such speaking to a small group of people, impossible. It is thought to be the most prevalent of all anxiety disorders with a lifetime prevalence of 13.3 percent and a 12-month prevalence of 7.9 percent. In addition, social phobia is the third most prevalent of all mental disorders, exceeded only by major depressive disorder and alcohol dependence.

Many factors can affect the onset and maintenance of a phobia. Among them are age and sex, and type of reaction to the object or situation. For example, the average age of onset for animal, blood, storm, and water phobias tends to be in early childhood.

Q What are the symptoms of someone who experiences a phobia?

When the object or situation that is the center of a phobia is encountered, the reaction is severe. Some features of a phobia follow.
- The individual understands that the fear is irrational and is totally out of proportion with the threat to his or her safety and well-being.
- Physical reactions can include rapid heartbeat, shortness of breath, fear, sweating, and a need to flee the object or situation.
- The individual feels persistent and irrational panic when the situation or object is encountered.
- The reaction is not voluntary, but automatic.
- The individual avoids the object or situation that is the focus of the phobia. Given that the object or situation itself does not pose a threat, it is easy to see how the reaction to a phobia can be debilitating.

Q How common are phobias?

Approximately 11 percent of the general population will experience a specific phobia sometime is his or her life. There is a lifetime prevalence rate for women having the disorder of about 15 percent compared to 7 percent for men. The average age for onset of a phobia is between 15 and 20 years.

Social phobia is thought to be the most prevalent of all anxiety disorders with a lifetime prevalence of around 13.3 percent and an occurrence in any one year of 8 percent of the general population. Social phobia is the third most prevalent mental disorder, exceeded only by depression and alcohol dependence. The average age of onset for social phobia is 15 years, and it most often begins before age 25.

Q What are some characteristics of agoraphobia?

Unlike specific phobias where the person knows to avoid an object or situation, agoraphobia is unpredictable and most often follows a panic attack. These panic attacks are unpredictable and can come at any time without any warning. Fear of a panic attack can be extremely anxiety-producing. A person develops a state of constant anxiety anticipating the next panic attack, which is then accompanied by an agoraphobic reaction.

Because of this unpredictability, the individual may avoid any place remotely associated with the original panic attack. As the attacks recur, more places become off limits until the individual excludes himself or herself from a large range of otherwise normal activities.

Q What is the most effective psychosocial treatment for specific phobias?

The treatment of choice for specific phobias is exposure-based procedures, particularly *in vivo* (or in real life exposure). The idea behind exposure-based therapy is that the patient confronts his or her fear and eventually adapts to it. In desensitization, the therapist carefully and gradually introduces an object or situation to the patient. Other than desensitization, flooding may be used. Here, the patient is exposed directly and immediately to the feared object or situation. The patient remains in the situation until the anxiety is reduced.

The desensitization method, for which the most well-designed studies have been conducted, includes the gradual exposure of the phobia-causing object or situation to the individual, accompanied by relaxation and breathing exercises. The exposure takes place *in vivo* rather than in a laboratory setting using imaginal exposure (where the patient just thinks of the phobia-related object or situation). For example, for a person who has a phobia of water, the first step *in vivo* might be visiting a swimming pool, the second sitting on the side, the third putting one foot in the water, and so on, all the while trying to concentrate on relaxing. The therapy attempts to gradually introduce the feared object or situation without any of the accompanying anxiety, threats, or danger posed by the original traumatic event. *In vivo* treatment is preferable, but if it is not possible, then imaginal exposure is acceptable.

In vivo exposure is deceptively simple. Therapists usually initiate exposure treatment within a few visits to the office. During these initial visits, the therapist collects information about the patient's feelings, thoughts, and behaviors concerning the object or situation. The system of exposure is explained to the patient, telling him or her that repeated exposure at increasingly "real" levels will allow him or her to become desensitized to the object or situation. A key point is that the exposure is under the control of the patient, and if the experience becomes too threatening, the patient can terminate the session. The patient is taught a variety of coping strategies such as relaxation and breathing exercises. The therapist and the patient then try to imagine a setting where a phobic reaction might become pronounced, and a treatment plan is formulated for how to deal with it.

An extensive amount of literature documents the effectiveness of exposure-based treatments of specific phobias for a wide range of objects or situations. In fact, the power of the treatment is in its applicability across settings, regardless of the feared object or situation.

Q Exposure-based treatments for specific phobias work, but these treatments vary. What are some of these differences?

Some of the factors that distinguish different types of *in vivo* exposure treatments are the duration and spacing of sessions, how involved the therapist is, and the use of additional treatment components.

In general, it appears that massive sessions (such as one long session) results in the most robust clinical improvement. In one study, a single 3-hour session left 90 percent of persons with animal or injection phobias to be much improved or recovered. Also, the more a therapist is involved, the more likely the phobia will be effectively dealt with. Patients who engaged in therapy with a therapist, as opposed to self-directed exposure therapy, were found to be free of the phobia at a much higher rate (71 percent compared with 6 percent) than those who did not have the assistance of a therapist.

Finally, some phobias benefit from an exposure-based procedure plus additional treatment strategies. For example, one of these additional strategies is useful for blood-injury phobias (where the individual panics at the sight of blood). In such a phobic reaction, heart rate and blood pressure increase in anticipation of confrontation with the feared object or situation. Then the heart rate and blood pressure drop dramatically, sometimes producing fainting. The applied tension technique is often used to sustain blood pressure levels until the crisis has passed. This technique includes tensing and relaxing all the large muscle groups, thereby forcing blood back to the extremities and not allowing blood pressure to drop.

Q What are some directions for research into the psychosocial treatment of specific phobias?

There is no doubt that specific phobias can be reduced if not eliminated, but there is also much to be learned. For example, little is known about the different characteristics of the five subtypes of specific phobias. If such information were available, more effective treatments could be designed. For example, the applied-tension technique works best with the blood-injection phobia. Perhaps other types of ancillary treatments would be as effective for other types of specific phobias.

Q What are the most effective psychosocial treatments for social phobias, and how effective are they?

The most common psychosocial methods used to treat social phobias are social skills training, relaxation techniques, and exposure-based methods (like those used to treat specific phobias), all used in conjunction with cognitive-behavioral therapy.

- Social skills training is based on the rationale that people with social phobias are deficient in their verbal and nonverbal social skills. There has been so little systematic research testing the effectiveness of this treatment that it is impossible to say whether it is effective.
- Relaxation training aims to reduce the aroused state that someone with a social phobia experiences. Once again, the little research that does exist does not make the case for this being an effective strategy for treating social phobias.
- Exposure-based and cognitive therapy seems to be an excellent and effective combination for treating social phobias. Here, the patient confronts the situation he or she fears until the anxiety is gradually reduced. These exposure sessions are conducted *in vivo*, where the feared event is continually confronted. The cognitive element of the treatment addresses the role of negative evaluation (embarrassment or reconstructing the environment to fit the needs of the patient). Right before a meeting with seventeen other people, rather than thinking, "Oh-oh, I'm in trouble now," the patient learns how to take the time needed to readjust his or her thinking about that task at hand. This combination of exposure and cognitive therapy has been shown to be superior to any other psychosocial treatment.

Q What developments are expected in the psychosocial treatment of social phobias?

Although exposure-based treatment for social phobias is effective, the number and type of studies that have been conducted limit the strength with which mental health professionals can recommend this treatment. More research is needed before any consensus can be reached. Consequently, the agenda for future work in the area of social phobias is better-controlled and well-documented research projects.

Q *What medications are used to treat phobias, and how effective are they?*

Social phobias have been treated successfully with medication, although it is clear that more research will strengthen confidence in this approach.

- Monoamine oxidase inhibitors, such as phenelizine (Nardil), are effective in treating social phobias, but there can be significant side effects including hypertension, weight gain, insomnia, and sexual dysfunction.
- Beta blockers have been tried but have not been proven to be effective in the treatment of social phobia.
- Benzodiazepines, such as clonazepam (Klonopin), have been effective in reducing social anxiety, interpersonal insensitivity, and general level of disability. Keep in mind, however, that this class of drugs can be difficult to discontinue.
- Selective serotonin reuptake inhibitors, such as paroxetine (Paxil), are useful in the treatment of social phobias based on the results of well-controlled and well-designed studies.

Q *Where Can I Find More Information About Anxiety Disorders?*

Books

Anxiety & Depression: The Best Resources to Help You Cope edited by Rich Wemhoff. Resource Pathways, 1998. ISBN 0965342468.
   A listing of resources on and about depression and anxiety.

Anxiety and Related Disorders edited by Benjamin B. Wolman and George Stricker. John Wiley & Sons, 1993. ISBN 0471547735.
   An academic text that goes into great detail on the origin and treatment of anxiety disorders. Experts write about the various types of anxiety disorders and how they are treated.

Shy Children, Phobic Adults: Nature and Treatment of Social Phobia by Deborah C. Beidel and Samuel M. Turner. American Psychological Association, 1997. ISBN 1557984611.
   An extensive discussion on this disorder and how it is treated.

Social Phobia: From Shyness to Stage Fright by John R. Marshall. Basic Books, 1995. ISBN 0465078966.

A comprehensive overview of the causes, symptoms, impact, and treatment of social phobias.

Anxiety and Its Disorders: The Nature and Treatment of Anxiety and Panic by David H. Barlow. Guilford Press, 1988. ISBN 0898627206.

A detailed and informative review of the treatment of both general anxiety disorder and panic disorder.

Internet Sites

The Anxiety Network
(at http://www.anxietynetwork.com/) includes general information about generalized anxiety disorder, panic disorder, and phobias. It has specific pages for each disorder and links to other sites on anxiety.

The Panic Disorder Home Page
(at http://www.mentalhealth.com/dis/p20-an01.html) of the Internet Mental Health network contains diagnostic information, a description of the disorder, a discussion of treatment, and extensive print and on-line resources.

The Anxiety/Panic Resource
(at http://www.algy.com/anxiety/) offers an extensive collection of anxiety-related topics.

Doc Wiberg's Panic Page
(at http://www.usinternet.com/users/ccwiberg/panic.html-ssi) is a somewhat lighthearted approach to this serious topic and includes lots of links for panic and anxiety disorders plus information about pharmacological treatment of anxiety disorders.

Center for Stress & Anxiety Treatment
(at http://www.stressrelease.com/) advertises books and other treatments but also has useful information about stress and anxiety as well as a list of resources.

The following newsgroups contain dialogue about anxiety disorders and are open for contributions: alt.support.anxiety-panic and alt.recovery.panic-anxiety.self-help.

Where to Write

National Panic/Anxiety Disorder Association
1718 Burgundy Place, Suite B
Santa Rosa, CA 95403
707-527-5738

Anxiety Disorders Association of America
11900 Parklawn Drive, Suite 100
Rockville, MD 20852
301-231-9350

Women Helping Agoraphobics, Inc.
P. O. Box 4900
South Framingham, MA 01701

Chapter 9

Obsessive-Compulsive Disorder: Over and Over

Everyone has his or her peculiarities. Some people care about how their hair is done, how their eggs are scrambled, or that their daily routine proceeds without disruption. John cares too much and knows it. He has to turn each lock on his apartment door three times every time he enters, otherwise he will experience unendurable anxiety about someone breaking in. He has to have all the spices aligned on the kitchen window in alphabetical order and perfect rows, has to tie both shoelaces when only one is untied, and must touch each floor-indicator button in the elevator for fear that the car otherwise will fall 10 floors. And there are more of these strong "must do's."

John suffers from obsessive-compulsive disorder. He is driven by thoughts that bad things will happen unless he performs rituals like those described above. The anxiety he has about his fears is temporarily reduced by these repetitive actions; these behaviors would not be bad if they were just habits that didn't interfere with his everyday life. But they have becoming so consuming of time and energy that his work and his relationships suffer.

John's treatment for this disorder includes a rather scary but orderly and systematic exposure to the things that prompt him to act compulsively, such as unlocked doors, untied shoelaces and medication. He is taking a prescribed medication as well. After months of therapy, he can now face these uncomfortable situations without having to perform the burdensome rituals. He no longer aligns all his folders on his desk or checks to make sure that exactly the same number of pants and shirts hang in both sides of his closet. His treatment is working. He is more relaxed around situations that would have previously driven him to maintain order and has more time and energy for the things that he enjoys.

Q What is obsessive-compulsive disorder, and how common is it?

The hallmark signs of an obsessive-compulsive disorder are the presence of frequently intrusive and unwanted thoughts (obsessions) and repetitive behaviors (compulsions). In general, the anxiety created by the obsession is relieved through acting out the compulsive behavior. The individual becomes enmeshed in a cycle of feeling anxious over and over, and each time feeling as if he or she has to undertake a particular behavior to relieve the anxiety. These obsessions (and subsequent compulsions) are so disturbing that they interfere with everyday functioning including work, school, and relationships with others. The person who has an obsessive-compulsive disorder knows that the thoughts and the need for repetitive actions are excessive and time-consuming and reflect far more than simple concerns about everyday responsibilities and situations. This *intact insight*, knowing that these thoughts are not normal, is a characteristic of an obsessive-compulsive disorder.

The lifetime prevalence of obsessive-compulsive disorder in adults is about 2.5 percent. For children, the number is about the same. Slightly more than half of the adults suffering obsessive-compulsive disorder are female, meaning that the male-female ratio is approximately equal. Among children, however, about twice as many males as females have the disorder.

The age of onset ranges from early adolescence to young adulthood with earlier onset in males (about 13-15 years of age) than for females (about 20-24 years). One-third to one-half of adults with obsessive-compulsive disorder report that it started during childhood.

Q I have heard that obsessive-compulsive disorder is difficult to diagnose. Is this true?

Studies have found that it takes an average of 17 years from the time obsessive-compulsive disorder begins for people to obtain appropriate treatment. This situation may be due to several reasons.

First, people with obsessive-compulsive disorder are secretive about their illness and don't want to acknowledge the presence of the symptoms or disorder. While it may take a great deal of effort, the disorder can be hidden or be characterized as being merely overly concerned about certain aspects of one's everyday life. Second, physicians and other healthcare workers are not familiar with this disorder (as with many other mental disorders) and continue to look for overt physical problems (none of which are present). And, as is always the case with mental disorders, many people don't have access to treatment because it is not available or they cannot afford it.

Q When does a worry, a doubt, or a superstition become characterized as part of an obsessive-compulsive disorder?

Making sure that your hands are clean or that the doors are locked is normal. Saying prayers before you go to bed each night is not excessive. When activities or beliefs, however, are out of proportion with need or reality, they can be characterized as part of an obsessive-compulsive disorder. For example, washing hands 100 times a day and never touching anything that others have touched for fear of contamination is far out of proportion to any threat of disease. So is spending an hour each day making sure that the paperweights on the mantle are all aligned perfectly.

Q What are some classic obsessions and classic compulsions?

Obsessions and compulsions most often occur together in an obsessive-compulsive disorder, but an individual with an obsessive-compulsive disorder may sometimes have only one or the other. Classic obsessions include violent, religious, and sexual themes as well as preoccupation with contamination, pathological doubting or uncertainty, concerns with symmetry, and a general sense that something bad will happen if a particular ritual is not performed in precisely the right manner. Classic compulsions included washing, cleaning, counting, checking, repeating, and arranging behaviors.

For the most part, though, an obsessive-compulsive disorder manifests itself as multiple obsessions and multiple compulsions. Only when the thoughts and behaviors become excessive in intensity or duration is there some indication of a disorder.

At one time it was thought that all obsessions were mental events and that compulsions were acted out only as behavioral events. That view has changed. Compulsions can be either mental or behavioral. For example, a mental ritual (such as repeating a phrase to yourself over and over) is equivalent to a behavioral ritual and serves the same purpose, reducing the anxiety associated with an obsession.

Obsessions and compulsions almost always occur together. In fact, 90 percent of the patients in one study indicated that their compulsive behaviors aim to prevent harm associated with their obsessive thoughts. People with obsessive-compulsive disorder recognize the stress that an obsession creates and perform a behavior (that is compulsive in its frequency) to decrease the distress associated with the obsession.

Q What are some theories about the cause of obsessive-compulsive disorder?

Several different accounts suggest what might be the central cause of obsessive-compulsive disorder. One is that once a fear is acquired, avoidance patterns (or compulsions) develop and are maintained when they provide relief for the fear. Another is that obsessive-compulsive disorder is based on exaggerated fears ("If I don't do this, something bad will happen"). Another perception has to do with the way the person with obsessive-compulsive disorder organizes his or her thoughts. In this view, thinking of a behavior is the same as doing it (bad thoughts are the equivalent of bad behaviors), failing to prevent harm is the same as causing the harm, and responsibility for harm is not diminished by extenuating circumstances (such as being unable to help); thus, inappropriate thoughts should be controlled.

A person with an obsessive-compulsive disorder may even conclude that a situation is dangerous because he or she lacks evidence that it is not dangerous. In other words, the person assumes that a situation is something to fear because he or she draws incorrect conclusions about what is safe and what isn't.

Some studies suggest that obsessive-compulsive disorder is present more often in certain families than in others, although abnormal genes for the disorder have yet to be identified. Among parents, children, and siblings of patients who have obsessive-compulsive disorder, the rate of occurrence is about 10 to 15 percent, much higher than the average of 2.5 percent in the general population. Another biological perspective regarding the cause of this disorder concludes that it results from abnormal metabolism of certain brain chemicals, including serotonin.

Modern brain imaging studies have consistently identified abnormalities in patients with obsessive compulsive disorder. Most recently, an association has been found among children with obsessive compulsive disorder and an immunological marker for strep infection. This has raised the possibility that some cases of early onset obsessive compulsive disorder are caused by an abnormal antibody response to the bacteria that causes routine strep throats. These antibodies mistakenly attack cells in a particular region of the brain, causing obsessive compulsive disorder.

Q What are some of the early ways in which an obsessive-compulsive disorder was treated, and were any of these treatments successful?

Until the 1960s, there were no successful treatments for obsessive-compulsive disorder. A wide variety of psychosocial and pharmacological treatments were unsuccessful.

During the 1960s, an ingenious behavioral program was developed. The program required the prolonged exposure of patients to those cues in the environment that set off their obsessions and then a strict restriction on completing the ritual associated with the obsession. This therapy was called exposure and response prevention (also called response blocking). It was subsequently found to be very effective in ten of fifteen cases and somewhat successful in the remaining five. Of equal importance is that after 5 years, only two of fifteen patients relapsed.

About this same time, new medications were developed that were effective as treatments of obsessive-compulsive disorder. Since that time, researchers have tried to develop better psychosocial and pharmacological treatments. Today, although treatment of this disorder remains challenging, the effectiveness of both behavioral and pharmacological therapies has been significantly improved.

Q What is the exposure and response prevention technique, and how successful is it in treating an obsessive-compulsive disorder?

The most effective psychosocial treatment for an obsessive-compulsive disorder is exposure and response prevention. This treatment involves the patient's actually being exposed to a provocative setting or stimulus (such as touching a "contaminated" object like a toilet seat) and then refraining from carrying out the ritual compulsion of hand washing. It is hypothesized that anxiety will diminish after a person has enough contact with something that is feared without suffering a negative consequence. The two most important elements of exposure treatment is that it take place *in vivo* (in a real-life situation) and that the response actually be prevented, primarily by the patient's exercising great willpower and not performing the usual response. When it is not possible to have the patient experience the real object, the patient is asked to imagine the situation that brings on the compulsion to act.

Numerous, reasonably well-designed studies have shown exposure/ritual prevention to result in positive results in less than 1 month, with dropout rates of less than 20 percent. Even with this short duration of treatment, relapse rates are relatively low, with treatment gains being maintained for up to 5 years after active treatment was discontinued.

The effects of exposure/ritual prevention from different studies have been combined to examine the overall effectiveness of the treatment in different settings. The results of these "meta-analyses" suggest that the behavioral treatment is effective in controlling the symptoms of obsessive-compulsive disorder and superior to no treatment at all. But meta-analyses have shortcomings. First, since studies are combined, there is always a mixture of the specific study details such as the way in which treatments were implemented. Perhaps one study included exercises at home and another did not. Also, studies with different levels of control are included. Finally, studies differ in length, therapist involvement, strictness of ritual control, and the use of imaginal exposure (when *in vivo* treatment is impossible), leaving many reasons to believe that the results of meta-analyses are not conclusive.

However, regardless of any confusion about combining the results of several studies, it has been generally found that patients with obsessive-compulsive disorder improve when seeing a therapist weekly and then practicing exposure and response prevention on their own.

Perhaps the major limitation of exposure and response prevention is the generalizability of the results or the effect it has on the obsessive-compulsive disorder itself. For example, sometimes the treatment's effect is limited to the particular stimulus and compulsive behavior associated with it and does not generalize to other settings and other stimuli. This issue is still a focus of research.

Q What other factors need to be considered when judging the effectiveness of exposure/ritual prevention?

As is true with most therapies, efforts are always being made to find the best combination of treatments. In the case of obsessive-compulsive disorder, different combinations of elements have been tried with varying degrees of success. Following are the results of studies done with several ancillary treatments.

- In general, the use of imaginal exposure (where the patient imagines exposure to the stimulus) rather than *in vivo* exposure can be of some help in the reduction of symptoms and in the maintenance of treatment gains. However, it is not as effective as *in vivo* treatment.
- Self-instructional therapy, which includes information-getting and relaxation exercises, does not appear to have any positive effect on the symptoms associated with an obsessive-compulsive disorder.
- Another cognitive approach—rational-emotive therapy consisting of therapist-led sessions plus homework—produced some benefit, although less than the group receiving exposure and response prevention treatment alone.
- Individual versus group therapy seems to result in no difference in the reduction of obsessive-compulsive disorder symptoms. Both seem to be equally effective at the time of treatment as well as 6 months later. Group treatment is much less expensive and more efficient since it can reach a larger number of people for less cost.
- There is no difference in result whether patients are treated alone or with a family member involved. Obsessive-compulsive disorder severity is reduced

in both cases. However, exposure/ritual prevention when combined with a very intense family support program—including assistance with homework assignments, relaxation therapy, and participation in response prevention—resulted in increased improvement.

Q Given the effectiveness of exposure/ritual prevention, what are some other steps that might be taken to make it even more effective?

Many patients prefer the medical treatment of obsessive-compulsive disorder since the exposure/ritual prevention is so frightening, and 25 percent of patients refuse the latter type of treatment. After all, that treatment forces them to confront their fears, and why would they want to constantly be exposed? More studies are needed that examine the use of medication followed by training using exposure/ritual prevention eventually to reduce the obsession and associated compulsion. More studies are also needed that examine the factors that might contribute to the fear of participating in exposure and response prevention, especially since this method is by far the most effective way to treat an obsessive-compulsive disorder.

Q What are the first-line pharmacological treatments of obsessive-compulsive disorder?

Several levels of pharmacological treatment have been suggested for obsessive-compulsive disorders, beginning with the front-line strategy of serotonin reuptake inhibitors such as clomipramine (Anafranil), fluoxetine (Prozac), sertraline (Zoloft), fluvoxamine (Luvox), and paroxetine (Paxil).

There is consistent scientific evidence from well-designed and well-executed studies that support the efficacy of selective serotonin reuptake inhibitors in the treatment of obsessive-compulsive disorder. Large-scale studies have generally shown that approximately 40 to 60 percent of patients responded to these medications with average improvement of about 20 to 40 percent. Medication used in combination with exposure therapy constitute the regimen of choice as the first step in the treatment of obsessive-compulsive disorder.

Treatment using medication takes about 8 to 10 weeks for an adequate trial; serotonin reuptake inhibitors have been shown to be more effective than other types of antidepressants.

Q What are some side effects of the selective serotonin reuptake inhibitors?

This class of medication tends to be well-tolerated by most people, although there are some side effects associated with taking them. The side effects associated with fluoxetine, fluvoxamine, paroxetine, and sertraline include nervousness, insomnia, restlessness, nausea, diarrhea, and sexual problems. The use of clomipramine is associated with dry mouth, fatigue, dizziness, sexual problems, and weight gain. Clomipramine has also been associated with blood pressure and heart rate problems. See our discussion in the introduction to this book about what to do if side effects are a problem.

Q The various serotonin reuptake inhibitors have been shown to be equally effective treatments of obsessive-compulsive disorder, but which one should a patient try first? What if that one does not work?

All of the selective serotonin reuptake inhibitors have been shown to be effective in treating symptoms of obsessive-compulsive disorder. Since these drugs have been associated with fewer side effects than other medications, the selective serotonin reuptake inhibitors (such as fluoxetine, fluvoxamine, paroxetine, and sertraline) should be the first choice. Which specific one depends on the doctor's advice and the experiences that the patient or family members might have had with a specific medication.

After giving sufficient time for the treatment to work (at least 8 to 10 weeks, although some people see results after as few as 3 weeks), a different serotonin reuptake inhibitor could be tried. If that is not successful, it is time to move to some entirely different medication.

Q How effective are alternatives to these first-line treatment medications of obsessive-compulsive disorder?

If serotonin reuptake inhibitors fail to provide relief, second-line pharmacological approaches include additional medication to augment the action of the serotonin reuptake inhibitors. Researchers surmise that the minority of patients who do not respond favorably to serotonin reuptake inhibitors probably constitutes a highly varied group. As a result, subsequent treatment might be very effective for some of these patients but not generally for all.

Numerous agents have been used to augment the effects of the serotonin reuptake inhibitors. Among these other drugs are lithium (Eskalith) and buspirone (BuSpar), both relatively ineffective as treatments for obsessive-compulsive disorder. The most impressive augmentation data seem to result from the use of neuroleptics such as pimozide (Orap), or haloperidol (Haldol). Uncontrolled studies using the antipsychotic drug risperidone (Risperdal) have also yielded encouraging preliminary results. Numerous other agents have been tried in combination with selective serotonin reuptake inhibitors including clonidine (Catapres) and trazodone (Desyrel), as well as other antidepressants. Very little information about the effectiveness of this last set of medications has been systematically collected.

Q What about some of the other treatments for obsessive-compulsive disorder? What are they, and do they work?

If psychosocial and pharmacological treatments do not work, third-line treatment includes neurosurgery and electroconvulsive therapy, which are reserved for patients with debilitating cases of obsessive-compulsive disorder for whom no other treatment has worked. Electroconvulsive therapy rarely works and neurosurgery is clearly a "last resort." For example, in some recent studies, 45 percent of patients undergoing some type of neurosurgery did experience symptom reduction of at least 35 percent. For this small group of patients, this last resort can be of some help.

Studies using electroconvulsive therapy also lack any control data that allow a conclusion to be reached about its efficacy. Since there is a high degree of concurrence or comorbidity for obsessive-compulsive disorder and depression, and since electroconvulsive therapy has been shown to be an extremely potent treatment for depression (see Chapter 7), it is no surprise to learn that electroconvulsive therapy also is somewhat effective for symptoms of obsessive-compulsive disorder. That knowledge, however, does not reveal the efficiency of electroconvulsive therapy as a treatment for obsessive-compulsive disorder alone.

Q What future directions will treatment and research into obsessive-compulsive disorder take?

Future treatment directions for obsessive-compulsive disorder can be divided into two categories. The first are initiatives to assess and optimize the use of currently available treatments. The second direction is to develop new treatments. One potential avenue of investigation is the use of sophisticated neuroimaging techniques that have documented changes in brain activity following successful treatment with either serotonin reuptake inhibitors or exposure therapy. Such findings underscore the power of neuroimaging as it may be possible to predict who as well as how well patients will respond to treatment. Treatment for strep infection, including antibiotics and exchange transfusion, may also hold promise.

Q *Where Can I Find More Information About Obsessive-Compulsive Disorder?*

Books

The Boy Who Couldn't Stop Washing: The Experience and Treatment of Obsessive-Compulsive Disorder by Judith L. Rapoport. New American Library, 1997. ISBN 0451172027.

Tells, often in their own words, the stories of people who have obsessive-compulsive disorder.

Over and Over Again: Understanding Obsessive-Compulsive Disorder by Fugen A. Neziroglu and Jose A. Yaryura-Tobias. Jossey-Bass, 1997. ISBN 0669249971.

From a variety of perspectives, focuses on obsessive-compulsive disorder, its origin, treatment, and effects. The back material is especially interesting with 100 questions and guidelines for families coping with obsessive-compulsive disorder.

Obsessive Compulsive Disorder: A Guide by John H. Greist. Dean Foundation, 1997. ISBN 1890802034.

An easy-to-understand booklet on the treatment of obsessive-compulsive disorder. It's especially useful for patients and their families. Commonly asked questions plus some self-help materials add to its usefulness.

The Sky Is Falling: Understanding and Coping With Phobias, Panic, and Obsessive-Compulsive Disorders by Raeann Dumont and Aaron T. Beck. W.W. Norton & Company, 1996. ISBN 0393038483.

Includes pragmatic advice for recognizing "magic thinking" and setting both short-term and long-range goals. "Magic thinking" is defined as a conclusion being formed without a rational thought process.

Up from Insanity: One Man's Triumph over Obsessive-Compulsive Disorder by Reagan Smith. Emerald Publishing, 1997. ISBN 0965828808.

Focuses on one man's 30-year struggle with obsessive-compulsive disorder and how he finally overcame it.

Internet Sites

The Obsessive Compulsive Disorder Forum
(at http://www.nimbusnet.com/wwwboard/ocdboard.html) provides a venue for sharing stories, therapy successes and failures, and just about anything on the topic.

A fairly comprehensive recommended reading list about obsessive-compulsive disorder can be found at http://www.suncompsvc.com/ocd/reading.htm.

Teen OCD
(at http://www.angelfire.com/il/TeenOCD/) is a mailing list where teens can post messages and share thoughts and feelings with others.

AMI/NYC
(at http://www.schizophrenia.com/ami/) has schizophrenia in the title but is a huge resource for materials on several types of mental illnesses including obsessive-compulsive disorder.

From the Giant Merck Manual
(at http://www.merck.com/!!uYTk_1UKPuYTk_1UKP/pubs/mmanual/html/mhkighki.htm) is introductory material on the origins, symptoms, diagnosis, prognosis, and treatment of obsessive-compulsive disorder.

Obsessive Compulsive Disorder Bulletin Board
(at http://www.support-group.com/cgi-bin/sg/get_posts)

Where to Write

Anxiety Disorder Association of America
600 Executive Boulevard, Suite 513
Rockville, MD 20852
301-231-9350

OC Information Center
2711 Allen Boulevard
Middleton, WI 53562
608-836-8070

Obsessive Compulsive Foundation
P. O. Box 70
Milford, CT 06460
203-878-5669

Chapter 10

Post-Traumatic Stress Disorder

This isn't the first time that Sam has gotten entirely spooked when he heard the whoop-whoop-whoop sound of helicopter blades overhead. He can tell himself that it is only the Life Flight helicopter from the local hospital carrying an injured person for medical help, but he can't get out of his head the association of those sounds with his intensely frightening experiences in Vietnam. As an infantry soldier, Sam's travels in a helicopter were always to a site of conflict, and the helicopter never landed without being fired on. Sam was wounded on one such mission, and he often feels the pain and scarring although the wound is a long time healed. And he will never be able to forgot the terrible shock of seeing one of his closest friends in the company shot and killed beside him. Sam has reacted before to these sounds, but now, the cold sweat and racing heartbeat are too much, as is the unwanted reexperiencing of the event both as intrusive thoughts and recurrent dreams.

The post-traumatic stress disorder that Sam has developed is not uncommon among Vietnam veterans and others who have survived intense stress. Sam seeks help from a clinic that specializes in helping people who have been traumatized, be it from combat experiences, earthquake, fire, rape, or other physical assault. The psychosocial and pharmacological therapies that are available work; Sam finds himself in a group therapy setting. As the therapy takes hold, Sam finds that when he is again gradually exposed to the sounds that he used to fear, he no longer feels the panic, though some mild discomfort remains. Eight months later, Sam looks up to see a helicopter and listens for the sound; it still reminds him of hard times. But he's no longer overwhelmed by his fears and his memories.

Q What is post-traumatic stress disorder, and how common is it?

Post-traumatic stress disorder is an anxiety disorder wherein the individual *relives* a traumatic experience, including feeling the anxiety and discomfort of the original event. The reliving may occur as a flashback, nightmares, or increasingly intrusive thoughts, and any of these can be debilitating.

Q What types of traumatic events are associated with post-traumatic stress disorder, and how common is the disorder?

Just about any event that involves actual or threatened physical harm and where the individual's reaction includes intense fear or helplessness can prompt the disorder. Earthquakes, fires, floods, and storms are some of the naturally occurring events that might be associated with post-traumatic stress disorder. Human-made events such as automobile crashes, war, domestic abuse and violence, and the Holocaust are similarly related. If you think of the hundreds of thousands of people who experience such events, it's no surprise thousands and thousands of people suffer post-traumatic stress disorder or some of the associated symptoms.

The incidence of post-traumatic stress disorder is very high, with a lifetime prevalence of about 15 percent, accounting for 20 million cases. Many researchers believe that these estimates reflect the high level of interpersonal violence in American society. For example, in a random sample of young adults living in Detroit, more than one-third experienced threatening traumatic events such as rape, assault, or motor vehicle accidents. Among those who have experienced torture, such as concentration camp survivors and former prisoners of war, the prevalence of post-traumatic stress disorder can be very high, with some estimates between 50 and 75 percent.

Among war veterans, lifetime estimates for post-traumatic stress disorder are 30 percent. For survivors of natural disasters such as fires and earthquakes, the incidence ranges from 4 to 16 percent (but still high relative to the incidence of other mental disorders). Among American women, approximately 13 percent have been raped, and 31 percent of those women developed post-traumatic stress disorder following the assault. Interestingly, men report higher rates of exposure to traumatic events, but women experience post-traumatic stress disorder more often than men. Some reasons for this difference might be gender differences in depression (which can accompany post-traumatic stress disorder) and types of stressors to which women are exposed (such as sexual assault).

Q What symptoms accompany a diagnosis of post-traumatic stress disorder?

The symptoms of post-traumatic stress disorder are classified into three groups. Following is a brief overview of each group and what behaviors one might expect. Keep in mind that a defining diagnostic criterion for post-traumatic stress disorder is the experiencing of an event that is traumatic for the individual.

- Intrusive symptoms occur when thoughts about or recollections of a traumatic event intrudes into everyday life and activities. This intrusion might involve an unwanted memory of the event, disturbing dreams (that interfere with sleep), acting as if the event were recurring, or experiencing physical distress following the memory. Flashbacks can be so vivid that the person reacts as if he or she is actually experiencing the trauma again.

- Symptoms of avoidance severely affect several aspects of the person's everyday life. The individual with post-traumatic stress disorder avoids any remembrance of the trauma and also avoids establishing close emotional ties with family and friends, perhaps because such ties remind him or her of the traumatic event. This behavior is sometimes called numbing since emotions are absent, and actions are done in a mechanical and routine way. The person with post-traumatic stress disorder appears simply to not care. Characteristic behaviors include efforts to avoid thoughts, feelings, and even talk about the event, avoidance of any reminder of the trauma, and the inability to recall important aspects of the trauma. Also common are a diminished interest in normally significant activities, feelings of being detached from others, lack of feelings about things in general, and a sense of no future. Because they are so far emotionally removed, people with post-traumatic stress disorder can't work out the grief and anger they've experienced, and the trauma becomes the defining element in their behavior and their lives.

- Hyperarousal symptoms include an explosive reaction to anything related to the trauma, being on edge and irritable, difficulty concentrating, insomnia, and a constant fear that danger is near. Such a fear often leads to being easily startled.

In addition to the above criteria, symptoms must be present for at least 1 month and must be accompanied by a significant degree of impairment in functioning at home, work, or school. If the symptoms last for more than 3 months following the traumatic event, the diagnosis is one of chronic post-traumatic stress disorder, rather than acute post-traumatic stress disorder. If the symptoms begin 6 months or more after the event, then the disorder is called delayed post-traumatic stress disorder.

*Q Exposure to a traumatic event is necessary for the
development of post-traumatic stress disorder, but
what other factors are associated with an increased
risk for developing the disorder?*

Even though exposure to a traumatic event is necessary, not everyone who is
exposed to a traumatic event develops post-traumatic stress disorder. Other
factors that influence the development of symptoms include the severity of the
trauma, personal history of stress or abuse, history of psychological problems,
presence of other mental disorders, and subsequent exposure to events that
reactivate the fear associated with the original trauma.

To fully appreciate the factors involved in the development of post-traumatic
stress disorder, the following factors need to be considered: the traumatic event
itself, the context in which the event occurred, the resources and deficits that the
individual brought to the event, and the environment following the trauma. Much
research that has been done in the treatment of post-traumatic stress disorder has
tried to identify and better understand the relationship between these factors and
the disorder.

*Q Exposure therapy is the current psychosocial
treatment of choice for post-traumatic stress
disorder. How does it work, and how effective is it?*

You might remember that different types of exposure therapy are used to treat
other anxiety disorders, such as obsessive-compulsive disorder (Chapter 9). The
basic idea is the same here. The therapist teaches the patient to respond to aspects
of the traumatic event in a new way. For a Vietnam veteran who always recoils at
the sound of a backfiring car, for example, such therapy would mean learning to
associate the noise with pleasant or at least neutral events, thereby reducing the
power the noise and the accompanying emotions have over his life. This result is
achieved by gradually exposing the patient to the triggering event, such as a
backfiring car, immediately followed by a pleasant or neutral event.

Early research using only single subjects showed that systematic exposure to
memories of traumatic events experienced by combat veterans resulted in a
decrease of symptoms and a reduction in anxiety. The results of later, more
controlled group studies showed that imagery-based exposure therapy (where
images are used rather than re-experiencing the actual and original event) showed
reductions in post-traumatic stress disorder behaviors that were maintained at a 6-
month follow-up.

While this treatment has been shown to be effective, additional research needs to be done in two areas. First, most patients who participated in this type of therapy experienced rape or combat as the traumatic precipitating event, somewhat limiting the degree to which the findings might apply to patients with different precipitating events. Different traumatic events trigger different types of reactions in people, and the source of the trauma needs to be seriously considered in any future treatment research. Remember the importance of individual factors (such as context and history) in understanding the intensity of reaction to a traumatic event.

Second, information about occupational and social functioning needs to be gathered in future studies. For example, the degree of one's reaction to a specific event (which may precipitate this type of anxiety) can be affected by the social support system that exists for the individual.

Q How effective is anxiety management training in the treatment of post-traumatic stress disorder?

Anxiety management training involves teaching patients an assortment of behavioral and cognitive strategies to help increase the ability to manage the emotions (such as being fearful) and behaviors (such as being aggressive) associated with post-traumatic stress disorder. Examples of such skills might be relaxation techniques, breathing techniques, trauma education, and communication skills. In general, most anxiety management programs employ several techniques to reduce the anxiety associated with memories of the trauma, but some use a single technique as well. For example, in one study biofeedback significantly helped the group using only that single technique.

And what about the effectiveness of anxiety management training? Evidence shows that such a program reduces symptoms of post-traumatic stress disorder, although the data from various studies on the effectiveness of anxiety management training are not as convincing as those for exposure therapy.

Q If exposure therapy works well and anxiety management training is also effective, wouldn't it be logical to test the combination of the two?

Yes, and one study examined the effects of such a combination (called cognitive processing therapy) at 3 and 6 months after treatment was completed. The patients who received the combined therapy improved markedly over those who received nothing. In fact, most impressively, 6 months after treatment, none of the formerly diagnosed post-traumatic stress disorder patients met the criteria for post-traumatic stress disorder. This combined treatment, which is relatively new, is currently the focus of many different treatment studies.

Q *I've heard about a therapy that focuses on eye movements that has been applied to the treatment of post-traumatic stress disorder. How does it work, and is it effective?*

Eye-movement desensitization and reprocessing was first introduced in 1989, and uses a wide range of psychotherapeutic approaches along with eye movements to stimulate the brain's information-processing system. The treatment involves a series of steps including the recalling of the trauma, an evaluation of the negative characteristics of images or memories, the identification of an alternative interpretation of the memory, an examination of physiological response to the memory, and a set of directed eye movements while the patient focuses on the traumatic memories.

Examining the effectiveness of eye-movement desensitization and reprocessing is a challenge since the way it works is not at all well understood, and it isn't based on recognized theories of human behavior or learning. While some studies suggest that the treatment can be effective, others have found no difference between the patients who received eye-movement desensitization and reprocessing and those who did not.

Q *What are some of the first line pharmacological treatments used for post-traumatic stress disorder, and how effective are they?*

Many different types of medication have been used to treat post-traumatic stress disorder including monoamine oxidase inhibitors, selective serotonin reuptake inhibitors, and benzodiazepines.

- Monoamine oxidase inhibitors such as phenelzine (Nardil) were the first medications to be considered as a possible treatment for post-traumatic stress disorder. The first trial resulted in a dramatic level of improvement and an almost complete reduction in symptoms. In another study this medication was found to be particularly helpful with intrusive symptoms and insomnia, both core symptoms of post-traumatic stress disorder. This study was particularly well-conducted. Veterans were selected from an outreach program rather than from a hospital (indicating they are not chronic sufferers), all were employed, and none had any other mental disorder. A limitation of this treatment is that it does not appear to be particularly effective for intrusive symptoms, and it carries the danger of a reaction when the medication is taken with certain foods and other medications, plus other side effects. Such side effects accompanying the use of phenelzine are dizziness, erectile dysfunction, delayed ejaculation, delayed urination, constipation, dry mouth, blurred vision, and blackouts.

- Tricyclic antidepressants such as amitriptyline (Elavil) and imipramine (Tofranil) have been used. These antidepressants have been the most extensively studied medications for the treatment of post-traumatic stress disorder. In general, results of well-controlled studies have shown a moderate amount of success in treating intrusive and hyperarousal symptoms. The majority of studies have reported the efficacy of antidepressants in non-combat populations such as rape victims, motor vehicle accident victims, torture survivors, burn victims, and survivors of plane crashes. This range of patients is especially important since it contributes important information about the generalizability of this class of drugs across different populations.

- Selective serotonin reuptake inhibitors such as fluoxetine (Prozac) became popular as pharmacological treatments of depression and anxiety, and mental health professionals began to consider whether they would be effective for the treatment of post-traumatic stress disorder. In the majority of trials, this class of medications has been very effective in reducing the symptoms of post-traumatic stress disorder. A major advantage of this class of medication is that it has performed better than any other medication group in targeting all the symptoms of post-traumatic stress disorder rather than just any one of the categories of symptoms discussed earlier.

- Benzodiazepines such as diazepam (Valium) were initially tried in the treatment of post-traumatic stress disorder because of their usefulness in relieving the general symptoms of anxiety. They have shown a moderate level of success but should be used with caution. Patients with post-traumatic stress disorder also have a high rate of substance abuse. Consequently, these medications may not be wise because there is a risk for developing a dependency, and withdrawal symptoms are associated with discontinuation of this class of medication. These medications may work best at the early stages of post-traumatic stress disorder for a short period of time for individuals with no history of substance abuse.

Q What other medications have been used to treat post-traumatic stress disorder, and how effective are they?

Lithium (Eskalith) and anticonvulsants such as carbamazepine (Tegretol) have been shown to be helpful with certain symptoms of post-traumatic stress disorder such as impulsivity and explosiveness, but almost all the research done on these mood stabilizers has been with combat veterans suffering chronic post-traumatic stress disorder. These men were specifically selected because of the nature of their symptoms and problems with impulsivity and explosiveness. Consequently, the results of the treatment may not be generalizable to other groups. Beta blockers and serotonergic drugs have also been used to treat symptoms of post-traumatic stress disorder, but most information about their effectiveness is based on a small number of preliminary reports.

Q What directions should future research into the pharmacological treatment of post-traumatic stress disorder take?

The amount of information available about the pharmacological treatment of post-traumatic stress disorder is relatively small, and few studies have been well-controlled and well-documented. In addition, most studies have been done on populations of veterans.

Several directions need to be explored in future research into the development and refinement of medication to treat post-traumatic stress disorder. First, the characteristics of groups treated need to be significantly broadened beyond war veterans. Combat veterans are an ideal but limited group to study, and medications' effectiveness may be partially a function of the type of trauma, age at which the trauma occurred, sex of the individual, and several other factors known to contribute to the development of post-traumatic stress disorder.

Second, no single medication fully addressees the complex syndrome of post-traumatic stress disorder, although the selective serotonin reuptake inhibitors do a pretty good job. This observation raises the question of whether the disorder is so multifaceted that different medications need to be explored, or that medication in conjunction with other types of therapy is the treatment of choice. Undoubtedly, one aspect which mental health professionals will study is the interaction between medication and the psychosocial treatments.

Q Where Can I Find More Information About Post-Traumatic Stress Disorder?

Books

Coping With Post-Traumatic Stress Disorder by Carolyn Simpson and Dwain Simpson. Rosen Publishing Group, 1997. ISBN 0823920801.

Discusses stressful situations such as physical abuse, natural disasters, wars, and violence, and how responses relate to delayed reactions to trauma.

Everything You Need to Know About Natural Disasters and Post-Traumatic Stress Disorder by Richard S. Lee and Mary Price Lee. Rosen Publishing Group, 1995. ISBN 0823920534.
Explores the emotional trauma that results from post-traumatic stress disorder and shows how natural disasters can have long-term psychological effects on individuals.

Post-Traumatic Stress Disorder: The Victim's Guide to Healing and Recovery by Raymond B. Flannery, Jr. Crossroad Publishing Company, 1995. ISBN 0824514459.
Describes the disorder and discusses how to recover from its debilitating effects. In three parts, this book focuses on the nature of the disorder, the victims, and steps to recovery.

Straight Talk About Post-Traumatic Stress Disorder: Coping with the Aftermath of Trauma by Kay Marie Porterfield. Facts on File, 1996. ISBN 0816035520.
Uses four case studies to introduce the disorder. Cases are referred to throughout this discussion of history, research, causes, symptoms, and treatments. Special focus is on young people affected either primarily or secondarily by post-traumatic stress disorder.

The Harmony of Illusions: Inventing Post-Traumatic Stress Disorder by Allan Young. Princeton University Press, 1997. ISBN 0691017239.
Argues that traumatic memory is an artificial creation, and presents a case study of how this disorder was created as a cultural artifact.

Internet Sites

The National Center for Post-Traumatic Stress Disorder
(at http://www.dartmouth.edu/dms/ptsd/) offers links to databases, publications, and resources.

PTSD Research Quarterly
(at http://www.dartmouth.edu/dms/ptsd/RQ.html) contains review articles written by experts on various topics relating to post-traumatic stress disorder.

The Post-Traumatic Gazette
(at http://www.patiencepress.com/) is published six times a year and is targeted at trauma survivors, their families, friends, and therapists.

The International Society for Traumatic Stress Studies
(http://www.istss.com/) covers conferences, critical issues, publications, and links and resources to other sites.

David Baldwin's Trauma Information Pages
(at http://www.trauma-pages.com/) are an award-winning collection of resources and links to pages available in five different languages.

Where to Write

National Center for Post-Traumatic Stress Disorder
Rural Route 5
White River Junction, VT 05009
802-296-5132

International Society for Traumatic Stress Studies
60 Revere Drive, Suite 5000
Northbrook, IL 60062
847-480-9028

National Organization for Victim Assistance
1757 Park Road N.W.
Washington, DC 20010
202-232-6682

Chapter 11

Schizophrenia:
New Hope For A Severe Brain
Disorder

Ann knows what she went through with her own treatment of schizophrenia—and its treatment—and she is terrified that her daughter, who just graduated from college, will suffer the same way. Ann was diagnosed as having schizophrenia early in her marriage, when medication for this devastating psychosis had just been discovered. The medication reduced the frequency of the voices Ann heard and her feelings of always being watched, but the side effects were sometimes frightening. Her hands would shake uncontrollably, she gained weight, and she lost interest in sex. It took all her strength to take the medication twice a day. After all, who would voluntarily cause such problems? Eventually, after months of trials, the right type and amount of medication were determined. Since then, Ann has been largely symptom-free and as comfortable as possible under the circumstances.

Her daughter experienced upsetting thoughts lately. Stephanie isn't hearing voices, but has begun to sense that friends are ganging up against her. She also has suicidal feelings on occasion and recalls feeling that "none of my professors understand anything about what I am trying to say." Ann is quick to listen and suggests Stephanie see a mental health professional immediately. A visit to a psychiatrist leads to a diagnosis of schizophrenia and the prescription of one of the new medications for it. Happily, the new drugs have fewer side effects than those prescribed her mother years earlier. The doctor also prescribes a strict program of medication adherence and family support. Despite occasional setbacks, Stephanie is happy in her new job, dating a nice young man, and adjusting to life after college. Ann is relieved but vigilant for her daughter.

Q What is schizophrenia, and how often does it occur?

Schizophrenia is one of the most disabling of all the major mental disorders. Generally, it severely affects an individual's ability to think clearly, distinguish reality from fantasy, react in an emotionally appropriate way, and interact with others. Schizophrenia afflicts 2 million Americans. Each year, more than 300,000 acute episodes of schizophrenia occur in the United States. More than 100,000 patients with schizophrenia are hospitalized on any one day. In addition, approximately one-third of the homeless population in the United States suffers from schizophrenia.

These numbers are high, as are the costs of the disorder to society. Schizophrenia is a chronic illness that needs constant care and is especially debilitating. As a result, cost estimates of the disorder are more than $65 billion a year. Of this $65 billion, about $19 million is for treatment. The remaining costs are for such things as time lost from work and social and family services.

The lifetime loss of income for a male diagnosed as having schizophrenia early in adolescence is about $1 million. Much of this loss is due to unemployment. The disorder tends to strike between 18 and 35 years of age, the most important job training years. Such a young person is less likely than others to complete training for any job, and social and work skills suffer considerably. Society also must pay for the law enforcement and correctional systems that provide long-term institutionalization for people with schizophrenia who commit crimes. About 6 percent of all prisoners in correctional facilities have schizophrenia. It is important to note, however, that people with schizophrenia are no more likely to commit violent crimes than anyone else. However, about 10% of people with schizophrenia die by their own hand.

The good news, however, is that schizophrenia is treatable. With pharmacological treatment and rehabilitation tratment, the majority of symptoms of schizophrenia (such as hearing voices and unrealistic fears of persecution) can be controlled. The sooner treatment occurs after the first episode of schizophrenia, the better the prognosis.

Q How has schizophrenia been treated in the recent past?

The first empirical studies of psychosocial treatment for schizophrenia were conducted in the late 1950s and early 1960s. Students of the famous Harvard psychologist B.F. Skinner clearly demonstrated that what follows a behavior in large part controls whether that behavior occurs again. These studies were the first demonstration of a behavioral program used to treat an entire ward of patients with schizophrenia. Through the middle of the 1970s, the professional literature was abuzz with the results of these and other studies where several forms of behavior therapy were used effectively.

In the early 1970s, the second generation of behaviorally-oriented clinicians and researchers began to publish their work with people who had schizophrenia. The big difference between the methods of these scientists and their predecessors is the emphasis on teaching appropriate social behavior rather than just eliminating bizarre behaviors. If the goal is to have the institutionalized patient with schizophrenia leave the hospital and move to a community setting, the patient must learn to navigate the social world. In a community setting the patient must be able to lead a productive life, competently carry on conversations, and ask for directions. This teaching of prosocial behavior has evolved full force into the teaching of social skills, a helpful step on the way to integrating into the patient's community.

However, today, the main treatment for schizophrenia is antipsychotic drugs; psychosocial therapies play a secondary therapeutic role.

Q What are some of the major characteristics of schizophrenia?

Schizophrenia is characterized by two or more of the following behaviors:
- Delusions, that is, ideas and personal beliefs that are unrelated to reality. A person who believes in a conspiracy against him or her may be delusional. Such thoughts are usually based on feelings of grandeur (such as extraordinary abilities) or persecution (neighborhood residents conspiring to have the person thrown out of his or her house).
- Hallucinations, or hearing (and sometimes seeing) people and things that are not there.
- Disorganized thinking and speech, creating an inability to communicate clearly or carry on a meaningful conversation or an inability to concentrate, since thoughts come fast and furious.
- Inappropriate emotional expression, where the person exhibits what is sometimes called inappropriate affect, such as laughing uncontrollably upon stating that he or she is being persecuted.
- Lack of energy and motivation, where the person with schizophrenia has a low energy level, flat emotions, and generally no interest in everyday or even special things.

These characteristics can be organized into three symptom clusters:
- Positive symptoms comprised of delusions and hallucinations.
- Negative symptoms comprised of deficits in emotional and verbal expression.
- Disorganization symptoms reflected in disordered thinking and speech.

These characteristics or symptoms must impair social and occupational functioning for at least 6 months for a diagnosis of schizophrenia to be reached. Many other mental disorders (such as depression or bipolar disorder) can mimic schizophrenia. Consequently, other possible conditions—such as substance use disorder, brain abnormalities, mood disorders, and pervasive developmental disorders—must be ruled out through a complete physical and psychological examination before diagnosing schizophrenia.

Q Is schizoaffective disorder the same thing as schizophrenia?

You may see or hear the term *schizoaffective disorder* mentioned along with schizophrenia. Schizoaffective disorder has many of the same symptoms as schizophrenia but also involves a mood disturbance. Since both schizophrenia and schizoaffective disorder are treated similarly, most issues and findings related to the treatment of schizophrenia can be applied to the treatment of schizoaffective disorder as well.

Q What is the cause of schizophrenia?

It is unclear what factor or set of factors causes schizophrenia, but most experts believe that the disorder involves at least some irregularity in the brain. For example, new ways to examine living tissue (such as computerized axial tomography or CAT and magnetic resonance imaging or MRI) has allowed researchers to examine the brains of people who have schizophrenia and compare them with the brains of people who do not. One finding is that people with schizophrenia tend to have abnormal brain structures, such as large fluid-filled internal cavities. This indicates a decrease in brain tissue. Other brain imaging studies show abnormal activity of brain regions in schizophrenia.

Many mental health professionals organize the factors that may predispose one to schizophrenia into two categories:
- Vulnerability factors prominently include genetic predisposition. There are clear data to conclude that schizophrenia does run in families. For example, a child of a parent with schizophrenia has about a 12 percent chance of developing the disorder, while the child of non-schizophrenic parents has only a 1 percent chance.

  Approximate risks, given degree of relatedness are:
  - Individual unrelated to person with schizophrenia   1 percent
  - If a brother or sister has the disorder   8 percent
  - If one parent has the disorder   12 percent

- If a fraternal twin has the disorder — 14 percent
- If both parents have the disorder — 39 percent
- If an identical twin has the disorder — 47 percent
- Certain environmental exposures such as prenatal viral infection and early-life severe head injury.

The following factors influence severity of the disorder, and lead to repeat hospitalizations and prognosis:
- Stress factors include role expectations, daily responsibilities, major life events that demand adaptive changes, coping style, and trigger events (such as substance abuse) that can precipitate an episode where the disorder's symptoms are exacerbated.
- Protective factors, such as a supportive family, excellent treatment, and good social skills, help the vulnerable person with schizophrenia to buffer the negative effects of stress.

Q How do we know that abnormal genes, and not environment, cause the disorder to run in families?

Two types of studies have examined the degree of heritability of this disorder. The first type of study involved sets of identical twins, who share all their genes, compared to fraternal twins and siblings of different ages, who only share an average of 50 percent of their genes. The concordance rate for identical twins (or how often the same trait or characteristic occurs in both) is between 40 and 60 percent, much higher than for fraternal twins or other sibling pairs. While this rate shows a significant genetic effect operating, this value leaves a good deal of influence to the environment as well. The second kind of study, the adoptive study, addresses the role of the environment in the development of schizophrenia. Here, the adopted children of parents with schizophrenia were examined. If there were a strong genetic component, you would expect such children, who were adopted by non-schizophrenic parents, to develop the illness. Indeed that is the case. Even if there is little contact between a parent with schizophrenia and his or her biological child, the odds are higher that the child will develop schizophrenia than for the biological child of a parent who does not have schizophrenia.

Q At what age does schizophrenia usually begin, and are men or women more susceptible?

The onset of schizophrenia usually comes during adolescence or early adulthood. A small percentage of cases, however, begin in early childhood.

The disorder affects males and females equally, but males tend to be disproportionately represented in treatment settings. This may be the case because overt symptoms of the male with schizophrenia tend to be less tolerated by society and the patient's own family than similar symptoms displayed by a woman.

Q Over the long term, what patterns does the course of the disorder take?

Over the long term, schizophrenia tends to follow one of three patterns. The list is marked by one or two episodes of the disorder, with relatively rapid return to pre-episode functioning. This type is especially common in non-industrialized countries. The most common course of the illness is characterized by repeated acute psychotic relapses or experiences with partial remission between episodes. Finally, some sufferers are totally unresponsive to treatment. They make up about 15 percent of the total population of the people with schizophrenia and are very difficult to treat successfully.

Q The prognosis for many mental disorders is pretty good when treated properly. Is this the case with schizophrenia?

Schizophrenia is a challenging disorder to treat and takes constant efforts at maintenance to minimize the chances of relapse. There is good evidence, however, that many individuals with clearly diagnosed and even severe forms of schizophrenia can function fairly well after appropriate treatment. A great deal of evidence indicates that medication is the first line of treatment and is very effective. The key to assuring that the recovery is maintained is for the patient to be an active participant in managing symptoms and treatment, such as adherence to a medication routine, helping prevent or contain relapses (a very common occurrence with this disorder), and pursuing long-term social, personal, and occupational goals with the assistance and support of professionals and family.

The prognosis becomes worse when the patient abuses alcohol, stimulant drugs such as cocaine, or marijuana, or when episodes go untreated. If a therapist suspects that the person with symptoms of schizophrenia has been abusing drugs, the patient must be treated for substance abuse along with the prescription of antipsychotic medication. That is because the drug actions of illicit substances or alcohol can often exacerbate the symptoms or characteristics of schizophrenia.

Treating Mental Disorders

Other factors complicate the treatment and outcomes associated with schizophrenia. These factors include developmental disabilities, depression (a common occurrence and risk factor for suicide), and homelessness. Stressful environments, such as those where hostility or criticism is directed at the person with schizophrenia, may also increase rates of relapse.

Q How can you tell if a treatment program is effective?

Since schizophrenia is such a complex disorder, it is important to examine the different facets of an individual's life to evaluate whether a particular treatment is effective. Thus, in evaluating the effectiveness of a treatment, one must look at the level of bizarre and intolerable behaviors, difficulty in community living activities, level of social skills, ability to care for oneself when physically ill, ability to identify signs of relapse, quality of life, and involvement in recreational, social, and spiritual activities.

Q In general, how effective is medication in the treatment of schizophrenia?

The pharmacological agents used to treat schizophrenia are called antipsychotics. They help reduce the frequency and intensity of symptoms that we mentioned in the first part of this chapter. More than 100 controlled studies have demonstrated the effectiveness of antipsychotic medications in the treatment of schizophrenia. Moreover, these medications have been shown to significantly reduce the risk of relapse and rehospitalization when taken on a maintenance basis. These medications have been shown to be effective both for acute care and the chronic phases of treatment. The current thinking is that the medication works by correcting an imbalance in the chemicals responsible for communication between brain cells.

Given the nature of schizophrenia and the havoc it wreaks on individuals and their friends and families, the discovery and use of antipsychotics is a major milestone in modern psychiatry. Early claims that were critical of the efficacy of these mediations led to the eventual design of rigorous and well-controlled studies that allowed for the clear conclusion that these medications do work and above all, resulted in the development of new medications that work as well with fewer side effects.

Q *What are the two general types of antipsychotics used to treat schizophrenia, and how do they differ?*

Antipsychotic medications have been classified as typical (or conventional) and atypical (or novel). Chlorpromazine (Thorazine), a conventional medication, was introduced almost 50 years ago, and the novel medications such as clozapine (Clozaril) came later.

There is no agreed-upon definition of an atypical antipsychotic medication. The criteria used to define them generally include decreased side effects and increased efficacy (especially in treating the negative symptoms). Since the side effects that accompany some of the conventional antipsychotics can be severe and debilitating, the discovery of alternative medications that limit the side effects is important progress.

Besides Thorazine, conventional medications used to treat schizophrenia include fluphenazine (Prolixin), haloperidol (Haldol, the most commonly used antipsychotic during the past 30 years), thiothixene (Navane), trifluoperazine (Stelazine), perphenazine (Trilafon), and thioridizine (Mellaril). Other atypical medications used to treat schizophrenia include risperidone (Risperdal), quetiapine (Seroquel) and olanzapine (Zyprexa).

While both classes of medication are very effective, the newer antipsychotic drugs have fewer side effects. The decision as to which one is appropriate for any one patient is one that should be made by a psychiatrist.

Q *In general, how effective have conventional antipsychotics been in the treatment of acute symptoms of schizophrenia?*

The one hundred studies that have tested the effectiveness of conventional antipsychotics found that approximately 60 percent of treated patients, as compared with 20 percent of placebo-treated patients, demonstrated a nearly complete resolution of acute positive symptoms within a 6-week trial (the lower end of the recommended length of time to see if a medication works). Only 8 percent of patients treated with medication showed no improvement or worsened, whereas nearly 50 percent of placebo-treated patients did not improve at all or got worse. While all the symptoms associated with schizophrenia improved, the positive symptoms (delusions and hallucinations) seemed to respond to the greatest degree and most consistently.

Interestingly, despite the dozens of typical or conventional antipsychotics that have been available, they fail to distinguish themselves from one another in efficacy. In other words, they tend to work equally well. Perhaps the defining criterion for use is how well the patient can tolerate the side effects.

Q How long does it take an antipsychotic to work, and what happens if it does not?

The onset of any effect during the treatment of an acute episode usually takes 1 to 3 weeks, and most gains are noted by 8 weeks. However, some patients might need up to several months to achieve their full clinical benefits, including the remission of symptoms. The usual suggested wait time is 6 to 8 weeks.

When a patient fails to respond in that time period, the dosage can be increased, the patient can be switched to another antipsychotic medication, or treatment time can be extended. There is insufficient information to recommend any one of these strategies over another. The clinician might also try to find out if the patient has failed to comply fully with his or her medicine regimen. If non-compliance is found, injections of typical antipsychotics that come in depot form can be tried. These injections are given biweekly or monthly.

Q What are the atypical antipsychotic drugs, and how effective are they?

The atypical antipsychotics offer increased efficacy in the reduction of the symptoms mentioned earlier and a welcome reduction in burdensome side effects. Here is a brief review of the major atypical antipsychotics and their effectiveness.

Clozapine (Clozaril) was the first atypical antipsychotic and has been shown to be as effective in the treatment of schizophrenia as the conventional antipsychotics. In addition, clozapine has been found to be especially effective with patients who have failed to respond to other antipsychotic medications. Moreover, it does not produce the extrapyramidel side effects characteristic of conventional antipsychotics and is superior in treating negative symptoms. One serious side effect is agranulocytosis (a potentially dangerous drop in the white blood cell count) that occurs in about 1 percent of the patients who take the medication. This requires weekly blood tests, a burdensome and costly proposition.

Risperidone (Risperdal), the second atypical antipsychotic, has been found to outperform conventional antipsychotics in reducing the negative symptoms of schizophrenia. It has been at least equal to conventional antipsychotics in efficiency with a lower incidence of side effects at the lower dosage levels. It does not produce agranulocytosis.

Olanzapine (Zyprexa), the third atypical antipsychotic approved by the Food and Drug Administration for the treatment of schizophrenia, is a very promising new drug because of its efficacy and significant reduction in side effects. It is also superior to conventional antipsychotics and does not cause agranulocytosis.

Quetiapine (Seroquel) is a very new drug that has just received approval from the FDA to be used in the treatment of schizophrenia. It shares the favorable properties of the other antipsychotic drugs. Risperdal, Zyprexa and Seroquel are now considered first-line treatments for schizophrenia with Clozaril generally reserved for patients who do not respond to these three.

Q What are the possible side effects of antipsychotics?

Therapeutic doses of typical antipsychotics produce side effects at high rates, while the atypical medications result in substantially fewer side effects. Here is a list of possible side effects with the use of antipsychotic medication. Note that some side effects are for particular medications or typical antipsychotics in general.

- akathisia (feeling restless or jittery and needing to fidget or pace)—Typical antipsychotics
- akinesia (feeling slowed down and having no mental energy)—Typical antipsychotics
- anticholingeric effects (dry mouth, blurry vision, and constipation as well as memory difficulties and confusion)—Typical antipsychotics and clozapine and olanzapine
- agranulocytosis (a dramatic drop in the white blood cell count)—Only clozapine
- dystonia (muscle spasms)—Typical antipsychotics
- sexual and menstrual difficulties—Typical antipsychotics and risperidone but not olanzapine or quetiapine
- tardive dyskinesia (uncontrollable movements of the mouth, tongue, or hands)—Typical antispychotics but not clozapine
- tremors, such as shaking of the hands or other parts of body—Typical antispychotics
- weight gain—Typical and atypical antipsychotics but not risperidone

Given that the typical antipsychotics have much more severe side effects, why would anyone prescribe such a medication for a patient as opposed to an atypical antipsychotic? First, the patient is doing well on the medication and there is no reason to change and second, they are less expensive.

Q Can patients with schizophrenia ever stop taking their medication?

Currently, there's not enough information to answer this question. It has been well documented that patients with schizophrenia who are treated with antipsychotic medication and who have responded successfully will experience a worsening of symptoms and an increased rate of hospitalization when the medication is discontinued. Even among patients who have been successfully treated for years, some studies have shown that almost two-thirds will relapse when medication is discontinued. About 30 percent of patients who remain on their medication will relapse as well. So, maintenance is of the utmost importance. Unfortunately, a patient who begins to feel better may very well think it no longer necessary to take medication, leading to a reappearance of symptoms that are often more severe than the original episode and sometimes more resistant to treatment.

The benefits of maintenance, however, are somewhat tempered by the risk associated with long-term side effects such as the development of tardive dyskinesia, a neurological condition. The risk of developing tarkive dyskenesia appears to be dramatically reduced with atypical drugs and is virtually non-existent with clozapine.

Q *Are there any other medications besides antipsychotics that can help with schizophrenia?*

Yes. Since schizophrenia occurs with the symptoms of other mental disorders— such as depression, mood swings, and anxiety. Other types of drugs have been used to treat schizophrenia as well as to treat these concurrent problems as adjuncts to schizophrenia.

Here is a brief discussion of what other pharmacological treatments have been tried and their effectiveness.

Antianxiety medications in the form of benzodiazepines (such as Valium) have been used to treat patients with schizophrenia since the early 1960s. There is some evidence that these medications are helpful, but in the majority of studies some patients did better while some did not. The studies differ in their methodology so that it is difficult to compare results. However, there is stronger evidence that for patients who also have anxiety, depression, hostility, and irritability, these benzodiazepines may be beneficial but also may worsen some behaviors associated with schizophrenia.

Antidepressants have been used either alone or in conjunction with antipsychotics. Very few studies have found positive outcomes for patients with schizophrenia when treated with antidepressants alone. When used to treat depression (a frequent disorder occurring with schizophrenia), the antidepressants appear to be helpful but only when patients were stabilized on antipsychotic medication.

The use of mood stabilizers such as lithium (Lithonate) and carbamazepine (Tegretol) have resulted in mixed outcomes, with positive results seen in about one-half the studies that have been done. Some evidence supports use of carbamazepine in conjunction with antipsychotics for the treatment of schizophrenia, especially when the patient is aggressive and agitated. However, since this medication can have serious side effects, specific enzyme levels need to be monitored because of the potential for liver damage as a side effect

Dopamine agonists such as bromocriptine (Parlodel) have been associated with undesirable exacerbation of psychotic symptoms in a large proportion of schizophrenia patients who used these drugs. However, there is some evidence (although limited by the number of studies) that this medication can help control the negative symptoms of schizophrenia such as emotional flatness.

Finally, electroconvulsive therapy has been used as a treatment for schizophrenia and works best when patients are in the earliest stages. However, it is rarely used today except in the cases of patients who have frequent relapses or patients who fail to respond to all other therapies and cannot live outside of the hospital. It is never given, however, without the patient's full consent and understanding.

Q It is clear that medical approaches to treating schizophrenia are very effective. What are some of the psychosocial interventions that have been used to treat schizophrenia, and how effective are they?

Once the bizarre or psychotic behaviors are under control (through medication), a supportive environment in which the patient transacts his or her daily life becomes critical to continued success and the avoidance of relapse. Such a supportive environment includes adherence to a medication schedule and the development of social and work skills.

Among the different types of psychosocial treatments used to maintain these appropriate behaviors are supportive therapy, behavioral and social learning programs, cognitive therapy, educational therapy, social skills training, vocational therapy, and case management. Generally, the criterion for judging the effectiveness of these therapies is how quickly and effectively the person with schizophrenia can be integrated into his or her community.

Q How effective is supportive therapy in the treatment of schizophrenia?

Traditional psychodynamically oriented therapy has not been shown to be especially effective in the treatment of schizophrenia. However, the qualities that are characteristic of such an approach (such as a positive therapeutic relationship) are a necessary element of any successful psychosocial treatment approach. Supportive therapy is an approach that incorporates such important features with an emphasis on the reciprocity between the patient and the mental health professional. Supportive therapy can be individual or group in nature and is characterized by a positive, therapeutic alliance between the patient and mental health care workers, a focus on reality issues such as solving everyday life problems, an active role by the therapist, who uses his or her own life experiences as a model for the patient, encouragement, and education of the patient and the family in the proper use of antipsychotic medication.

Well-controlled studies have tested the efficacy of supportive therapy. While supportive therapy is popular, the evidence is unclear as to its effectiveness. In one study, individual supportive therapy led to worse outcomes at the 6-month follow-up, but for those who stayed past the first year and continued in supportive therapy, relapse rates and social functioning were improved at the 2-year follow-up. Another study found supportive therapy to be less effective than alternative treatments such as social skills training.

Q How effective are behavior therapy and social learning programs in the treatment of schizophrenia?

Behavior therapy has been used to manage the symptoms of schizophrenia ever since the initial demonstrations of the technique's effectiveness in the early 1960s. Hundreds of studies have examined the effectiveness of this approach. The studies usually evaluate the efficacy of reinforcement schedules, social modeling, and other principles of behavior analysis and social learning theory, two distinct theoretical approaches to understanding complex patterns of learned behaviors.

Behavior therapy and social learning program treatments have been shown to reduce the level of schizophrenic behaviors. For example, the most rigorous and well-controlled of the studies randomly assigned patients to several different treatment conditions including social learning therapy. On all measures of effectiveness, such as frequency and intensity of symptoms, activities of daily living, social behavior, community acceptance, and cost effectiveness, patients in the treatment condition did better than the patients in the control group.

Q How effective is cognitive therapy in the treatment of schizophrenia?

Historically, cognitive therapy has been very effective in the treatment of depression (Chapter 7) and anxiety disorders (Chapter 8). Only recently has the method been tried as a treatment for schizophrenia. Any cognitive therapy is based on the assumption that changing an individual's thoughts, attitudes, and perceptions can have favorable effects on the symptoms that accompany schizophrenia.

Different types of cognitive therapy offer assistance at different levels of cognitive functioning. The most specific type of cognitive therapy is called cognitive redemption. This approach focuses on improving or normalizing the most basic cognitive functions such as verbal learning, memory, and sustained attention behaviors. Each of these functions is abnormal in a large proportion of people with schizophrenia. The rationale for cognitive redemption is that by improving these basic cognitive skills, an individual will improve in his or her ability to learn broadly based, more applied relevant skills such as those associated with work and social settings.

In general, the evidence is not very supportive of cognitive therapy as a useful tool in treating schizophrenia. The primary reason is that many studies used questionable methods of diagnosis, and many patients participating in the study may not have been as seriously ill as initially thought. These methodological limitations restrict the generalizability of the findings to other cases.

Q How effective is educational therapy in the treatment of schizophrenia?

A number of studies suggest that the emotional climate of the family is one of the most powerful predictors of relapse in schizophrenia. Consequently, interventions have been designed and empirically tested that are aimed at engaging families as active participants in the treatment and rehabilitation of family members who have schizophrenia. Such interventions, generally referred to as educational therapy, have many different names such as family psychoeducation, behavior family management, family-aided assertive community treatment, and multiple family therapy.

All these methods of treatment have the following in common:
- structured and clear expectations for participation by the patient and family members
- outreach to family members to provide them with support
- practical education about the nature of schizophrenia
- assistance in treating schizophrenia and using community resources
- teaching better family communication skills and family problem solving
- encouraging family members to pursue their own goals

Several well-controlled studies have been conducted that support the use of family education as a therapy that is superior to medication alone or other psychosocial approaches. A key element of an effective family education program is its duration—a minimum of 9 months or a year of weekly and biweekly family sessions, a major commitment for the patient as well as the family. Using family education, relapse rates (a primary indicator of a treatment's effectiveness) have been reduced, but there are also studies showing that use of family education is not effective as a treatment.

Q How effective is social skills training in the treatment of schizophrenia?

Social skills training uses behavioral techniques that enable persons with schizophrenia and other disabling mental disorders to acquire social skills that enable them to negotiate with others. This treatment combines the effective features of behavioral therapy and educational approaches. The skills that are taught include appropriate use of antipsychotic medication, communication with mental health professionals, recognizing the early signs of relapse, developing a relapse prevention plan, coping with persistent psychotic symptoms, avoiding street drugs, and leisure and conversational skills.

A social skills training session is usually conducted one to three times per week with groups of four to ten patients in an office, a community mental health center, or an outpatient or inpatient hospital setting. To participate, a patient must adhere to his or her medication routine, be able to follow instructions and pay attention, and be able to tolerate a session lasting 45 to 90 minutes. During these sessions, role playing and positive reinforcement plus homework are used to encourage the development of appropriate skills. Mental health professionals look for the learning, durability, and use of the skills in real life settings, quality of life, and relapse rate to determine if social skills training programs are successful.

In general, the evidence is excellent that social skills training is an effective way to help people with schizophrenia integrate themselves into the community, especially in conjunction with family training programs like the kind just described. In fact, the results of one study that combined social skills training with family education resulted in no relapses of schizophrenia over a 1-year period.

Q How effective is vocational rehabilitation in the treatment of schizophrenia?

Several programs have been designed to assist people with schizophrenia in procuring and maintaining employment. Not only does this approach make sense from a public policy point of view (since, for example people who work pay more taxes), but it also can have a profound effect on the family climate. Unfortunately, most efforts at vocational training have taken place in sheltered community settings where there is little opportunity to learn employment skills that are useful in the community at large.

However, there have been exceptions. In the 1960s and 1970s, the Fairweather Lodge (named after its founder, George Fairweather) designed a rehabilitation program that brought together groups of personally compatible patients with serious mental disorders such as schizophrenia. The program trained the patients to be supportive of each other, organized the groups by interest, and emphasized work and independent living skills. The results of this program were very encouraging, with every outcome (work, relapse rate, etc.) showing substantially greater benefits for the participants than for those who did not. The program has been successfully used in more than 100 institutions around the United States and is still in use.

A variety of different forces—including the Americans with Disabilities Act, successful demonstrations of competitive employment for the mentally retarded, and community support programs—are operating to help vocational rehabilitation become an increasingly attractive alternative and supplemental method for helping reintegrate people with schizophrenia into the community. Vocational rehabilitation assumes it is an integral and not a separate component of psychiatric treatment and requires a team approach with specialists in job training, development, and placement. The goal of supportive employment is to place an individual in competitive employment in the community with training taking place on the job. Job coaching and supports from mental health and rehabilitation professionals—including ready access to psychiatric services, medication, and crisis services—are provided indefinitely, consistent with the knowledge that schizophrenia and other mental disorders are long-term disorders.

The development of vocational rehabilitation and supportive employment is so new that little information about their effectiveness is available. A slight variation of vocational rehabilitation is the job-finding club. This approach assumes that a client is ready for work but requires training and structured support in the job search process. Individuals set goals for the types of job for which they are qualified and participate in a 1- to 2-week program that offers training in creating a resume, finding job leads, telephoning, interacting with potential employers, going through a job interview, and maintaining the motivation for a complete job search. Although no controlled studies have tested this approach, results of informal studies show that 19 to 61 percent of mentally ill patients obtained competitive employment after an average of twent-five days.

Another approach, a psychosocial rehabilitation center or clubhouse (such as the Fountain House in New York) is very popular. Under this approach, an accepting, peer-oriented clubhouse de-emphasizes the role of patient and stresses the individual's own responsibility for rehabilitation. It offers a continuum of vocational opportunities ranging from training for jobs, unpaid work opportunities within the center, and transitional employment.

Q What is case management, and how effective is it in the treatment of schizophrenia?

The case management approach is based on the rationale that shorter hospital visits and intense oversight by treatment teams can result in better outcomes for the patient with less expense. A case manager is an individual who helps coordinate the delivery of services and also monitors the progress of the patient.

In one study using the case management approach, eleven days of hospitalization followed by day treatment produced better symptom outcomes than did 60 days of hospitalization plus outpatient follow-up. Case management recommends that patients with schizophrenia be discharged from the hospital when the symptoms are no longer present. In addition, therapists should attempt to ensure that appropriate continuity of care, social and family supports, and housing are all available before the patient is discharged to avoid the hospitalization-discharge-hospitalization cycle that afflicts many mentally ill people (including many of the homeless).

Three forms of case management have evolved, differing in the level of training and quality and amount of services that are directly delivered to the patient or client. These are the brokerage model, the clinical case management model, and the training in community living model.

In the brokerage model, services are arranged for by an agency and delivered to the client. This treatment has been found to be effective in treating and maintaining symptom reduction and in fulfilling the needs of the person with schizophrenia once hc or she has reentered the community.

The clinical case management model employs a case manager who has clinical training and skills and functions as the primary therapist, providing environmental supports in addition to counseling. This model has resulted in improvements in the subjective quality of life, but the case manager can easily become overburdened with responsibilities and suffer "burnout."

Finally, the training in community living model, which was developed more than 20 years ago, has been shown to be very effective in several well-controlled studies. This model organizes the service delivery system into multidisciplinary clinical treatment teams that serve different aspects of the patient's needs. Services are delivered in the patient's own environment and include assistance in managing the illness (e.g., medication), assistance with community living, and providing supportive employment activities.

Q What might the future hold for psychosocial approaches toward treating schizophrenia?

First, the efficacy of any of the treatments depends a great deal on the requirement that the patient be cognitively competent. In other words, patients should be able to pay attention, remember things, and solve basic problems. Since many people with schizophrenia cannot, one direction for future research focuses on developing a better understanding of how to overcome cognitive deficits.

Second, while many psychosocial programs are effective, these programs need to be detailed in treatment manuals so they can be easily replicated and administered whenever possible.

Finally, as the long-term effects of being on disability status become more apparent, work incentives and more efficient social interventions will become increasingly necessary and popular. Given that even the most severely mentally disabled individual can be gainfully employed, even if in a limited setting, programs that train and monitor the work habits of the mentally disabled are strongly in the public's and the individual's best interest.

Q Where Can I Find More Information About Schizophrenia?

Books

Conquering Schizophrenia: A Father, His Son, and a Medical Breakthrough by Peter Wyden. Knopf, 1998. ISBN 0679446710.

A story of a son's battle with schizophrenia as told by his father. A substantively accurate and inspiring book.

Surviving Schizophrenia: A Manual for Families, Consumers, and Providers by E. Fuller Torrey. Harper Perennial Library, 1995. ISBN 0060950765.

The third edition of a manual that details what patients, families, and professionals should know about schizophrenia.

Families Coping with Schizophrenia: A Practitioner's Guide to Family Groups by Jacqueline M. Atkinson and Denise A. Coia. John Wiley & Sons, 1995. ISBN 0471941816.

A comprehensive guide to setting up educational groups to help deal with schizophrenia as well as information about the political issues surrounding the provision of services and treatment alternatives.

My Mother's Keeper: A Daughter's Memoir of Growing Up in the Shadow of Schizophrenia by Tara Elgin Holley and Joe Holley. William Morrow & Company, 1997. ISBN 0688133681.

The story of a woman's struggle to care for her mentally ill mother, tracing the effects of the illness on both the woman and her family. The author, who at 16 became her mother's legal guardian, tells the story of how she learned to deal with her mother's schizophrenia.

Schizophrenia: The Facts by Ming T. Tsuang, Stephen V. Faraone, and Peter. Johnson. Oxford University Press, 1997. ISBN 0192627600.

A collection of information about the disease, including what schizophrenia is, meeting the challenge of schizophrenia, caring and coping in a changing social environment, and family and patient support groups.

Internet Sites

Doctor's Guide to Schizophrenia
(http://www.pslgroup.com/SCHIZOPHR.HTM) contains medical news and alerts, information about the disorder, and a listing of other related sites. Over 30 drug companies sponsor this site.

Internet Mental Health Schizophrenia
(http://www.mentalhealth.com/dis/p20-ps01.html) contains a description of the disorder and information on diagnosis, treatment, research, personal accounts, and a listing of printed resources.

The Schizophrenia Home Page
(at http://www.schizophrenia.com/) is perhaps the most active page on the Web dealing with schizophrenia and provides patient information, as well as information for families, friends, researchers, professionals, and students.

National Alliance for Research on Schizophrenia and Depression
(at http://www.mhsource.com/advocacy/narsad/schiz.html and which also is available in Spanish) is an excellent introduction to the illness, important issues, and current treatment alternatives.

An electronic mail discussion group about schizophrenia
(listserv@vm.utcc.utoronto.ca) is available by subscription. To subscribe enter SCHIZOPH [your_first_name] [your_last_name] in the subject line of an e-mail message, and send the message.

Where to Write

NARSAD RESEARCH
60 Cutter Mill Road, Suite 404
Great Neck, NY 11021
800-829-8289

Schizophrenia Society of Canada
75 The Donway West, Suite 814
Don Mills, Ontario M3C 2E9

National Alliance for the Mentally Ill
200 North Glebe Road, Suite 1015
Arlington, VA 22203-3754
800-950-6264

Chapter 12

Personality Disorders: More Than Just Being Different

If you didn't know better, you would think that Rick's preoccupation with detail was just an eccentricity, part of his personality and nothing more. He is an accountant by training, and it's understandable why he pays a great deal of attention to the little things; it's part of his job. That's what his girlfriend thought before she moved in with Rick. However, since then, she's learned how his preoccupation with detail affects his coworkers, his neighbors, and now, his girlfriend. Once, the next-door neighbor borrowed a tool and, when he returned it, placed it in the garage in a location different from where it was originally stored. Rick became very upset when he couldn't find the tool, although it wasn't clear whether he was upset because he couldn't find it or because the tool was not in the right place. Rick's girlfriend has also concluded that her response to Rick's passion for order sometimes interferes with the other kind of passion.

So, for his girlfriend, being together with Rick has become so demanding and, more often than not, so unpleasant that she has decided she is ready to move out. When she informs Rick, he agrees to see a therapist, who undertakes a combination of exposure therapy and social skills training, which if things go well, may save the day— and Rick's romance.

Q What is a personality disorder, and how often does it occur?

A personality disorder is present when a personality characteristic significantly impedes social or occupational functioning and distresses the person with the characteristic. A personality trait, such as being talkative or aggressive, is an enduring pattern of how a person relates to the world. When such a trait or combination of traits starts working against the individual and causes him or her distress, the trait is considered a personality disorder.

Everyone, at one time or another, is irritable or fails to plan ahead. But, for most people, such behaviors are neither consistent nor extreme. It's when these otherwise normal behaviors become a part of one's personality that concern arises about whether a personality disorder is present.

Although personality disorders are relatively common compared with other mental disorders, precise estimates of prevalence are difficult to obtain because the assessment tools to identify personality disorders are inadequate. Nevertheless, the best estimates indicate that the lifetime prevalence rate for personality disorder is a very substantial 6 to 10 percent. Another difficulty in estimating the number of affected people is that in spite of personality disorders' relatively high level of occurrence, relatively few affected individuals seek treatment. Because society tends to encourage people to tolerate personality faults in others ("Oh, he's just a bit demanding"), the individual who is acting far out of proportion to social and personal expectations often does not get appropriate feedback.

Another reason for the lack of an accurate estimate of prevalence is that people with personality disorders don't have the overt symptoms of a mental disorder and few around them (such as family or friends) see any need for treatment. In fact, the disorder often does not even trouble those suffering from these disorders, so they may well represent a significantly undeserved portion of people with mental disorders.

Interestingly, personality disorders often occur with one or more additional mental disorders. For example, half the people diagnosed with the personality disorder called avoidant personality disorder also are diagnosed with schizotypal personality disorder. In two studies, almost 40 percent of patients with personality disorders also had bulimia nervosa.

Q Personality disorder is a very general term. Are there more specific categories of personality disorders?

There are three clusters of personality disorders, and within each cluster is a set of specific disorders. Following is a description of each of the personality disorders within each cluster:

The odd cluster contains the paranoid, schizoid, and schizotypal personality disorders.

- Paranoid personality disorder is characterized by a distrust and suspicion about other people's motives. Specifically, the individual with the disorder suspects that others are trying to harm him or her, is suspicious of the faithfulness of spouses, bears grudges, is generally "looking for a fight," looks for and finds hidden meanings, and won't confide in others.
- Schizoid personality disorder is characterized by being detached from relationships with others including family, friends, and coworkers. Specific characteristics are disinterest in activities, indifference to judgments of others, lack of desire for close relationships, focus on solitary activities, and lack of affect or emotion.
- Schizotypal personality disorder is characterized by poor interpersonal relationships and eccentric behavior. Specific characteristics include inappropriate emotions or affect, odd behaviors, odd beliefs, general suspiciousness, and lack of close friends.

The dramatic cluster includes histrionic, narcissistic, antisocial, and borderline personality disorders.

- Histrionic personality disorder is characterized by excessive emotionality and attention-getting behavior. Specific characteristics include melodramatic behaviors, shallow emotions, discomfort when not the center of attention, high suggestibility, eccentric dressing to bring attention, and seductive or sexually inappropriate behavior with others.
- Narcissistic personality disorder is characterized by a need for admiration and a pattern of grandiose thinking and behaving. Specific characteristics include a preoccupation with success as defined (for example) by money or beauty, a need for excessive admiration, arrogant behaviors toward others, taking advantage of others, believing that he or she is entitled to attention and rewards, and a self-focus on his or her being "special."
- Antisocial personality disorder is characterized by a disregard of other people's rights. Specific characteristics include aggressive and impulsive behavior, lying, lack of remorse, and failure to conform to social expectations including respect for laws.
- Borderline personality disorder is characterized by a lack of stability in interpersonal relationships. Specific characteristics include difficulty controlling anger, a pattern of unstable personal relationships, impulsivity, recurrent suicidal behavior, a missing or incomplete sense of self, and efforts to avoid real or imagined abandonment.

The anxious cluster includes avoidant, dependent, and obsessive-compulsive personality disorders.

- Avoidant personality disorder is characterized by a pattern of feelings of inadequacy and overreaction to any criticism. Specific characteristics include reluctance to take personal risks because of potential embarrassment, inhibitions, an unwillingness to get involved with other people, and the avoidance of activities that involve personal contact because of fears of criticism. This last trait provides the general basis for much of the behavior of the person with this type of personality disorder.

- Dependent personality disorder is characterized by a need to be taken care of, which leads to clinginess and a fear of separation. Specific characteristics include the inability to make everyday decisions, fear of being left on one's own, lack of initiative, inability to assume responsibility for one's own life, refusal to express disagreement with others because of fear of losing support or friendship, and going to extremes to get support from others.

- Obsessive-compulsive personality disorder is preoccupied with orderliness and control. Specific characteristics include stubbornness, inflexibility, preoccupation with detail, rules, and lists, a level of perfectionism that interferes with the completion of the task, hoarding, and reluctance to delegate tasks to others unless the tasks are done exactly as designated.

Q What are some of the causes of personality disorders?

Little is known about the cause of personality disorders. The fact that personality disorders occur so often with other types of mental disorders makes it more difficult to separate what causes what. While not as debilitating, personality disorders also share some of the same symptoms as other mental disorders, such as schizophrenia and bipolar disorder. There is, however, some evidence that personality disorders, like the more serious disorders they resemble, may reflect in part a genetic predisposition.

Q A personality disorder is a fairly common type of mental disorder. What is the general status of psychosocial treatments for these different disorders?

Despite the relatively high prevalence of personality disorders, few outcome studies have systematically assessed the efficacy of psychosocial treatments. In addition, there have been no comprehensive reviews of treatments that have been tried. This may be because there are so many types of personality disorders, all having distinct characteristics, that drawing conclusions about treatments' effectiveness is difficult. However, some limited information is available about the effectiveness of psychosocial treatments for the avoidant and borderline personality disorders.

Treating Mental Disorders

Q What is the most effective psychosocial treatment for avoidant personality disorder?

The only well-designed and well-controlled study of avoidant personality disorder compared several types of behavioral treatments such as exposure, social skills training, and intimacy-focused training (as separate treatments) with a wait-list control group. Each of the treatments was better than nothing, but no difference was found between treatments. While the differences between the treatment and control groups were statistically significant, the patients in the treatment group were still not functioning at the level of a group without the disorder. Other studies that have been completed lacked the necessary control of extraneous influences, so it's impossible to draw any useful conclusions about the treatments used.

Q What is the most effective psychosocial treatment for borderline personality disorder?

The most thorough study done on the psychosocial treatment of the borderline personality disorder examined a relatively new treatment called dialectical behavior therapy. The therapy uses a complex and eclectic combination of weekly individual and group sessions. Dialectical behavior therapy consist of two parts. First, there are weekly individual therapy sessions in which problematic events are explored in detail beginning with the chain of events that led to the behavior the patient is trying to change, and including how the problem might be solved, and what prevented the patient from solving the problem. The second part of the therapy consists of group sessions in which interpersonal issues are explored.

In this study, the effects of treatment or no treatment on forty-four suicidal women were examined. The treatment group had a greatly reduced dropout rate (17 percent compared to 58 percent for the women who did not receive the treatment but continued to be treated in the community) and showed fewer and less severe episodes of suicide-related behavior and fewer days of hospitalization. However, no differences between the treatment and no-treatment groups were found in depression, hopelessness, or suicidal thoughts.

The basic assumption underlying dialectical behavior therapy is that some individuals react abnormally to otherwise normal stimulation because of negative aspects of their past or present environment (such as sexual abuse as a child). For these individuals, the level of emotional arousal goes up quickly and takes more time to return to normal. People with this disorder have highly variable emotional states that can shift rapidly. The general focus of dialectical behavior therapy is on high-risk suicidal behaviors, behaviors that interfere with the quality of life, goals that are set by the patient, and enhancing self-respect and self-image.

While dialectical behavior therapy shows promise, clearly, much more research must be done before concluding that it is an effective treatment for borderline personality disorder.

Q How effective are psychosocial treatments for other personality disorders?

No controlled studies have been conducted for histrionic, dependent, schizotypal, schizoid, narcissistic, antisocial, or paranoid personality disorders, so there is not enough information to conclude that these personality disorders can be effectively treated. However, one controlled study examined a sample of patients with mixed personality disorders. In this study, eighty-one patients with personality disorders received either no treatment or brief dynamic therapy. The treatment produced substantial improvements including better general adjustment and a reduction in patient complaints. And, also of importance, the gains were maintained upon testing $1^{1}/2$ years later.

Q Given what we know about treating personality disorders, what does the future hold for new treatment directions?

The systematic study of personality disorders is, at best, just beginning. Compared with advances made in treating many other mental disorders, the treatment of personality disorders is in its infancy. With few high-quality controlled studies having been done, it's difficult to make any recommendation with even a modest degree of confidence. Also, when other types of mental disorders are present, the conventional types of behavior therapy for a personality disorder will usually fail.

However, developments are promising. First, a continuing refinement of the definition of a personality disorder may provide a clearer picture of what treatment might be appropriate. For example, if the concurrence of drug abuse and avoidant personality disorder tends to be high (which it is), then perhaps the results of research should define and treat both as one type of disorder, at least for treatment and research purposes. Second, given the complexity of the different types of personality disorders, matching treatments to patients may be effective. For example, instead of antisocial personality disorder being a patient's diagnosis and determining his or her treatment, perhaps the behaviors underlying that diagnosis (anger and impulsivity, for example) should become the focus of treatment. And finally, perhaps psychosocial approaches to therapy will become better integrated to meet the individual demands of particular patients. For example, there might be both behavioral and dynamic psychotherapeutic elements to treatment, depending upon the issues faced by the patient.

Q The use of medication to treat personality disorders is relatively new. What are some of the uses of medication to treat a personality disorder?

Medication as a treatment for personality disorders might be the least well understood use of medication for mental disorders. Little research has been done.

Just as in the case of psychosocial treatment, there are methodological hurdles to performing studies on the effectiveness of treating personality disorders with medication. First, even within each personality disorder (such as borderline personality disorder), there is a high degree of heterogeneity, meaning that the cause of the disorder and its expression are highly varied from person to person. Second, personality disorders more often than not are accompanied by other mental disorders. Finally, the tools used to assess the behavior of someone with a personality disorder have limited reliability such that they do not give a consistent or an accurate picture of the patient's true state.

Treating personality disorders with medication relies upon clearly distinguishable symptoms and definitions that allow a distinction between one personality disorder and another. Without this distinction it is very difficult to accurately target pharmacological efforts.

Q What is the general status of pharmacological treatment of personality disorders?

Again, the entire group of personality disorders offers a challenge to the mental health professional in providing treatment because personality disorders frequently occur along with other disorders. Thus, it is not clear which disorder is actually responding to medication. Also, a personality disorder is often a less extreme (and often less noticeable) case of another disorder. For example, some have portrayed the schizotypal personality disorder as a relatively mild form of schizophrenia. In general, much of the same treatment for a specific mental disorder such as schizophrenia would be used to treat the comparable personality disorder, schizotypal personality disorder in this case.

Q What medications have been used in the treatment of the odd cluster personality disorders, and how effective are they?

Of all the personality disorders in this cluster, schizotypal personality disorder has been the most carefully studied. The commonalties between schizotypal personality disorder and schizophrenia have led to tests of the effectiveness of antipsychotic medications in treating schizotypal personality disorder.

The findings of several studies suggest that antipsychotic medications such as haloperidol (Haldol) may be beneficial in treating schizotypal personality disorder. The use of haloperidol led to improvements, including a decrease in depression and impulsivity in hospitalized patients, especially if the symptoms were severe. Also, knowing the efficacy of antipsychotic medications for treating schizophrenia, investigators have studied antipsychotics' effect on schizotypal personality disorder and found that the schizotypal personality disorder population is somewhat responsive to low doses of antipsychotic medication. Other medications that have been used are thiothixene (Navane), also an antipsychotic, and tranylcypromine (Parnate), an antidepressant.

Q What medications have been used to treat dramatic cluster personality disorders, and how effective are they?

Within this cluster, borderline personality disorder has received the most attention. Antidepressants such as amitriptyline (Elavil) have been found to decrease depression scores and the frequency of impulsive behaviors in a group of borderline personality patients, but worsen impulsivity, aggression, and paranoia. Other antidepressants, however, such as fluoxetine (Prozac) have been shown to decrease impulsivity and improve symptoms such as anger and irritability. Lithium has been shown to be another useful agent in treating some cases of borderline personality disorder. The effectiveness of antipsychotics in the treatment of borderline personality disorder is mixed. Their use has shown global, but modest, improvements.

Q What medications have been used in the treatment of the anxious cluster personality disorders, and how effective are they?

Several studies have shown the strong relationship between anxious personality disorders and other anxiety disorders such as social phobia. For example, one recent study of fifty patients diagnosed with social phobia found symptoms of avoidant personality disorder in 89 percent of the patients. Consequently, personality disorders in this cluster have tended to be treated with the same types of medication used to treat social phobias. The problem is that there have been very few studies that have investigated anxious types of personality disorders. In two controlled trials, the monoamine oxidase inhibitor phenelzine (Nardil) has been shown to decrease symptoms of avoidant personality disorder for patients with social phobia and to be associated with a marked increase in the patients' ability to socialize. Tranylcypromine (Parnate), another MAO inhibitor, had similar effects on socialization behavior. Finally, the benzodiazepines clonazepam (Klonopin) and alprazolam (Xanax) have been shown to decrease measures of avoidance.

Q What future steps might be taken to better use medications in the treatment of personality disorders?

The most important step in the pharmacological treatment of personality disorders is to better understand the biology of such disorders and to clarify the distinction between the different personality disorders and other major mental disorders. This clarification would allow for more controlled clinical studies and greater precision in the use of medications to treat personality disorders.

Q Where Can I Find More Information About Personality Disorders?

Books

Handbook of Antisocial Behavior edited by David M. Stoff, James Breiling, and Jack D. Maser. John Wiley & Sons, 1997. ISBN 0471124524.

Expensive, but a very comprehensive discussion of antisocial behavior. This book contains a discussion of the psychological, social, and biological causes that lead to violence and concrete guidelines for the clinical and social treatment of antisocial behavior.

Borderline Personality Disorder: The Latest Assessment & Treatment Strategies by Melanie A. Dean. Compact Clinicals, 1997. ISBN 1887537090.

A detailed discussion of what is currently available for the assessment and treatment of borderline personality disorder.

Narcissism and the Interpersonal Self (Personality, Psychopathology, and Psychotherapy: Theoretical and Clinical Perspectives) edited by John Fiscalini and Alan L. Grey. Columbia University Press, 1993. ISBN 0231070101.

A comprehensive discussion of narcissism from a psychoanalytic perspective and examination of the cultural, philosophical, and psychological dimensions of this disorder.

Conspiracy: How the Paranoid Style Flourishes and Where It Comes From by Daniel Pipes. Free Press, 1997. ISBN 0684831317.

An examination of conspiracy theory in general and the people who start and maintain such beliefs.

The Impulsive Client: Theory, Research, and Treatment edited by William G. McCown, Judith L. Johnson, Myrna B. Shure. American Psychological Association, 1996. ISBN 1557982082.

An anthology of perspectives in practice and theory on the impulsive personality, exploring why people differ in impulsivity and the implications for psychological treatment.

Internet Sites

BPD Central or Borderline Personality Disorder Central
(at http://members.aol.com/BPDCentral/) contains information about new books on borderline personality disorder as well as links to other borderline personality disorder sites.

Mental Health Net's All About Personality Disorders Page
(at http://personalitydisorders.cmhc.com/) discusses symptoms, treatment, on-line resources, and organizations.

alt.support.personality is a newsgroup with frank discussions about personality disorders.

You can automatically subscribe to several mailing lists on borderline personality at http://personalitydisorders.cmhc.com/guide/person.htm.

Where to Write

National Alliance for the Mentally Ill
200 North Glebe Road, Suite 1015
Arlington, VA 22203-3754
800-950-NAMI (6264)

Division of Mental Disorders
National Institute of Mental Health, National Institutes of Health
5600 Fishers Lane, Room 18C-26
Rockville, MD 20857
301-443-5047

Chapter 13

Disorders of Aging: Alzheimer's Disease, Depression, and Anxiety

Sandra spent her professional life as a scientist who did enough research to publish over 200 professional papers during a 35-year career. How ironic, given her distinguished career, that the first sign that something was wrong was when she developed problems remembering even the simplest facts about her everyday activities such as her own phone number or the time of an appointment. Over the course of a year or more, her memory gradually became worse, becoming so bad that she unfortunately could no longer even remember the reason why she had entered another room in her apartment. Her loss of memory was very disturbing for her since she always valued "the life of the mind" and clearly recognized the loss that was taking place. Sandra continued to decline, both in her physical health and her cognitive skills, eventually requiring full-time care when she could no longer perform the most simple of self-care basics such as dressing and bathing.

Sandra suffers from a type of dementia called Alzheimer's disease and she is being cared for and kept as comfortable as possible. She will not get better.

Q *What is Alzheimer's disease, and how common is it?*

Alzheimer's disease is a form of dementia initially characterized by a progressive deterioration in memory. Symptoms include:
- a loss in short-term memory ("What did you just eat?")
- problems with abstract thinking

- poor judgment
- difficulty performing familiar tasks
- disorientation as to time and place, including wandering off
- a change in personality
- a loss of long-term memory ("Where were you born?")

These symptoms begin to severely interfere with the patient's quality of life and certainly have an impact on home and work activities.

Alzheimer's disease is the most common form of dementia that occurs in the elderly. It is three times more prevalent in women then men, probably because women live longer. Alzheimer's accounts for 70 percent of patients suffering from dementia and affects about 2.5 million people in North America. About 5 to 10 percent of the population over 65 years of age has some of the symptoms listed above, and the number and severity of symptoms increase as people age. About 10 percent of all people over the age of 65 have Alzheimer's, and between 33 and 50 percent of adults over age 85 suffer from the disorder. However, Alzheimer's disease has been diagnosed in people as young as their 50s, so it is not exclusively a disorder of advanced age.

It's important to note that while forgetfulness is a normal part of aging, the loss of memory that characterizes Alzheimer's is different: it increases over time, is not reversible, and ultimately results in profound memory loss.

Q Is Alzheimer's disease the only type of dementia?

Not at all. Dementia is the general class of cognitive impairment, and Alzheimer's disease is by far the most common form of dementia. Other causes of dementia are strokes (referred to as vascular dementia—a series of mini-strokes) and dementia related to Parkinson's disease, depression, or other less common medical conditions.

Q What causes Alzheimer's disease, and how is it diagnosed?

It's unclear what causes Alzheimer's disease, but it's very clear that it is accompanied by a major change in the neuroanatomy of the brain. Autopsies of patients with Alzheimer's disease show specific kinds of diseased, non-functional neurons in the brain, nerve endings that have deteriorated, and other damage to the nerve cells. Whether these changes are the cause or the result of the disorder is not known.

We do know, however, about some factors that predispose people to Alzheimer's disease. For example, people who possess one or more of several particular types of mutations on a specific gene are at a higher risk to develop Alzheimer's disease than are people who do not have these mutations.

The only conclusive diagnosis of Alzheimer's disease is by an autopsy, so doctors make a tentative diagnosis (which can be up to 90 percent accurate) of Alzheimer's by excluding other possible causes such as stroke, the side effects of medication, and such other medical conditions as tumors, vitamin deficiencies, and thyroid disorders. Diagnosis by exclusion has its advantages in that this process demands an examination of all physical and psychological systems, some of which may need attention anyway. Recent research has identified some ways to improve diagnostic accuracy during the patient's lifetime, including brain imaging studies and genetic analysis.

Q What types of medication have been used to treat Alzheimer's disease, and how effective are they?

Several different types of medication have been used in the treatment of Alzheimer's disease, and some show modest promise to date, although none are curative. No drug can reverse the dementia process or restore functioning that has been lost: rather, the target is to slow the rate of deterioration.

The most common class of drugs focuses on enhancing the transmission of signals from neuron to neuron, with the hope of abating whatever deterioration or confusion is present. In particular, tacrine (Cognex) and donepezil (Aricept) have been used with some success to slow down the disease's progression, although they do not reverse the course of the disease.

Tacrine and donepezil (which has almost replaced tacrine) have received the most attention. In one study, patients taking tacrine were significantly less likely to enter a nursing home than similarly-aged patients who were taking a placebo or a very small dose of tacrine. This medication also has been found to have positive effects on the behavioral symptoms associated with Alzheimer's disease. While the best-designed studies using tacrine found some positive effects, there is concern about side effects. The more common ones are nausea, vomiting, diarrhea, and lack of coordination. The less common, but far more serious, side effects are changes in liver function. In addition, the drug might lose its effectiveness if taken over an extended period. One other disadvantage of the drug is that it needs to be taken four times a day, making compliance more difficult. Donepezil represents a new generation of drugs in the same class as tacrine (called cholinesterase inhibitors) but shows fewer side effects and is less expensive.

Q *What other medications have been used to treat Alzheimer's disease, and how effective are they?*

Medication developers have focused their Alzheimer's treatment efforts on drugs that enhance the transmission of impulses from one nerve to another through a change in the chemistry of the connection between nerve cells. However, other courses of action also exist.

In particular, some research shows that anti-inflammatory drugs help reduce the amount of neuronal damage. In fact, patients who have been taking anti-inflammatories, such as aspirin or ibuprofen, for other conditions have been found to have a lower risk for Alzheimer's disease than other people.

Estrogen also seems to slow the progression of Alzheimer's disease, possibly by preventing the twisting and tangling of neurons. It's not clear how or why this occurs, but post-menopausal women taking this hormone appear to be at less risk for Alzheimer's disease. The results are promising with women who underwent estrogen treatment showing improvements in measures of memory, attention, and concentration. Some of the same studies have also suggested the benefits of vitamin E and gingko boloba.

Q *I know elderly people suffer mental disorders besides dementia. How are depression and anxiety different for the elderly than they are for younger patients?*

As with younger people, depression and anxiety disorders in late life are serious public health concerns. They are not a normal part of the aging process. Rather, depression and anxiety disorders represent significant sources of disability, increased dependency, and premature death. Although depression and anxiety are diagnosed in the same way for older as for younger patients, depressed older adults may not experience or acknowledge sadness or guilt to the same extent as younger patients. Also, certain symptoms—such as lack of interest in normal pursuits, deterioration in self-care, and actual or perceived problems with memory and attention—may predominate among older adults. In addition, the much higher incidence of chronic and severe medical conditions is an important factor in diagnosis and care since such illness and depression usually coexist in a significant percentage of depressed patients.

Depression and anxiety disorders in later life can be chronic and recurring. Some studies done in a naturalistic setting (where there is very little experimental control) find that a quarter to a third of depressed older adults may fail to achieve a complete recovery, and the risk of relapse among those who recover following treatment increases over time.

Q How common are depression and anxiety among the elderly?

Although most older Americans lead healthy and fulfilling lives, approximately 15 percent over 65 years of age (or 5 million people) experience persistent and serious symptoms of depression. For those who are cared for in a nursing home, the rate jumps to between 15 and 25 percent. One explanation is that as people get older, they realize how their physical and mental disorders restrict their behavior and prevent them from doing things they think they should be able to do. Such recognition can contribute to the development of depression.

For anxiety disorders, the combined 1-month prevalence among persons 65 years or older has been found to be 5.5 percent, with phobias (see Chapter 8) being the most common. Generalized anxiety disorder is probably the next most frequent anxiety disorder. The total cumulative percentage for all anxiety disorders in the elderly is about 20 percent.

Q How important is the age of onset for depression and anxiety?

The age at which a depression or anxiety disorder begins is very important and has major implications for treatment. For example, late onset depression appears to be linked more frequently than average to structural changes in the brain, cognitive impairment, and medical conditions. The elderly are also subjected to an increasing number of real-life stressors that are related to anxiety and depression, such as caring for another elderly person, financial problems, and other illnesses. It has been established that individuals who care for patients with dementia (who are often elderly spouses of the patient) are at a greatly increased risk, sometimes as high as 50 percent in some studies, for depression.

Unfortunately, age plays another important role in the treatment of depression and anxiety. In the presence of medical illness, symptoms of these two mental disorders are often overlooked. The elderly often focus more on the physical symptoms of their illnesses, rather than on the depression or anxiety itself or on the interaction between the medical illness and the mental disorder. Also unfortunately, many physicians, who are primarily trained to look for underlying physical disease, fail to recognize the concurrence of depression or anxiety along with a medical condition. In fact, up to 70 percent of individuals aged 80-85 who successfully attempted suicide had seen their primary care physician in the month prior to death, but their depression generally went unrecognized and untreated. Since the elderly have the highest suicide rate of any age group (double the overall rate for the 80-85 age group), detection and treatment take on special importance.

Q What are the psychosocial treatments of choice for depression in the elderly, and how effective are these treatments?

In general, psychosocial treatments are effective in treating major depressive disorders in the elderly. The treatments that have been shown to work are cognitive-behavioral, psychodynamic, interpersonal, and educational. For example, in one study 70 percent of elderly depressed patients receiving cognitive, behavioral, and psychodynamic treatments showed significantly reduced depression over 6 weeks relative to a control group. At the 1-year follow-up 58 percent remained symptom-free, and at the 2-year follow-up 70 percent remained without symptoms.

For special populations—such as people who are undergoing treatment for medical conditions, are in nursing homes, or have physical impairments—there are some limitations in the power or duration of the benefits. The psychosocial treatments may work initially, but improvement varies with the initial condition of the patient. For example, in one study only the non-disabled patients continued to improve beyond a 6-month period.

Q What's the pharmacological treatment of choice for depression among the elderly, and how effective is it?

Antidepressant medications effectively treat depression, and approximately 30 well-designed and well-controlled studies have shown this effectiveness for acute depression that begins in later life. The primary classes of medication for which strong evidence exists are the tricyclic antidepressants, selective serotonin reuptake inhibitors, and monoamine oxidase inhibitors. The effectiveness of most of these medications is thought to be generally comparable for older and younger adults. About 60 percent of elderly patients show improvement between 4 and 12 weeks of treatment. However, one limitation of such studies is that 25 to 30 percent of all subjects drop out before treatment is completed.

There are characteristics about the elderly that make treating them different and perhaps more difficult than treating young patients. First, elderly people respond to treatment more slowly than younger patients and may simply need more time. For example, in one study, extending treatment to an elderly group by 2 weeks produced added benefits. Second, compliance to the schedule of medication is as important with the elderly as with any group but often fraught with difficulties. Older people are simply more likely to forget. Finally, the elderly are much more vulnerable than young people to side effects. Various antidepressant medications can impair attention and concentration, memory, and other aspects of cognitive functioning including judgment. It becomes necessary but difficult to differentiate between symptoms of the disorder and side effects of medication.

Following is a brief review of the different types of antidepressants and the evidence for their effectiveness.

- Tricyclic antidepressants have been used in about two dozen well-controlled studies. The effectiveness of tricyclic antidepressants, including the two most frequently studied, nortriptyline (Pamelor) and desipramine (Norpramine), has been established in treating depression among the elderly. However, patient acceptance of this class of antidepressants tends to be highly variable because of side effects such as dry mouth, constipation, and increased heart rate. In addition, these medications may introduce more serious medical side effects, such as an irregular heartbeat.

- The efficacy of selective serotonin reuptake inhibitors such as fluoxetine (Prozac), paroxetine (Paxil), citalopram (Celexa), and sertraline (Zoloft) has been examined in more than twenty well-controlled studies as treatment for depressed elderly patients. They have been found to be as effective as the tricyclic antidepressants but with much more tolerable side effects. Nausea may develop when one of these drugs is used, but it usually resolves itself in a week or two.

- Finally, the newest antidepressants are also effective in elderly people with depression including venlafaxine (Effexor) and nefazodone (Serzone).

Q What other treatments for depression in the elderly have been tried, and with what degrees of success?

Electroconvulsive therapy is clearly effective in the treatment of depression, including the elderly.

About one-third of patients treated with electroconvulsive therapy are elderly, and patients older than 60 constitute the age group most likely to receive electroconvulsive therapy as a treatment for depression since they manifest more of the indications that call for this mode of therapy. For example, elderly people may have a history of poor response to medication or of good response to electroconvulsive therapy. In general, studies show that electroconvulsive therapy is effective as a short-term treatment of depression in the elderly. In some cases, for example, when an elderly depressed patient refuses to eat or is suicidal, electroconvulsive therapy can be a life saver.

Q *What types of treatments are available for anxiety disorder in older patients, and how successful have they been?*

Unfortunately, controlled studies of treatment for late-life anxiety disorders are lacking. For the most part, available information is based on studies with younger patients. However, anxiety has been recognized as often accompanying depression in later life and has also been found to be responsive to the same treatments.

As far as psychosocial interventions, cognitive-behavioral therapy and supportive psychotherapy have both been found to be effective in the treatment of generalized anxiety disorder in patients who were 55 years of age or older and who reported to have had the anxiety disorder for more than 35 years. Relaxation methods, rational-emotive therapy, and anxiety management training have also been found to be effective.

Pharmacological treatments for anxiety in the elderly formerly overemphasized the use of benzodiazepines such as diazepam (Valium) and chlordiazepoxide (Librium). The few studies that have been done have shown this class of drugs to be effective in alleviating anxiety symptoms, with no benzodiazepine superior to any other. However, a large number of studies have indicated both that the use of benzodiazepines is associated with some degree of cognitive impairment even for younger patients, and that the elderly are at increased risk for these side effects. Most clinicians now believe that antidepressants and buspirone (BuSpsar) are better choices for elderly anxious patients.

Q *Where Can I Find More Information About Mental Disorders Of Aging?*

Books

Alzheimer's & Dementia : Questions You Have…Answers You Need by Jennifer Hay. People's Medical Society, 1996. ISBN 1882606574
  A straightforward collection of questions and answers about this disorder of aging.

Alzheimer's: A Complete Guide for Families and Loved Ones by Howard Gruetzner. John Wiley & Sons, 1997. ISBN 0471198250.
  Updated and revised, this guide shows that caring for the Alzheimer's patient can be more positive than ever. Explores the latest advances and presents them in an easy-to-understand and immediately useful way.

When Someone You Love Has Alzheimer's: The Caregiver's Journey by Earl A. Grollman, and Kenneth S. Kosik. Beacon Press, 1997. ISBN 0807027219.

A nicely written, personal, and accurate description of what happens to people when they have Alzheimer's.

"Depression in the Elderly: A Multimedia Sourcebook," Bibliographies and Indexes in Gerontology, Number 36 by John J. Miletich. Greenwood Publishing Group, 1997. ISBN 0313301131.

An extensive source of information from many different sources (books, tapes, etc.) about depression in the elderly that covers topics such as etiology, epidemiology, diagnosis, memory, cognition, dementia, physical illnesses, disability, and sensory impairment, among others.

Internet Sites

Depression in the Elderly
(at http://www.psycom.net/depression.central.elderly.html) covers diagnosis and treatment, recent developments in understanding the disorder, and a discussion of depression in the elderly who also have dementia.

The Anxiety Network
(at http://www.anxietynetwork.com/) includes general information about generalized anxiety disorder, panic disorder, and phobias. It has specific pages for each disorder and links to other sites on anxiety.

Some newsgroups devoted to a discussion of depression are alt.support.depression, alt.support.depression.manic, soc.support.depression.misc, and soc.support.depression.treatment.

Where to Write

The Alzheimer's Association
919 North Michigan Avenue, Suite 1000
Chicago, IL 60611-1676
312-335-8700

Anxiety Disorders Association of America
11900 Parklawn Drive, Suite 100
Rockville, MD 20852
301-231-9350

Index

depressive and bipolar disorders,
101-120
  description 102
  frequency of occurrence 102
  symptoms 102
disorders of aging 193-202
dissociative amnesia
  causes 94
  characteristics 94-95
  description 95
  treatment 95
dissociative disorders 93-101
  description 94
  types 94
dissociative fugue
  causes 95
  effectiveness of treatment 96
  treatment 96
dissociative identity disorder
  characteristics 96
  description 96
  different treatment 98
Division Of Mental Disorders 191
depression and aging, frequency of
  occurrence 197
dramatic cluster personality disorder
  188-189
dyspareunia, treatment 60
dyssomnia 44
dysthymic disorder
  description 109
  treatment 109

E
eating disorders, 25-40
educational therapy, treatment
  schizophrenia 174
electroconvulsive therapy
  description 108-109
  depression, treatment of 108
erectile dysfunction
  causes of 56
  effectiveness of treatment 58

erectile dysfunction cont.
  treatment 57
exposure and response prevention
  description 143
  effectiveness 143
eye movement desensitization 156

F
factitious disorder, description 92
female orgasmic disorder, treatment 59
functional family therapy
  effectiveness 18
  how it works 19

G
generalized anxiety disorder
  description and occurrence 122
  symptoms 122-123
  treatment 123
generic and trade medications
  xxiii-xxiv
gold standard of research, xii

H
heroin dependency, pharmacological
  treatment 83
hyperactivity and attention deficit
  hyperactivity disorder 3
hypoactive sexual disorders,
  treatment 55
hypochondria
  description 91
  treatment 91

I
impotence 56
insomnia
  behavioral treatment 47-48
  characteristics 42
  combined treatment 49
  description 41
  diagnosis 43
  different types 43